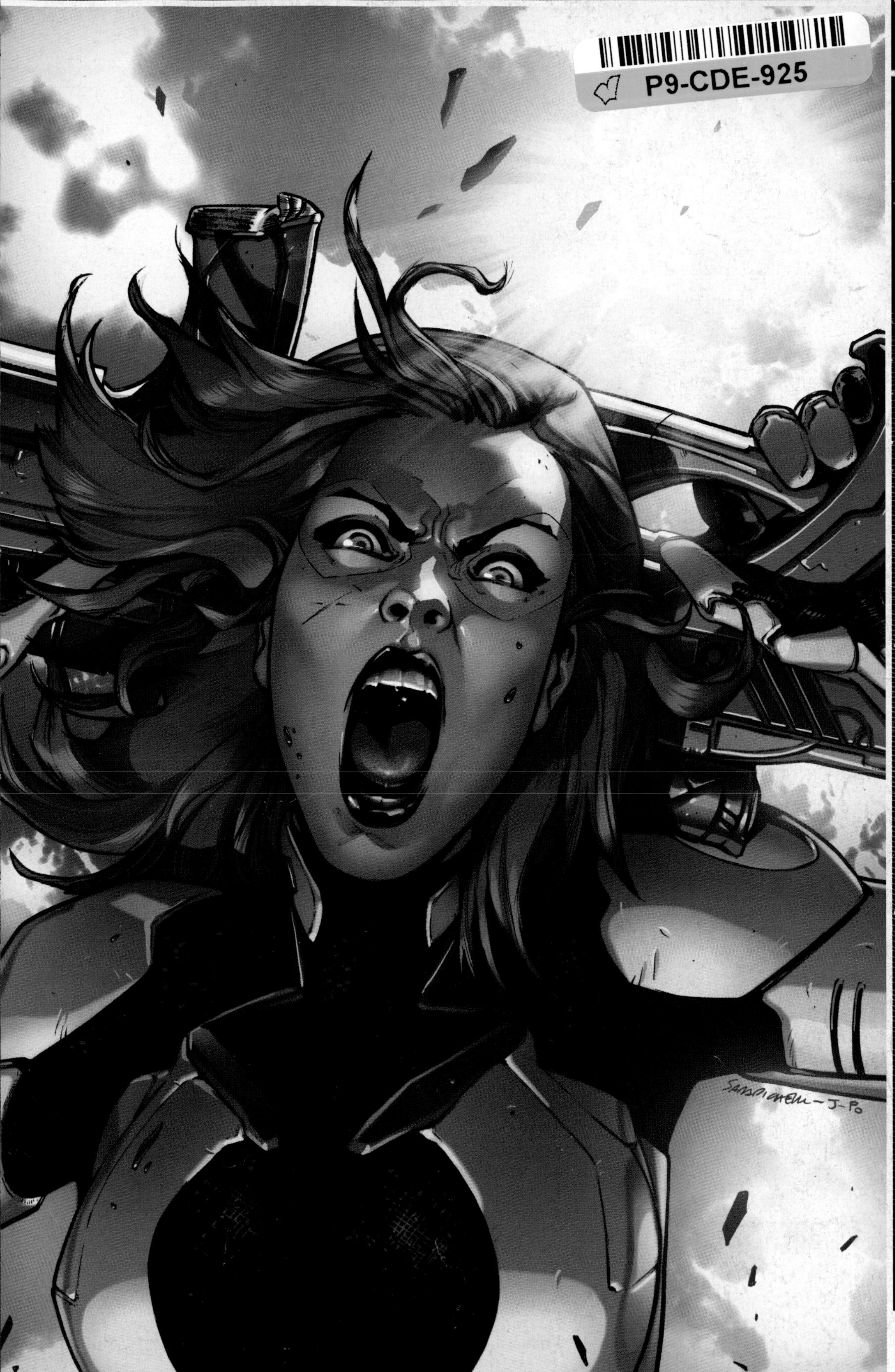

4

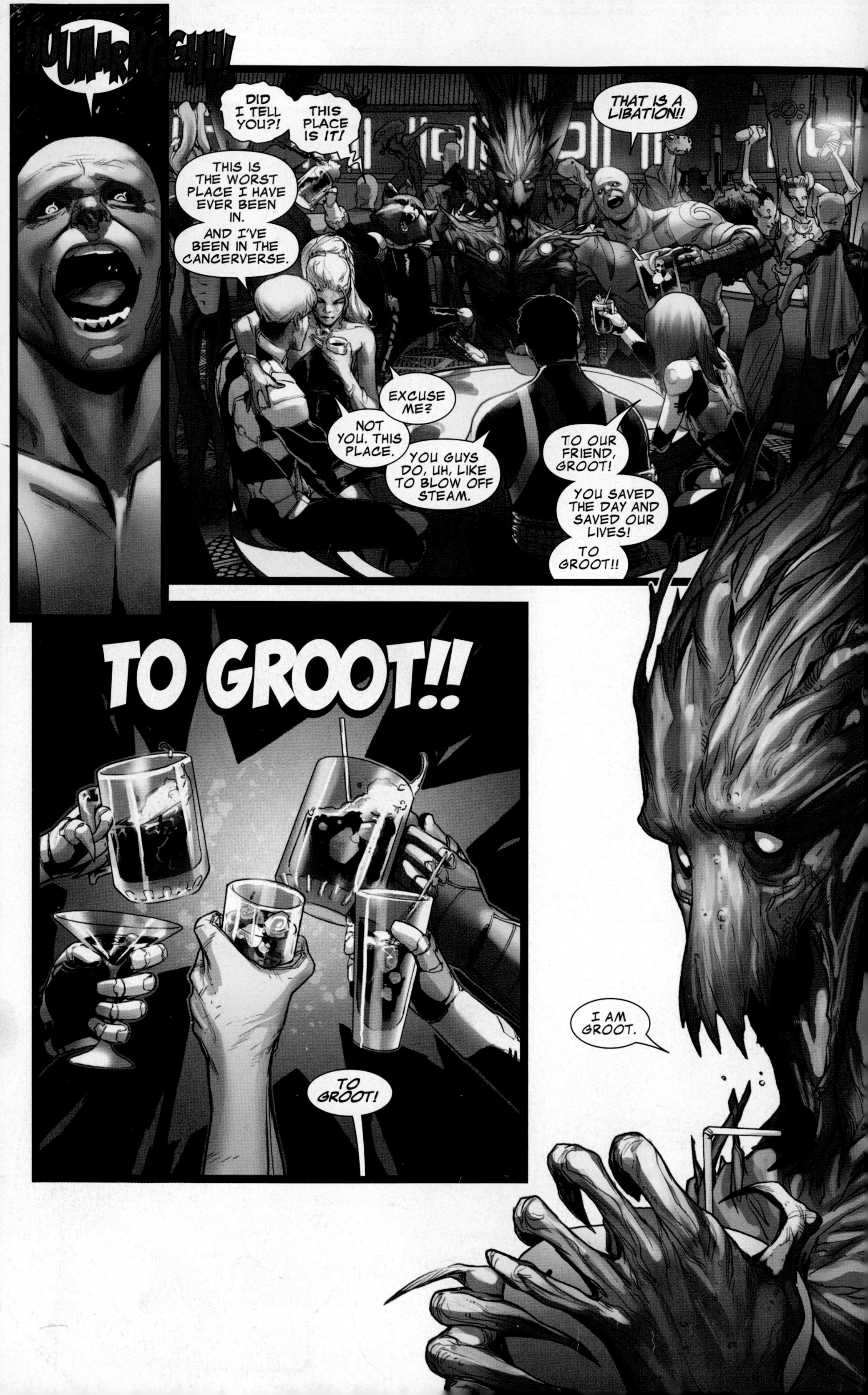
DID I TELL YOU?!
THIS PLACE IS IT!
THIS IS THE WORST PLACE I HAVE EVER BEEN IN.
AND I'VE BEEN IN THE CANCERVERSE.
THAT IS A LIBATION!!
EXCUSE ME?
NOT YOU. THIS PLACE.
YOU GUYS DO, UH, LIKE TO BLOW OFF STEAM.
TO OUR FRIEND, GROOT!
YOU SAVED THE DAY AND SAVED OUR LIVES!
TO GROOT!!
TO GROOT!!
TO GROOT!
I AM GROOT.

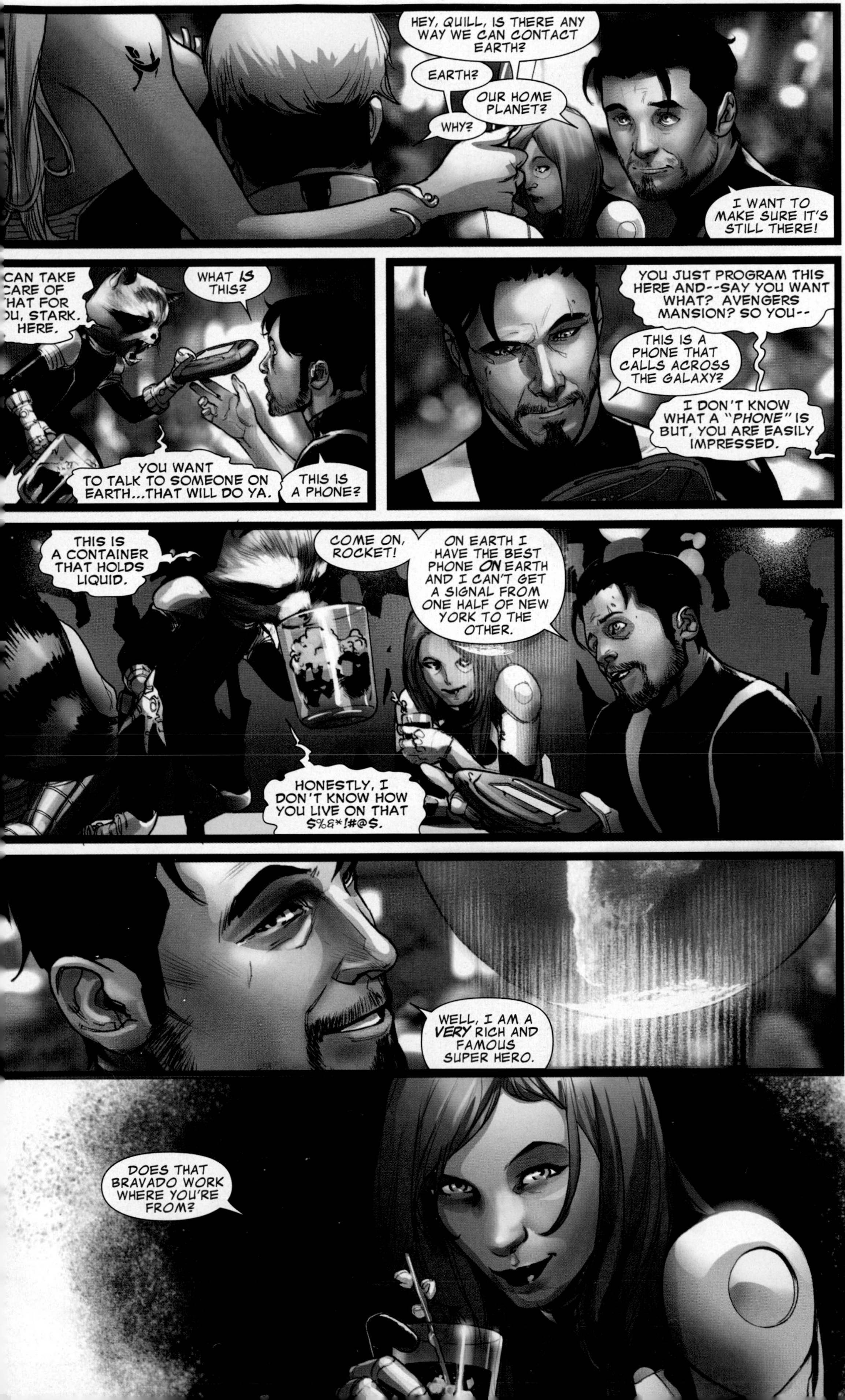
HEY, QUILL, IS THERE ANY WAY WE CAN CONTACT EARTH?
EARTH?
OUR HOME PLANET?
WHY?
I WANT TO MAKE SURE IT'S STILL THERE!
CAN TAKE CARE OF THAT FOR OU, STARK. HERE.
WHAT IS THIS?
YOU WANT TO TALK TO SOMEONE ON EARTH...THAT WILL DO YA.
THIS IS A PHONE?
YOU JUST PROGRAM THIS HERE AND--SAY YOU WANT WHAT? AVENGERS MANSION? SO YOU--
THIS IS A PHONE THAT CALLS ACROSS THE GALAXY?
I DON'T KNOW WHAT A "PHONE" IS BUT, YOU ARE EASILY IMPRESSED.
THIS IS A CONTAINER THAT HOLDS LIQUID.
COME ON, ROCKET!
ON EARTH I HAVE THE BEST PHONE ON EARTH AND I CAN'T GET A SIGNAL FROM ONE HALF OF NEW YORK TO THE OTHER.
HONESTLY, I DON'T KNOW HOW YOU LIVE ON THAT $%&*!#@$.
WELL, I AM A VERY RICH AND FAMOUS SUPER HERO.
DOES THAT BRAVADO WORK WHERE YOU'RE FROM?

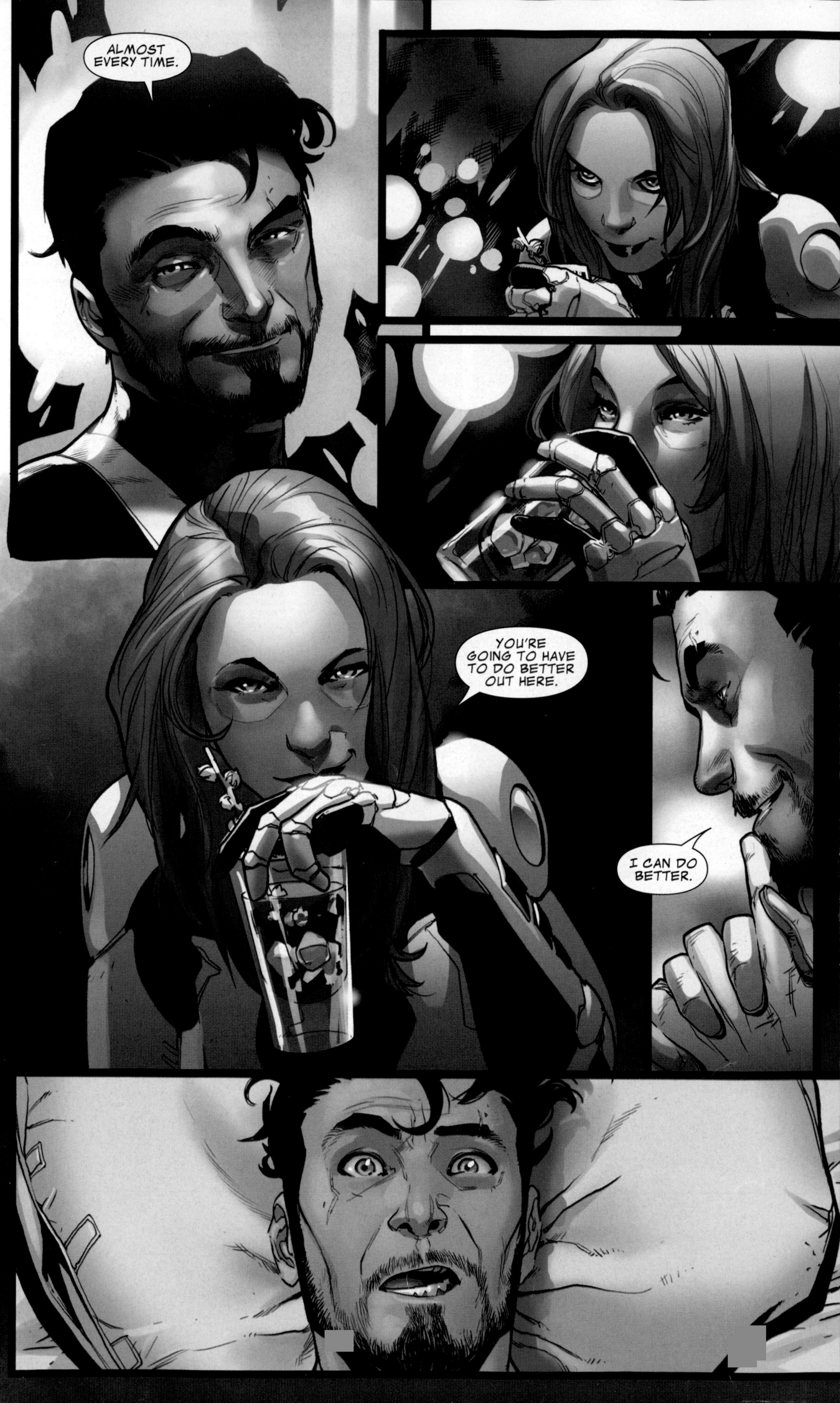
ALMOST EVERY TIME.
YOU'RE GOING TO HAVE TO DO BETTER OUT HERE.
I CAN DO BETTER.

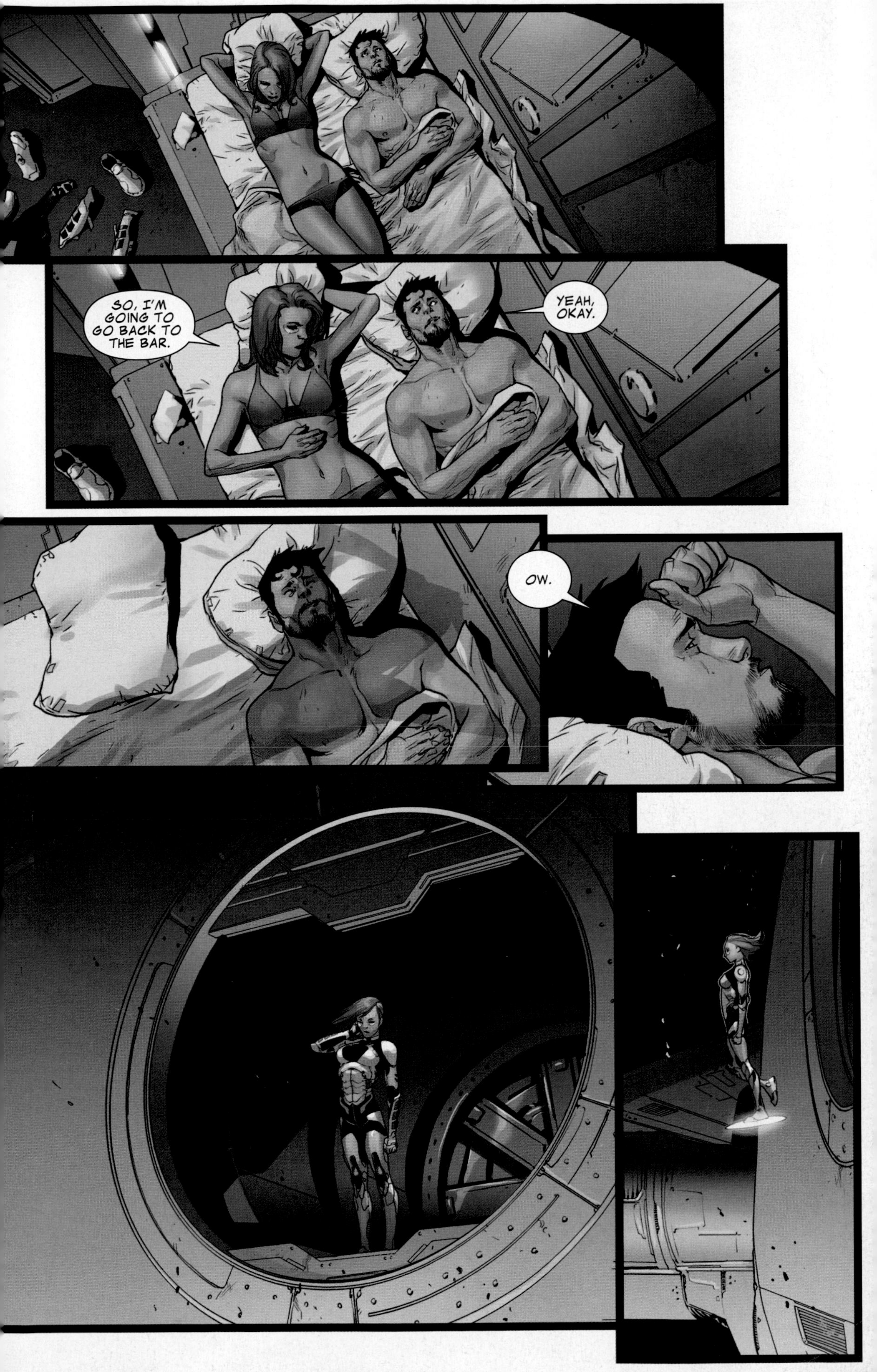
SO, I'M GOING TO GO BACK TO THE BAR.
YEAH, OKAY.
OW.

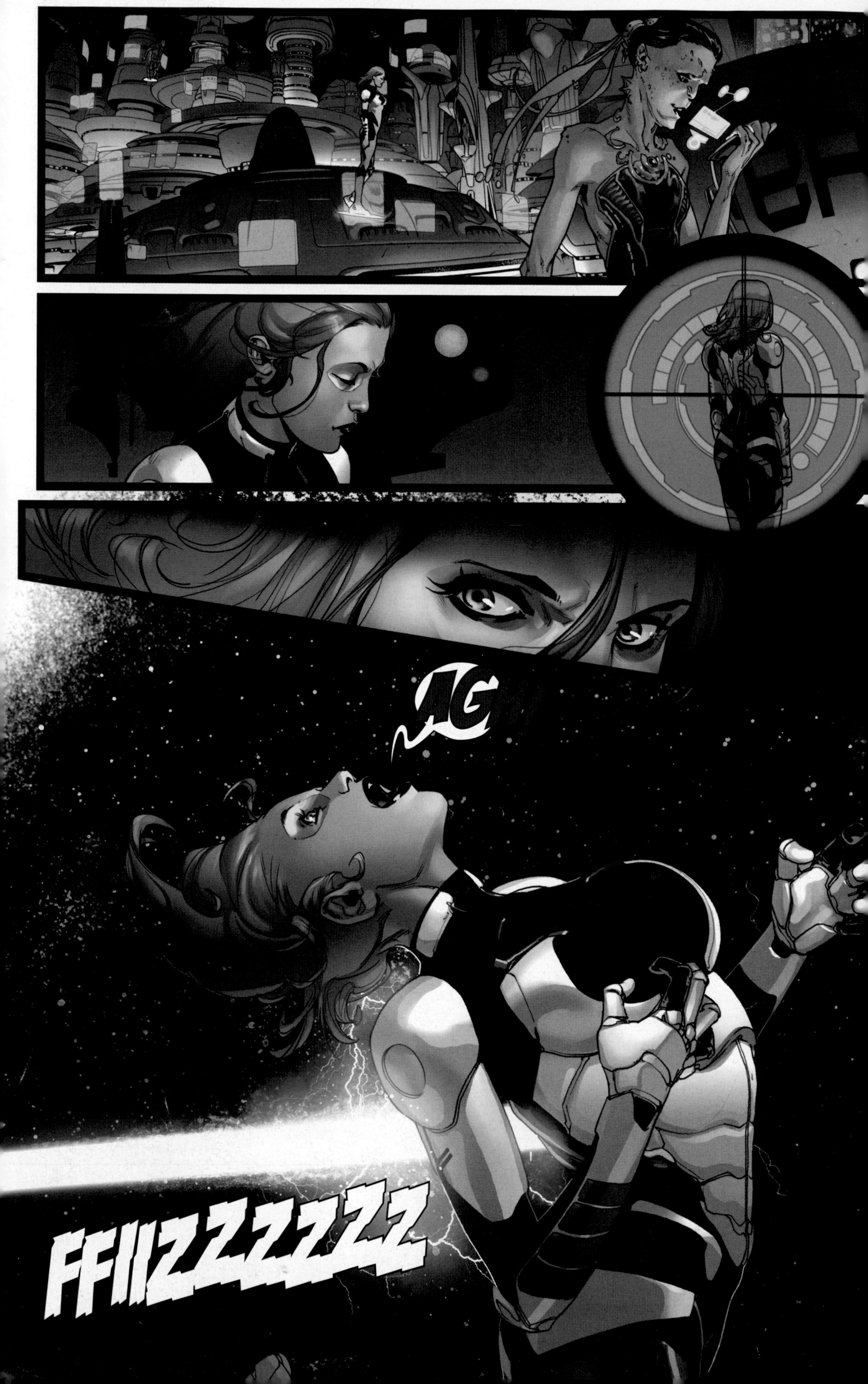
AG
FFIIZZZZZZ

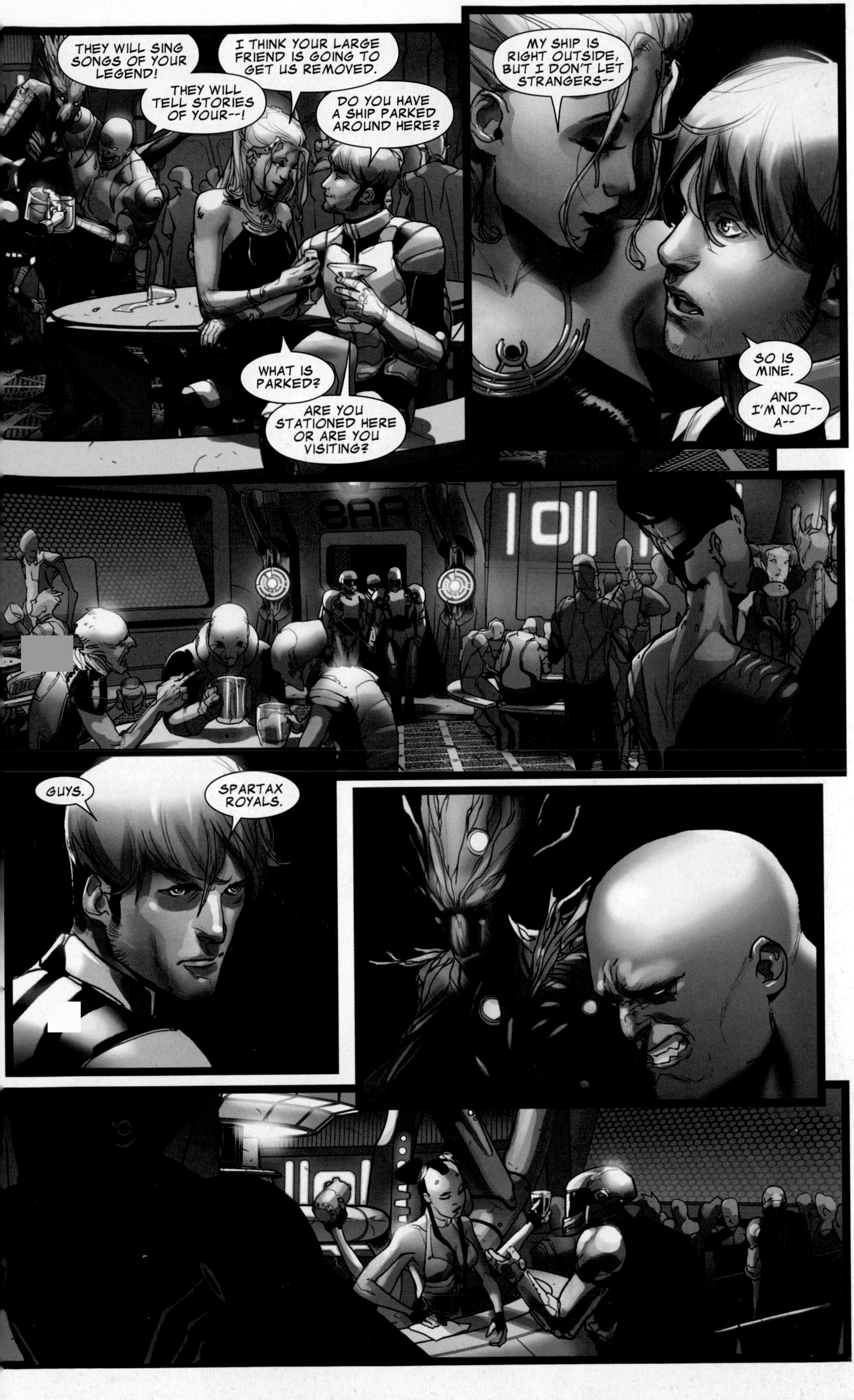
THEY WILL SING SONGS OF YOUR LEGEND!
THEY WILL TELL STORIES OF YOUR--!
I THINK YOUR LARGE FRIEND IS GOING TO GET US REMOVED.
DO YOU HAVE A SHIP PARKED AROUND HERE?
WHAT IS PARKED?
ARE YOU STATIONED HERE OR ARE YOU VISITING?
MY SHIP IS RIGHT OUTSIDE, BUT I DON'T LET STRANGERS--
SO IS MINE.
AND I'M NOT-- A--
BAR
GUYS.
SPARTAX ROYALS.

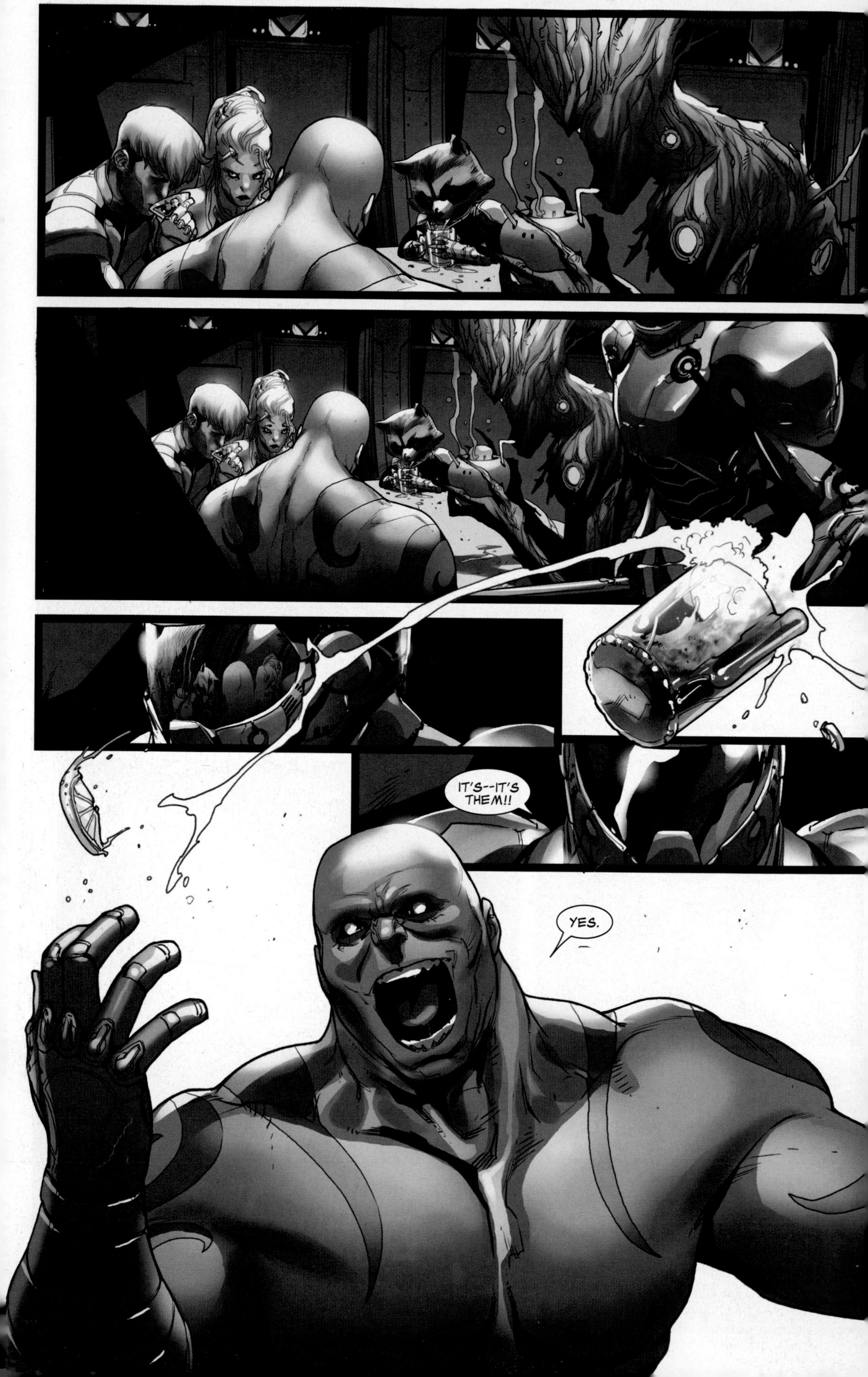
IT'S--IT'S THEM!!
YES.

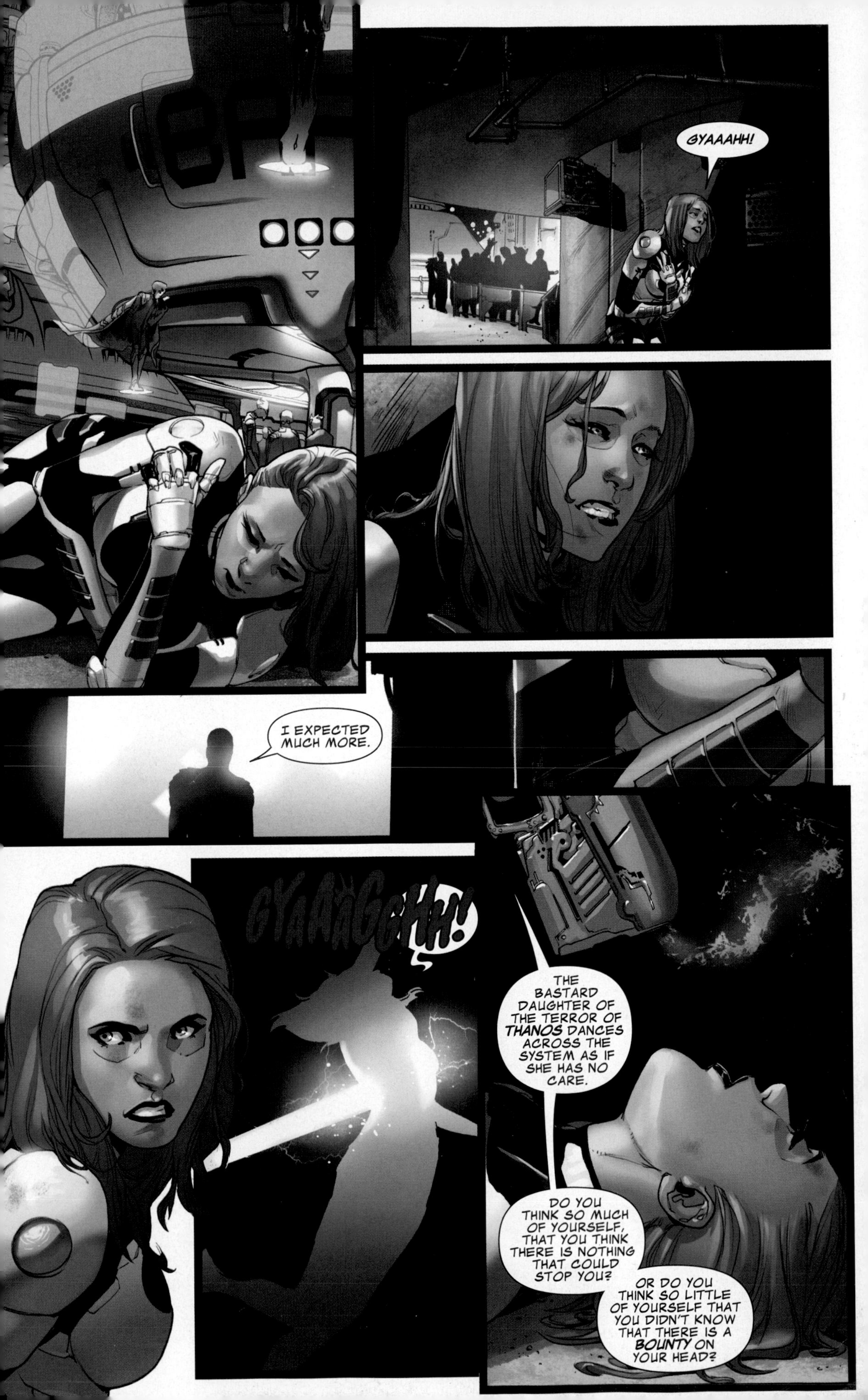
GYAAAHH!
I EXPECTED MUCH MORE.
GYAAAGGHH!
THE BASTARD DAUGHTER OF THE TERROR OF THANOS DANCES ACROSS THE SYSTEM AS IF SHE HAS NO CARE.
DO YOU THINK SO MUCH OF YOURSELF, THAT YOU THINK THERE IS NOTHING THAT COULD STOP YOU?
OR DO YOU THINK SO LITTLE OF YOURSELF THAT YOU DIDN'T KNOW THAT THERE IS A BOUNTY ON YOUR HEAD?

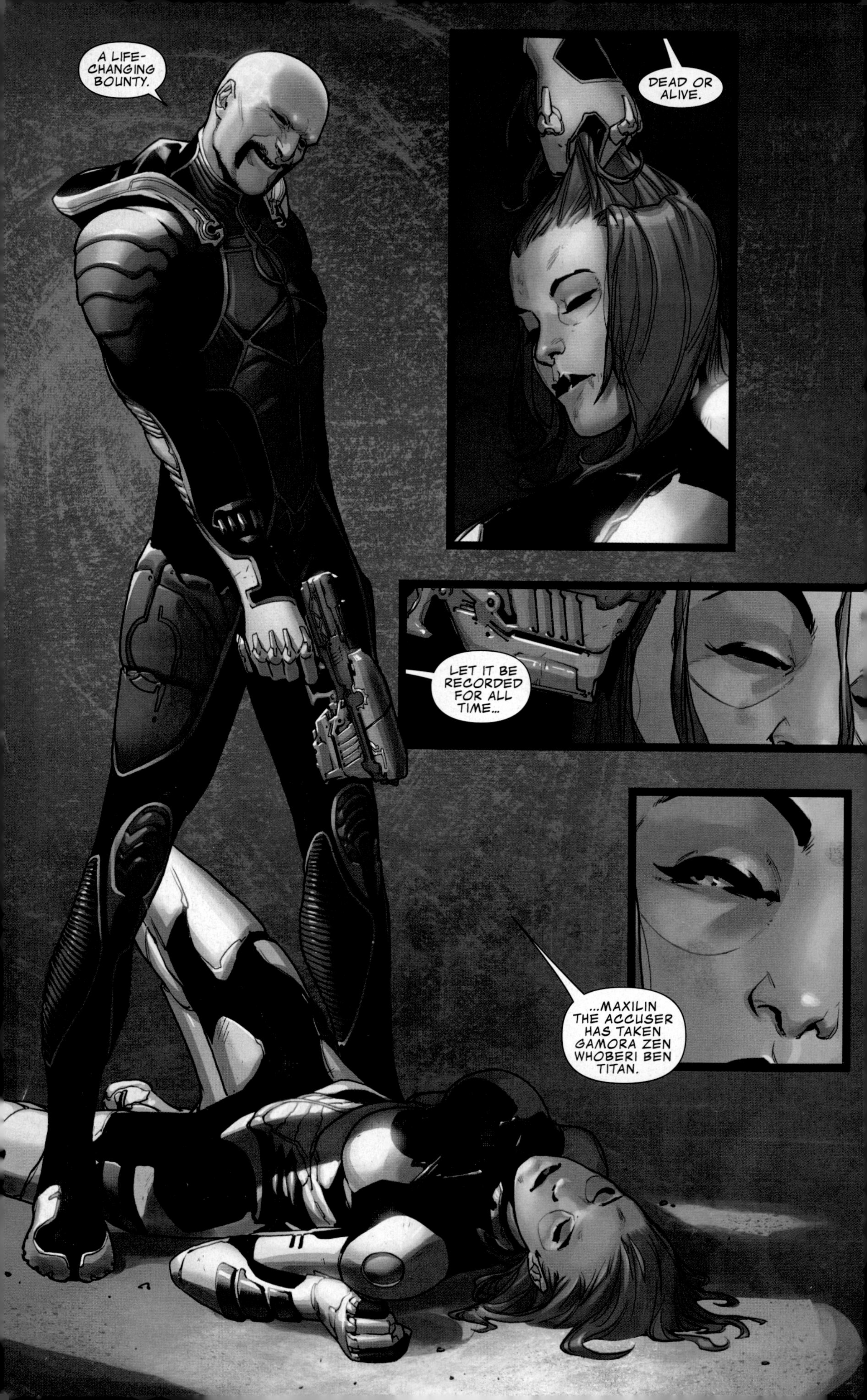
A LIFE-CHANGING BOUNTY.
DEAD OR ALIVE.
LET IT BE RECORDED FOR ALL TIME...
...MAXILIN THE ACCUSER HAS TAKEN GAMORA ZEN WHOBERI BEN TITAN.

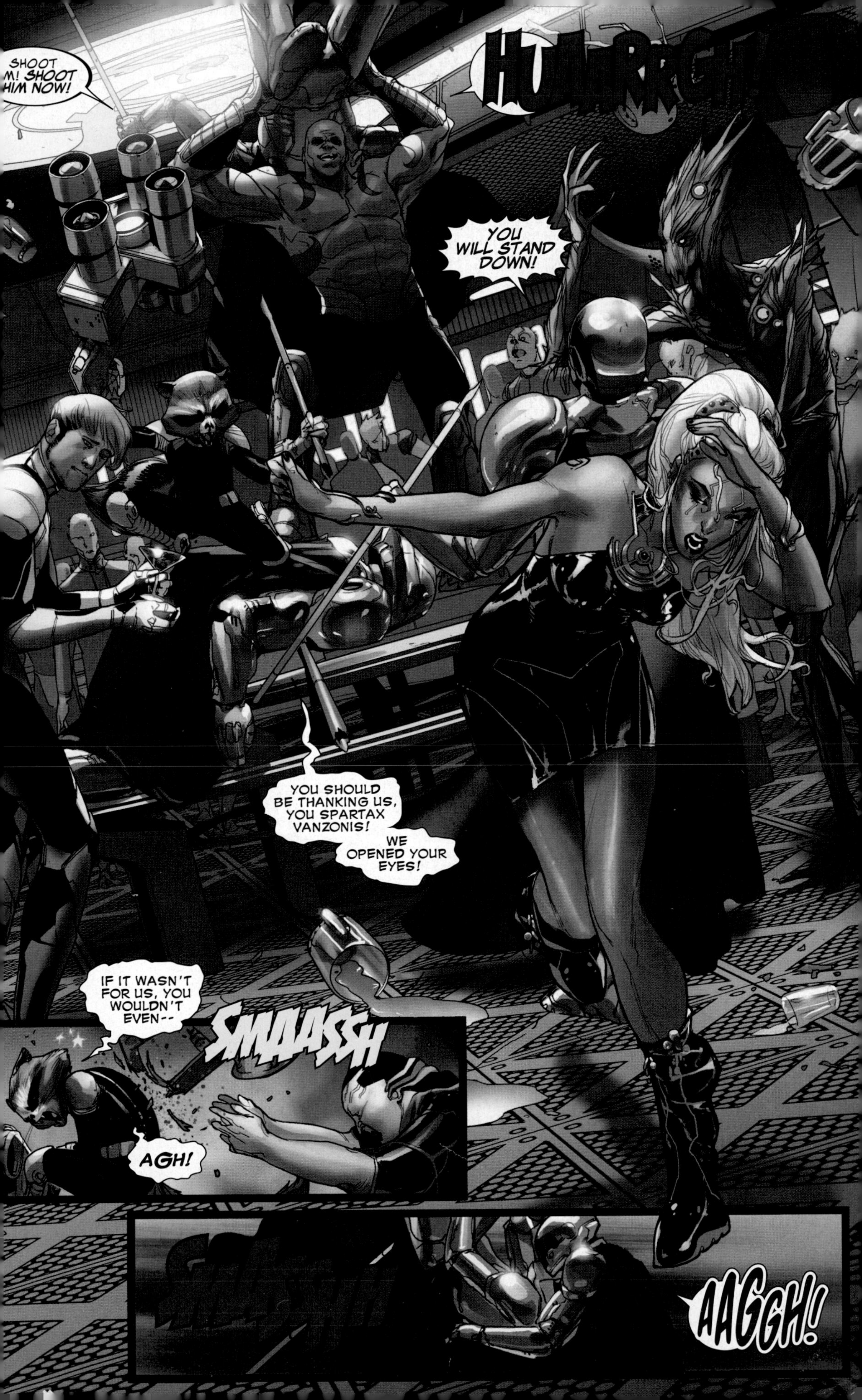
SHOOT M! SHOOT HIM NOW!
HUNRRGH
YOU WILL STAND DOWN!
YOU SHOULD BE THANKING US, YOU SPARTAX VANZONIS!
WE OPENED YOUR EYES!
IF IT WASN'T FOR US, YOU WOULDN'T EVEN--
SMAASSH
AGH!
AAGGH!

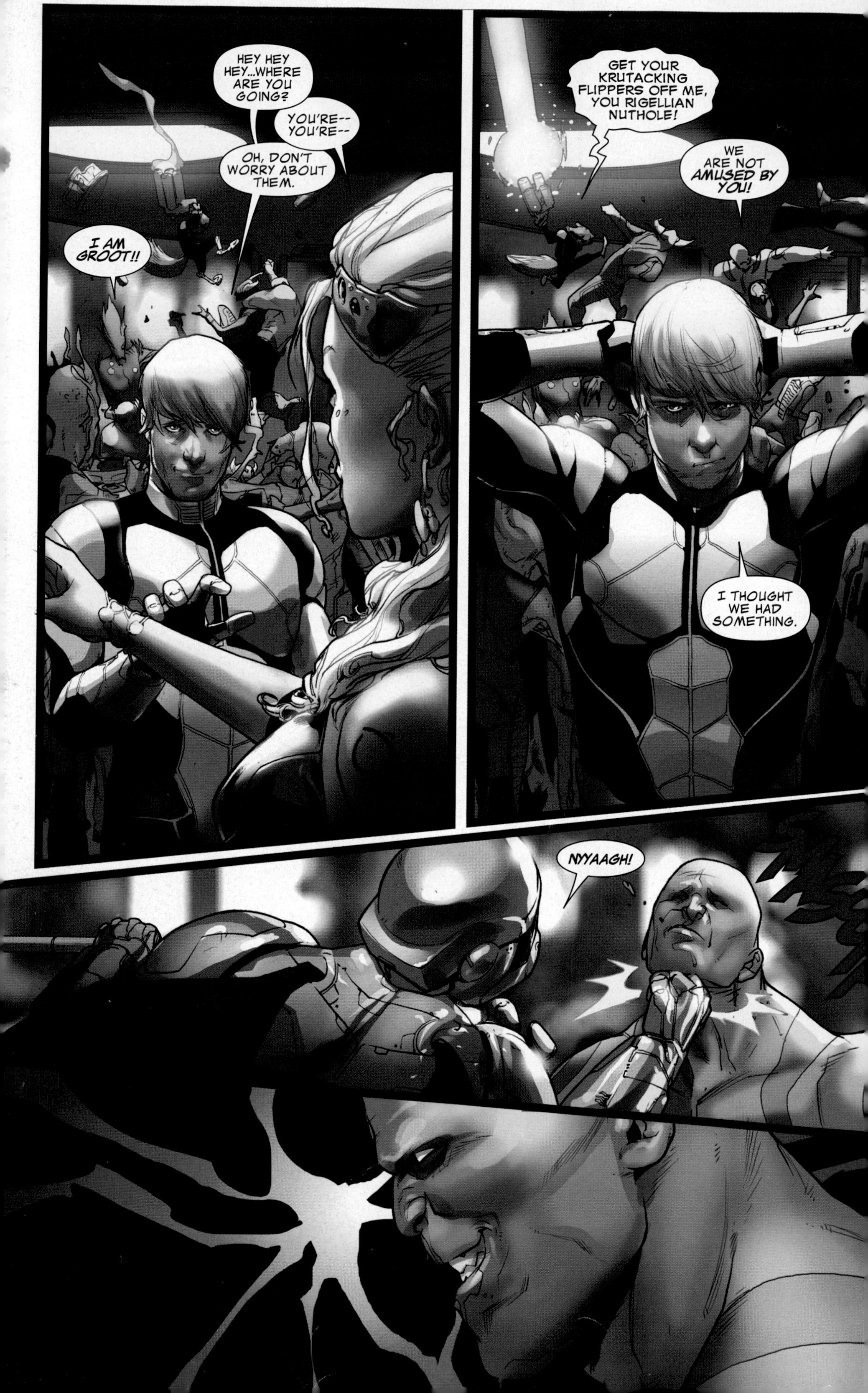
HEY HEY HEY...WHERE ARE YOU GOING?
YOU'RE-- YOU'RE--
OH, DON'T WORRY ABOUT THEM.
I AM GROOT!!
GET YOUR KRUTACKING FLIPPERS OFF ME, YOU RIGELLIAN NUTHOLE!
WE ARE NOT AMUSED BY YOU!
I THOUGHT WE HAD SOMETHING.
NYYAAGH!

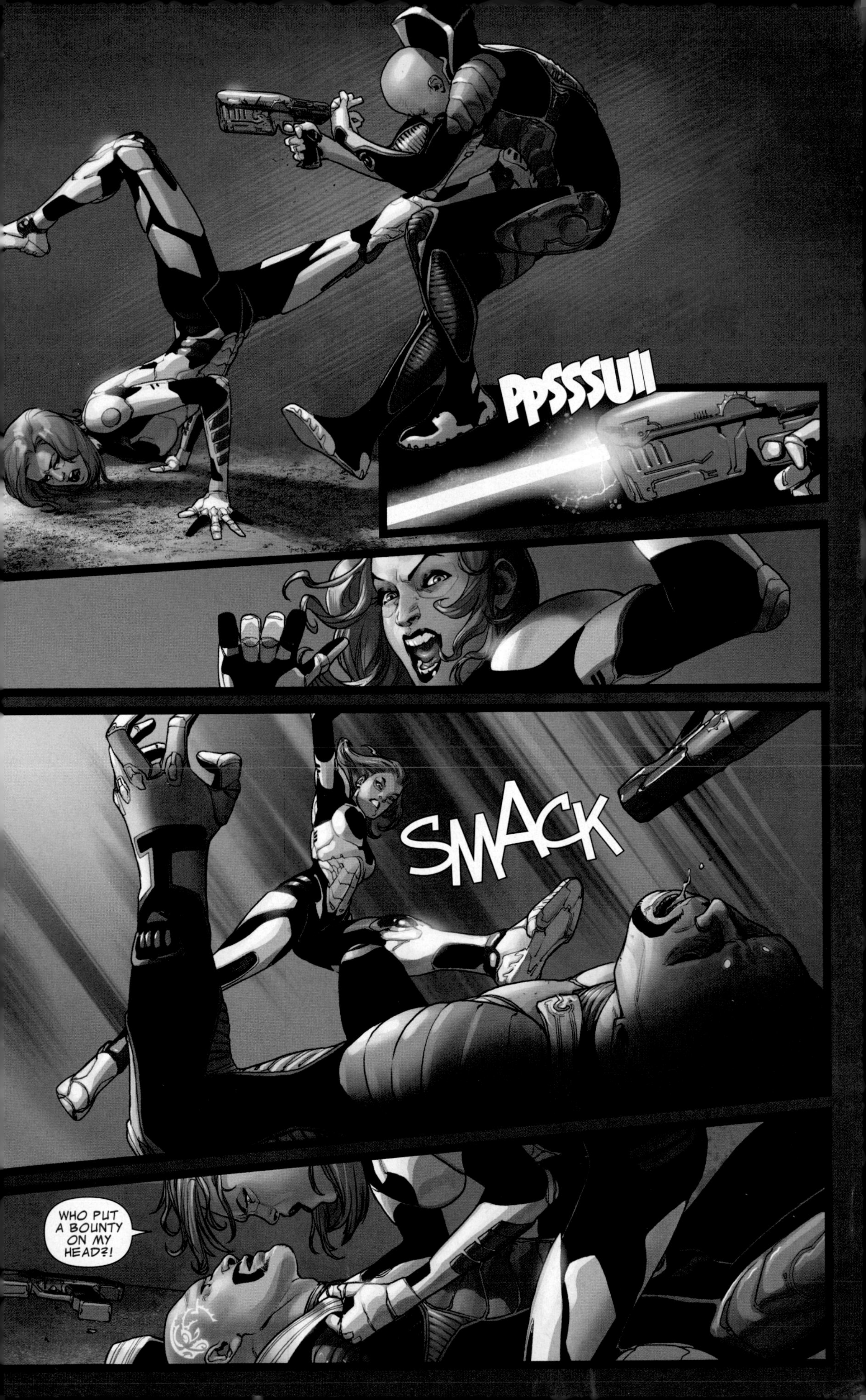
PPSSSUII
SMACK
WHO PUT A BOUNTY ON MY HEAD?!

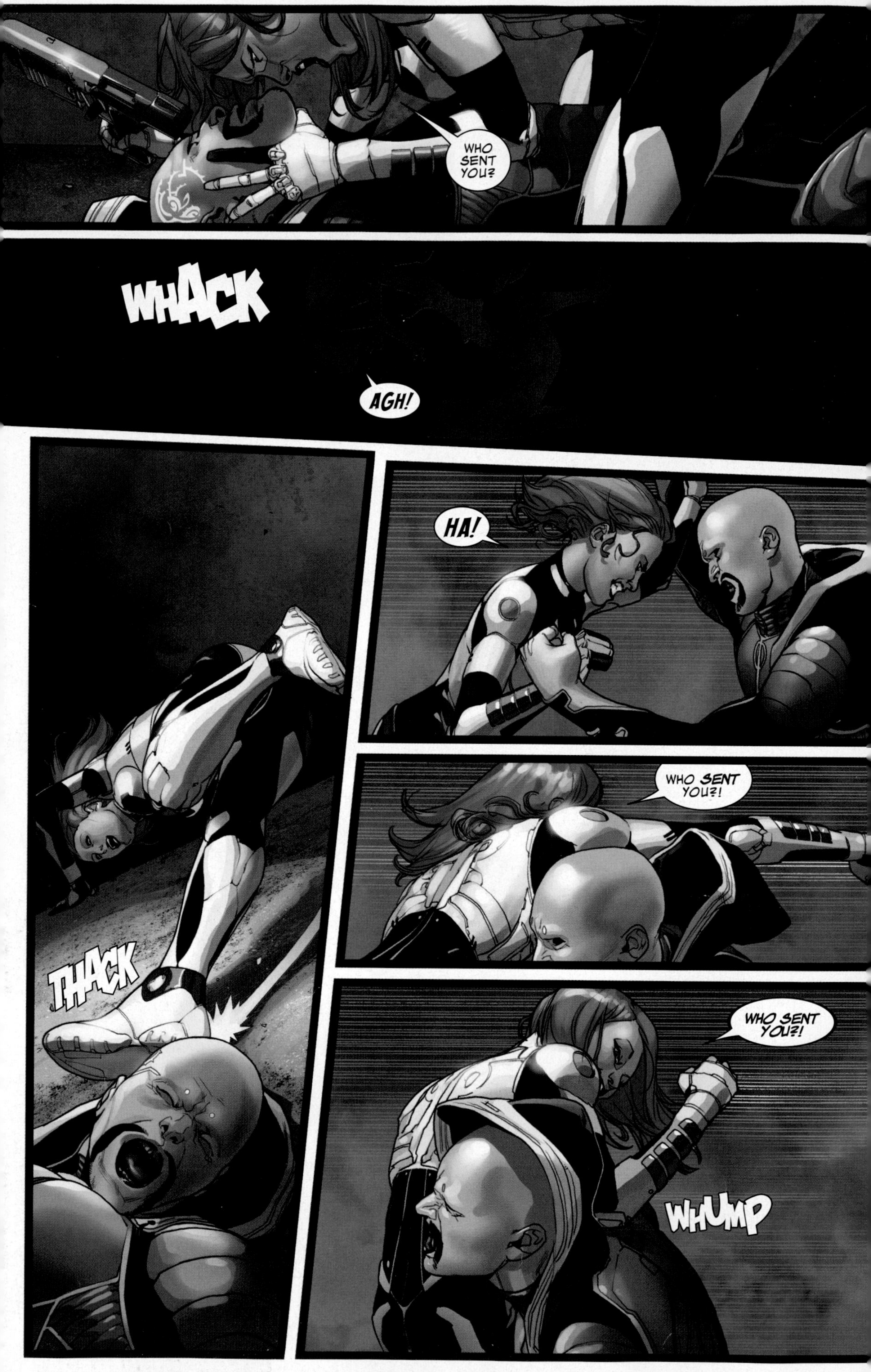
WHO SENT YOU?
WHACK
AGH!
HA!
THACK
WHO SENT YOU?!
WHO SENT YOU?!
WHUMP

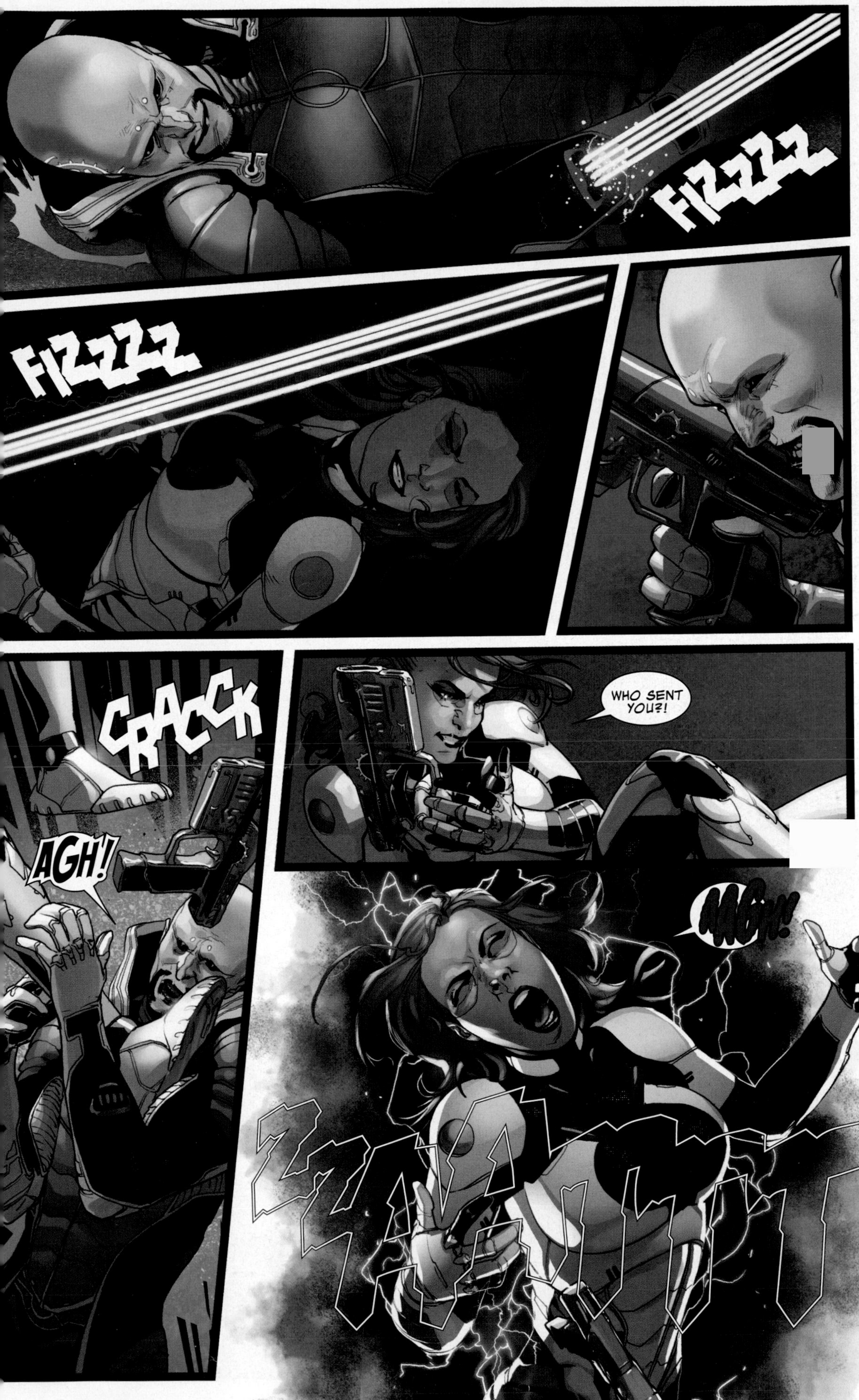
FIZZZZ
FIZZZZ
CRACCK
AGH!
WHO SENT YOU?!
MGH!

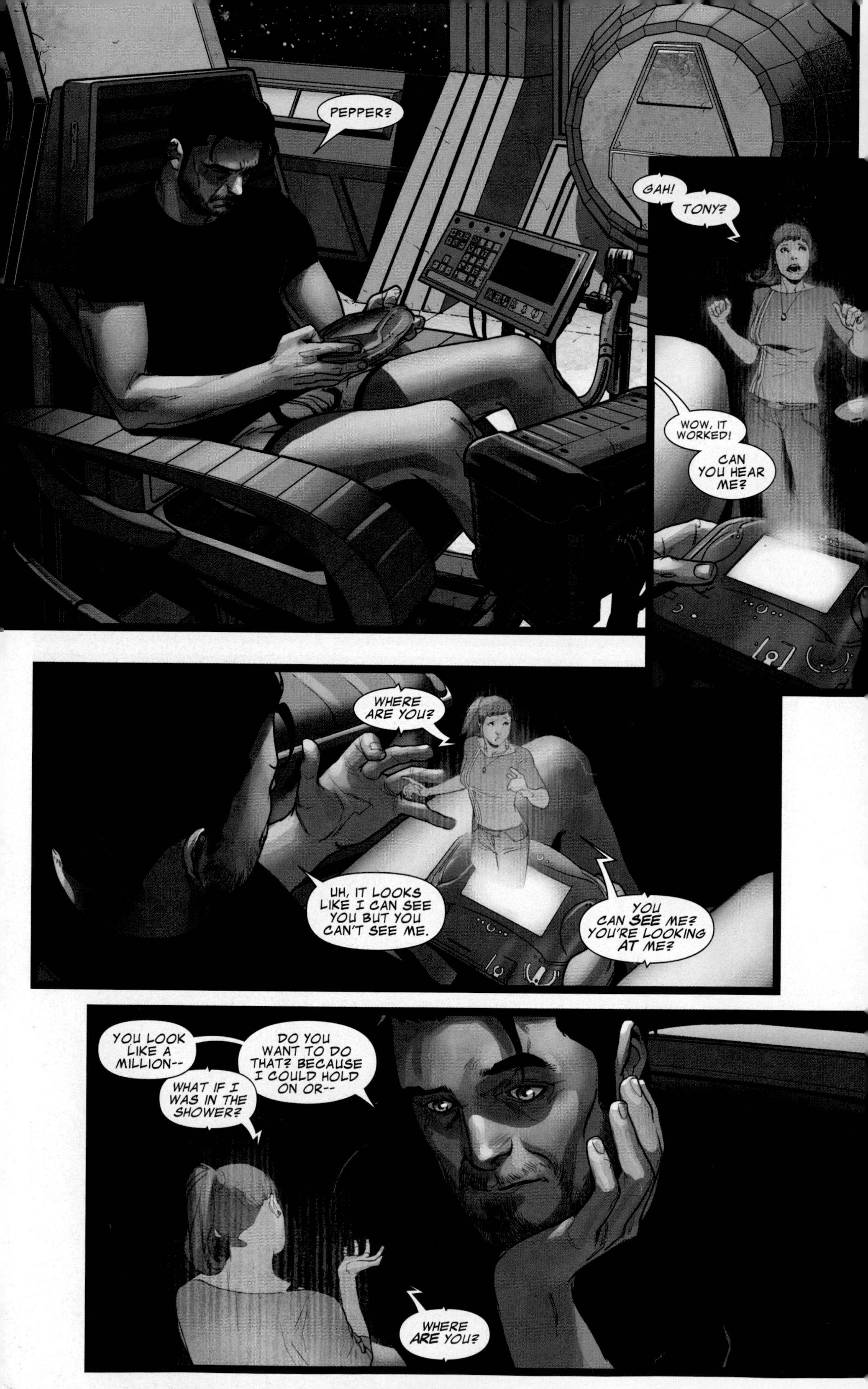
PEPPER?
GAH!
TONY?
WOW, IT WORKED!
CAN YOU HEAR ME?
WHERE ARE YOU?
UH, IT LOOKS LIKE I CAN SEE YOU BUT YOU CAN'T SEE ME.
YOU CAN SEE ME? YOU'RE LOOKING AT ME?
YOU LOOK LIKE A MILLION--
WHAT IF I WAS IN THE SHOWER?
DO YOU WANT TO DO THAT? BECAUSE I COULD HOLD ON OR--
WHERE ARE YOU?

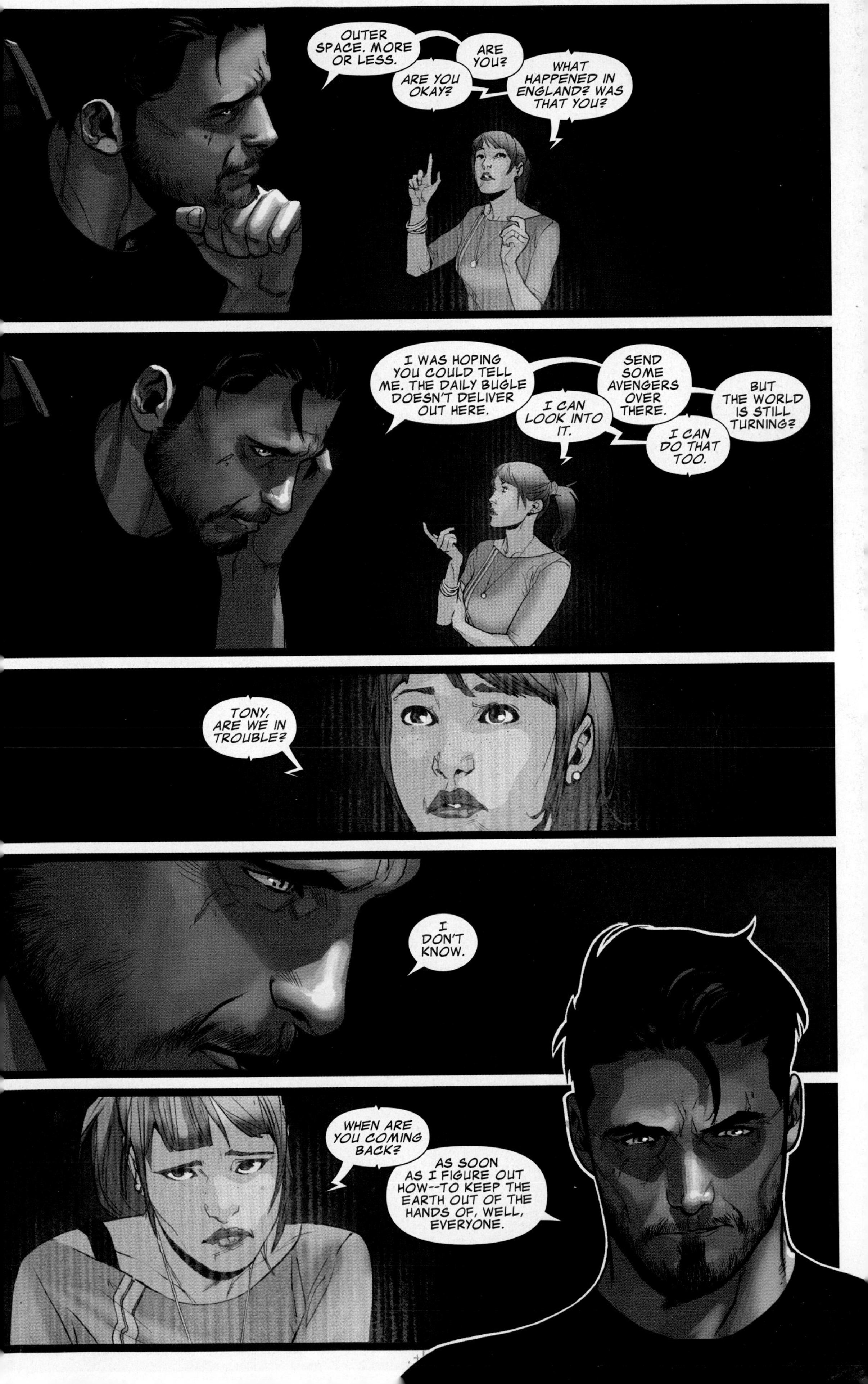

OUTER SPACE. MORE OR LESS.
ARE YOU?
ARE YOU OKAY?
WHAT HAPPENED IN ENGLAND? WAS THAT YOU?
I WAS HOPING YOU COULD TELL ME. THE DAILY BUGLE DOESN'T DELIVER OUT HERE.
I CAN LOOK INTO IT.
SEND SOME AVENGERS OVER THERE.
I CAN DO THAT TOO.
BUT THE WORLD IS STILL TURNING?
TONY, ARE WE IN TROUBLE?
I DON'T KNOW.
WHEN ARE YOU COMING BACK?
AS SOON AS I FIGURE OUT HOW--TO KEEP THE EARTH OUT OF THE HANDS OF, WELL, EVERYONE.

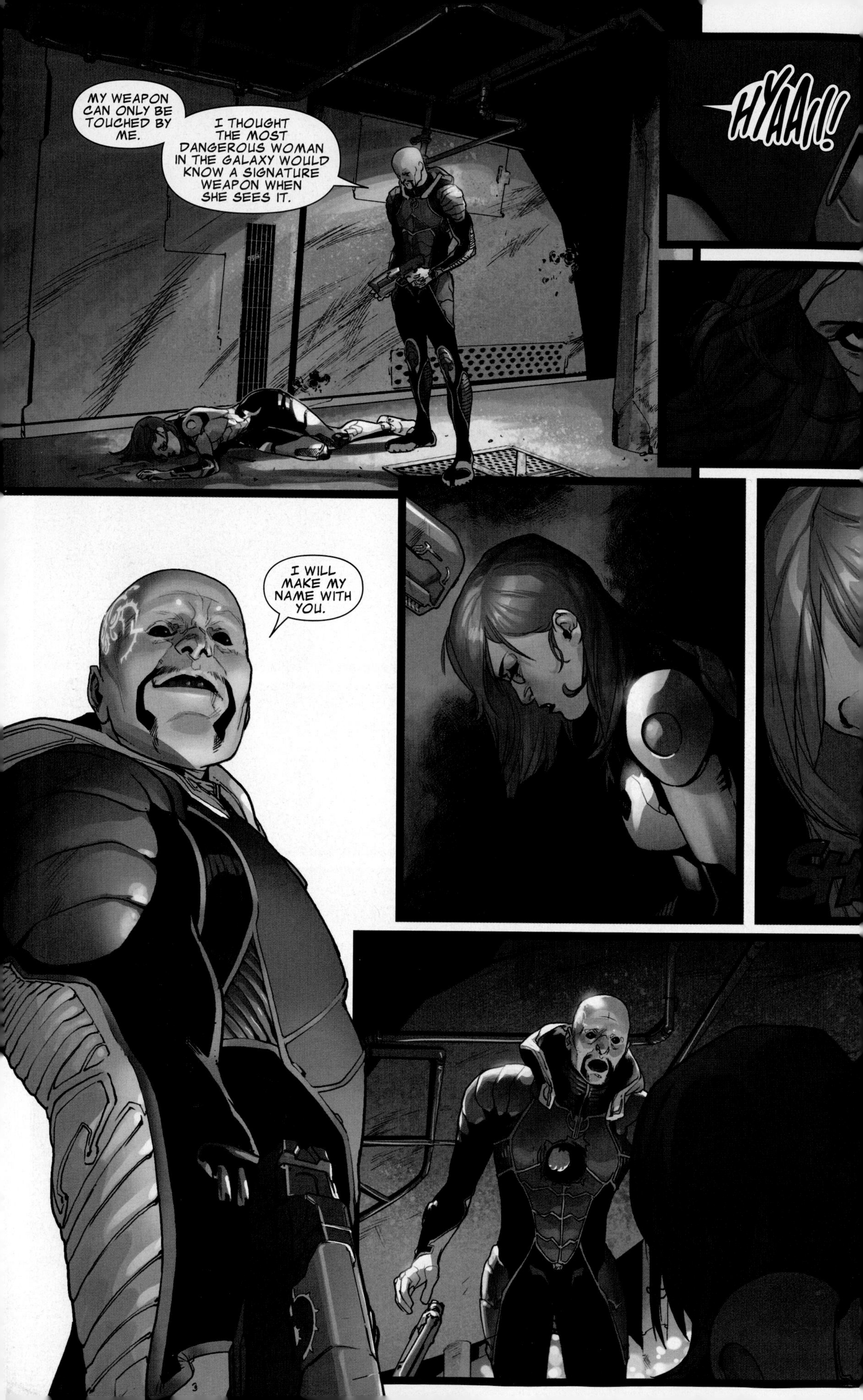
MY WEAPON CAN ONLY BE TOUCHED BY ME.
I THOUGHT THE MOST DANGEROUS WOMAN IN THE GALAXY WOULD KNOW A SIGNATURE WEAPON WHEN SHE SEES IT.
HYAAH!!
I WILL MAKE MY NAME WITH YOU.

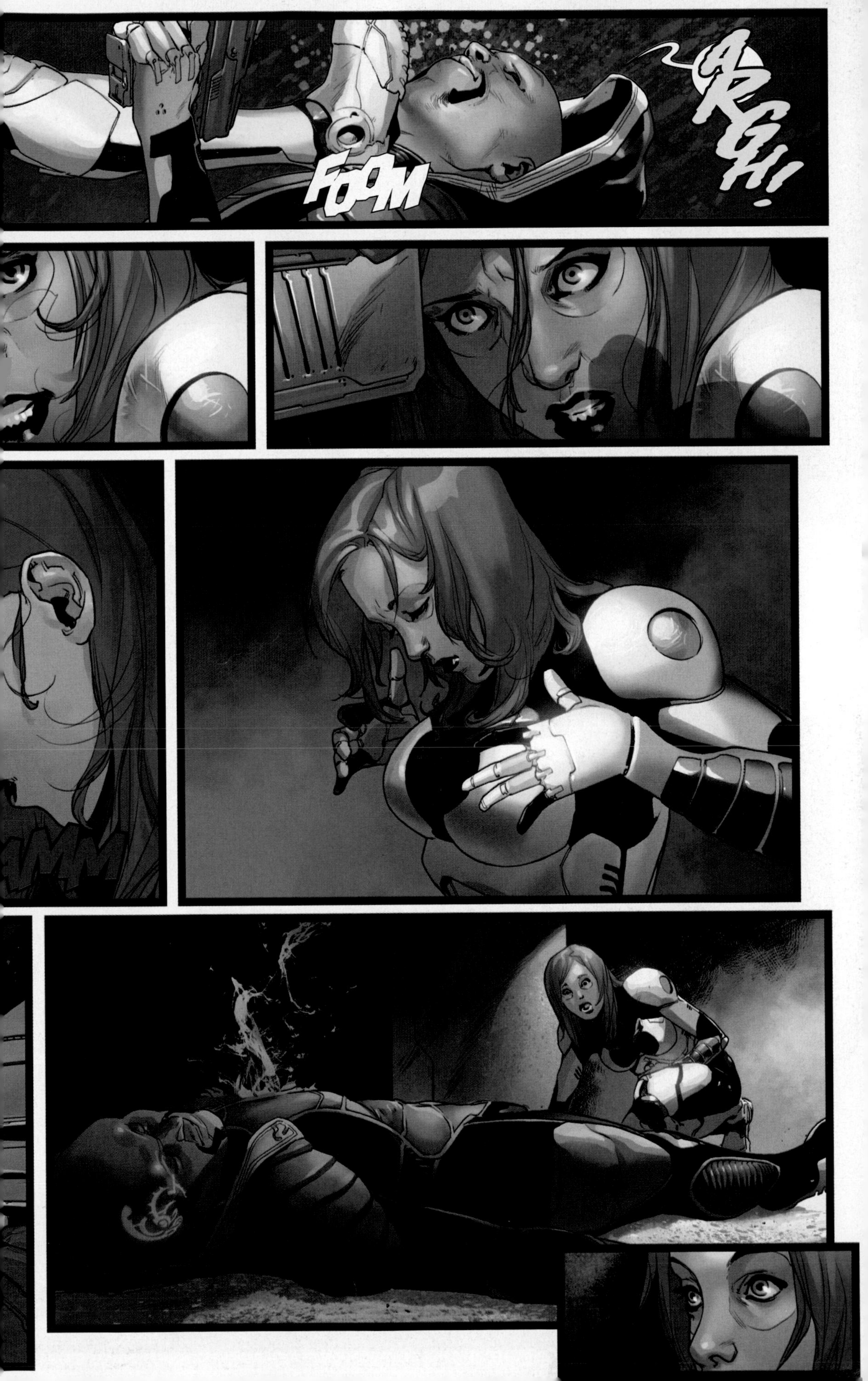
FOOM
ARGH!

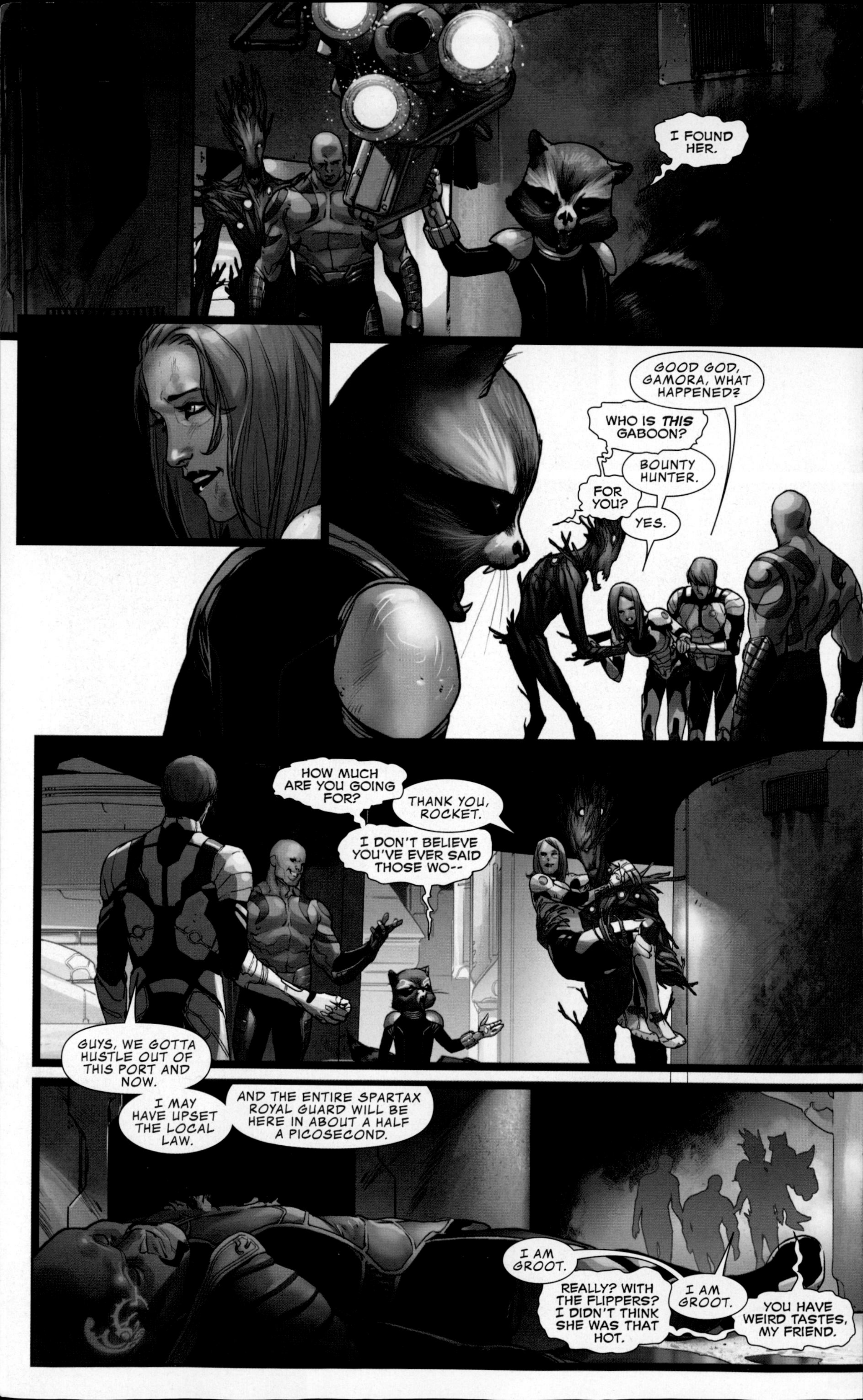
I FOUND HER.
GOOD GOD, GAMORA, WHAT HAPPENED?
WHO IS THIS GABOON?
BOUNTY HUNTER.
FOR YOU?
YES.
HOW MUCH ARE YOU GOING FOR?
THANK YOU, ROCKET.
I DON'T BELIEVE YOU'VE EVER SAID THOSE WO--
GUYS, WE GOTTA HUSTLE OUT OF THIS PORT AND NOW.
I MAY HAVE UPSET THE LOCAL LAW.
AND THE ENTIRE SPARTAX ROYAL GUARD WILL BE HERE IN ABOUT A HALF A PICOSECOND.
I AM GROOT.
REALLY? WITH THE FLIPPERS? I DIDN'T THINK SHE WAS THAT HOT.
I AM GROOT.
YOU HAVE WEIRD TASTES, MY FRIEND.

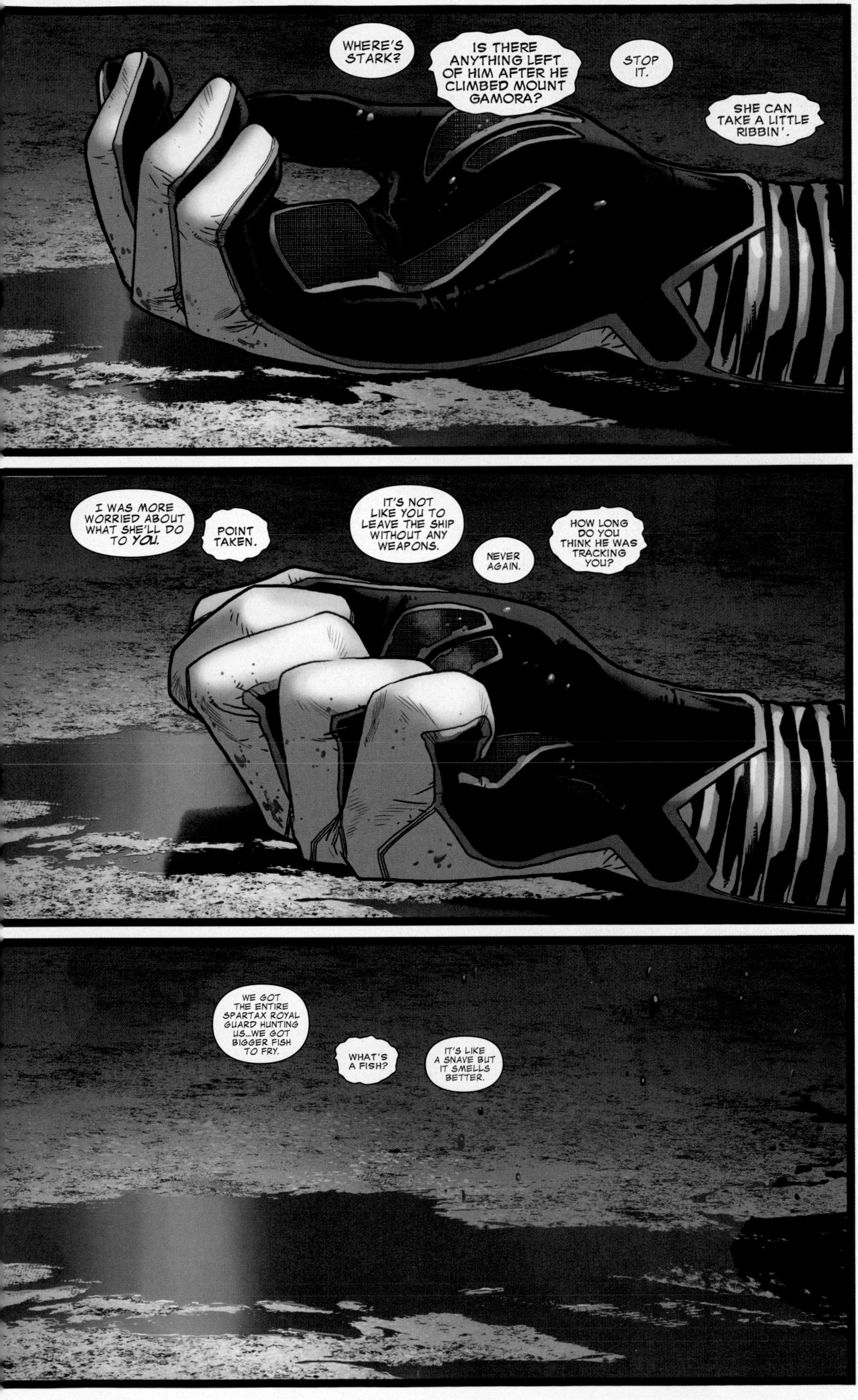
WHERE'S STARK?
IS THERE ANYTHING LEFT OF HIM AFTER HE CLIMBED MOUNT GAMORA?
STOP IT.
SHE CAN TAKE A LITTLE RIBBIN'.
I WAS MORE WORRIED ABOUT WHAT SHE'LL DO TO YOU.
POINT TAKEN.
IT'S NOT LIKE YOU TO LEAVE THE SHIP WITHOUT ANY WEAPONS.
NEVER AGAIN.
HOW LONG DO YOU THINK HE WAS TRACKING YOU?
WE GOT THE ENTIRE SPARTAX ROYAL GUARD HUNTING US...WE GOT BIGGER FISH TO FRY.
WHAT'S A FISH?
IT'S LIKE A SNAVE BUT IT SMELLS BETTER.

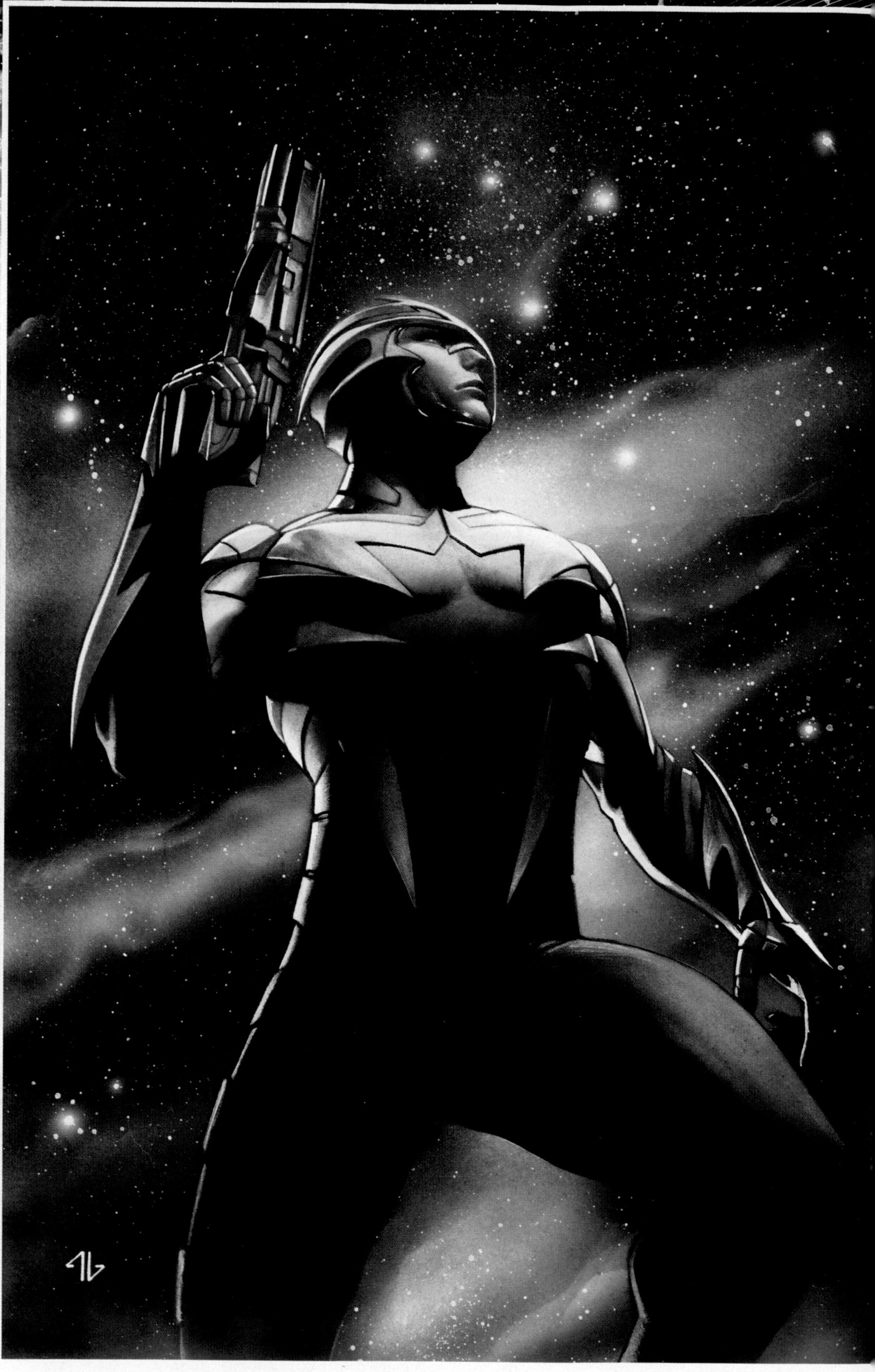

#4 VARIANT BY ADI GRANOV

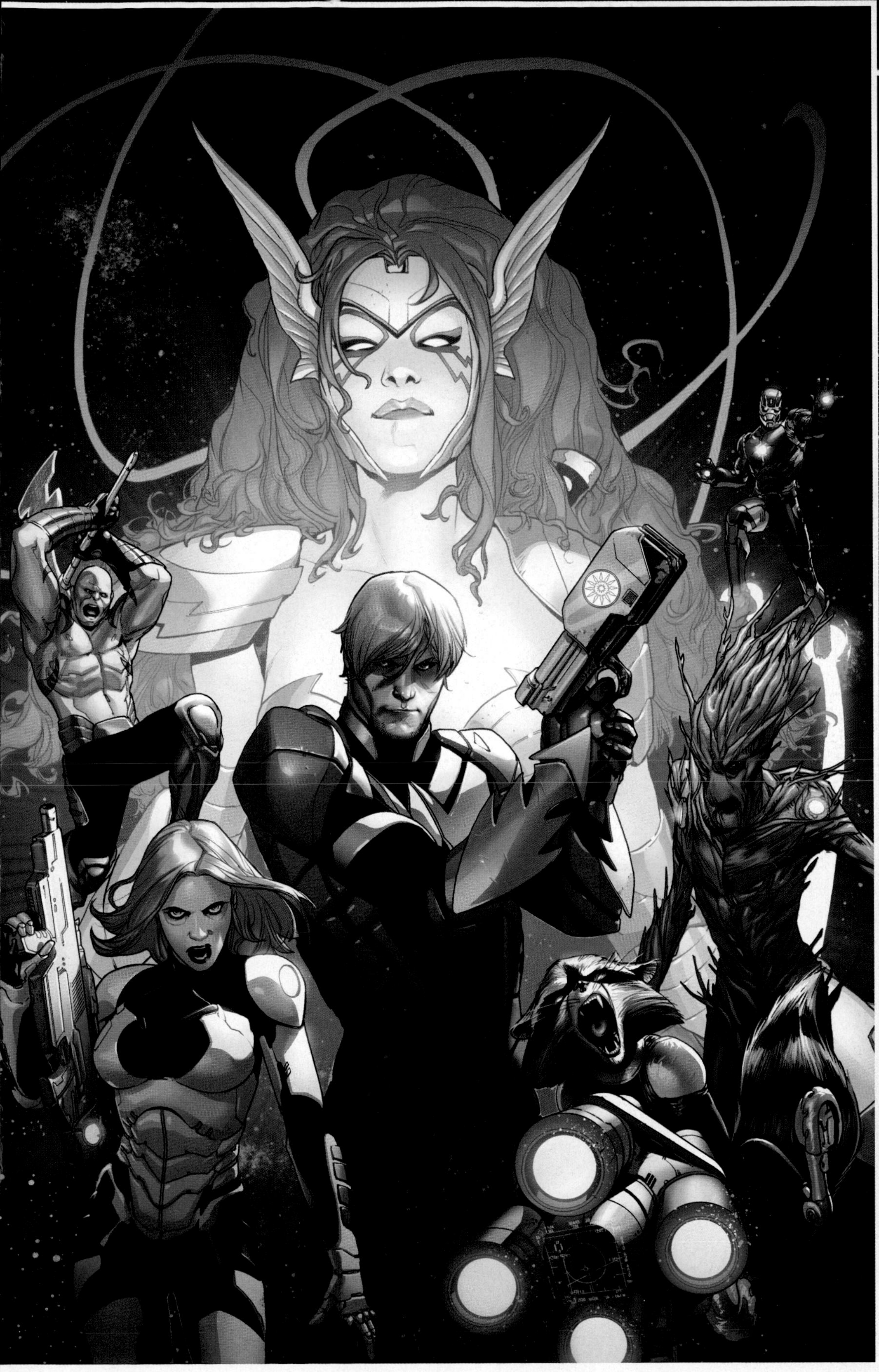

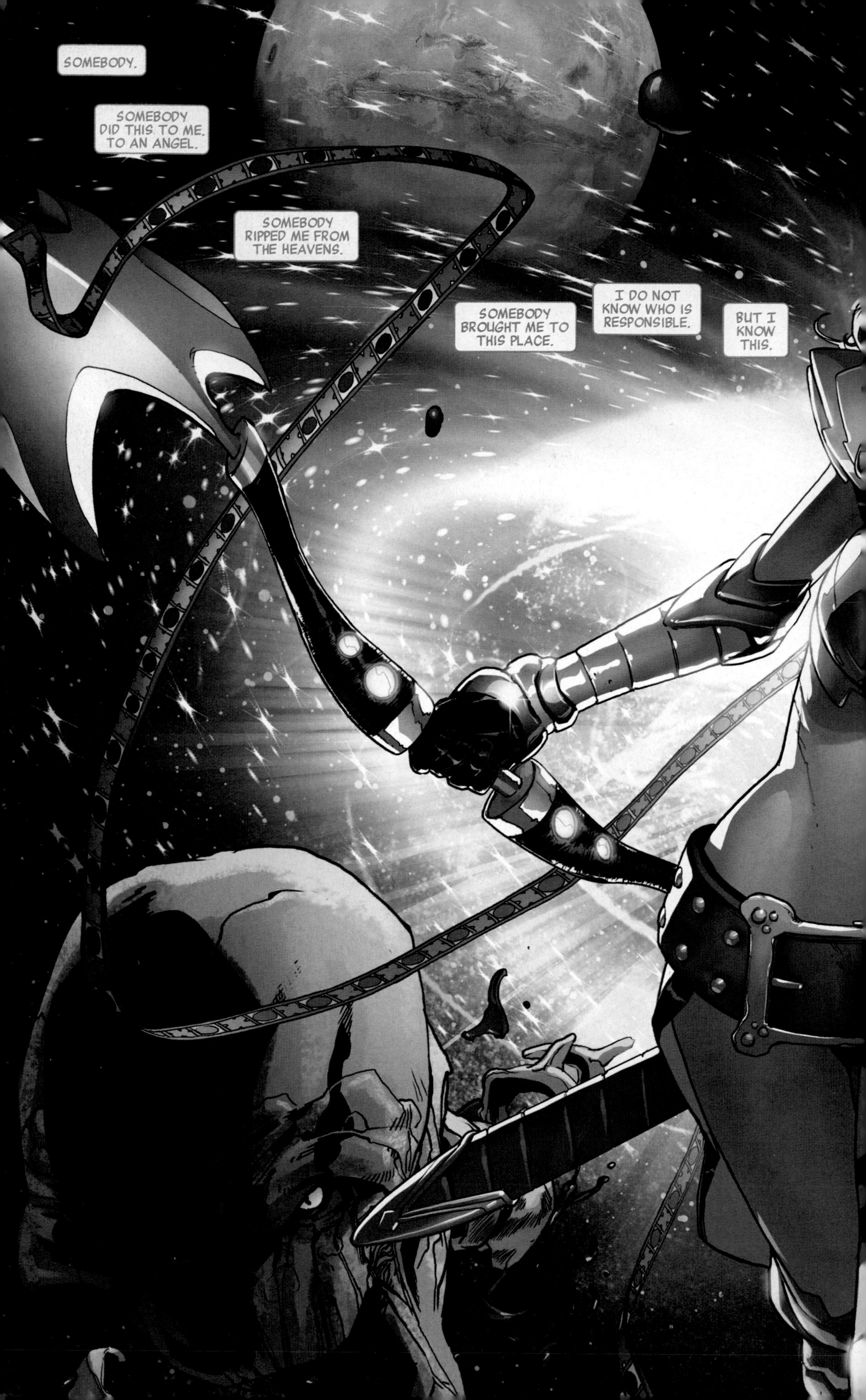
SOMEBODY.
SOMEBODY DID THIS TO ME. TO AN ANGEL.
SOMEBODY RIPPED ME FROM THE HEAVENS.
SOMEBODY BROUGHT ME TO THIS PLACE.
I DO NOT KNOW WHO IS RESPONSIBLE.
BUT I KNOW THIS.

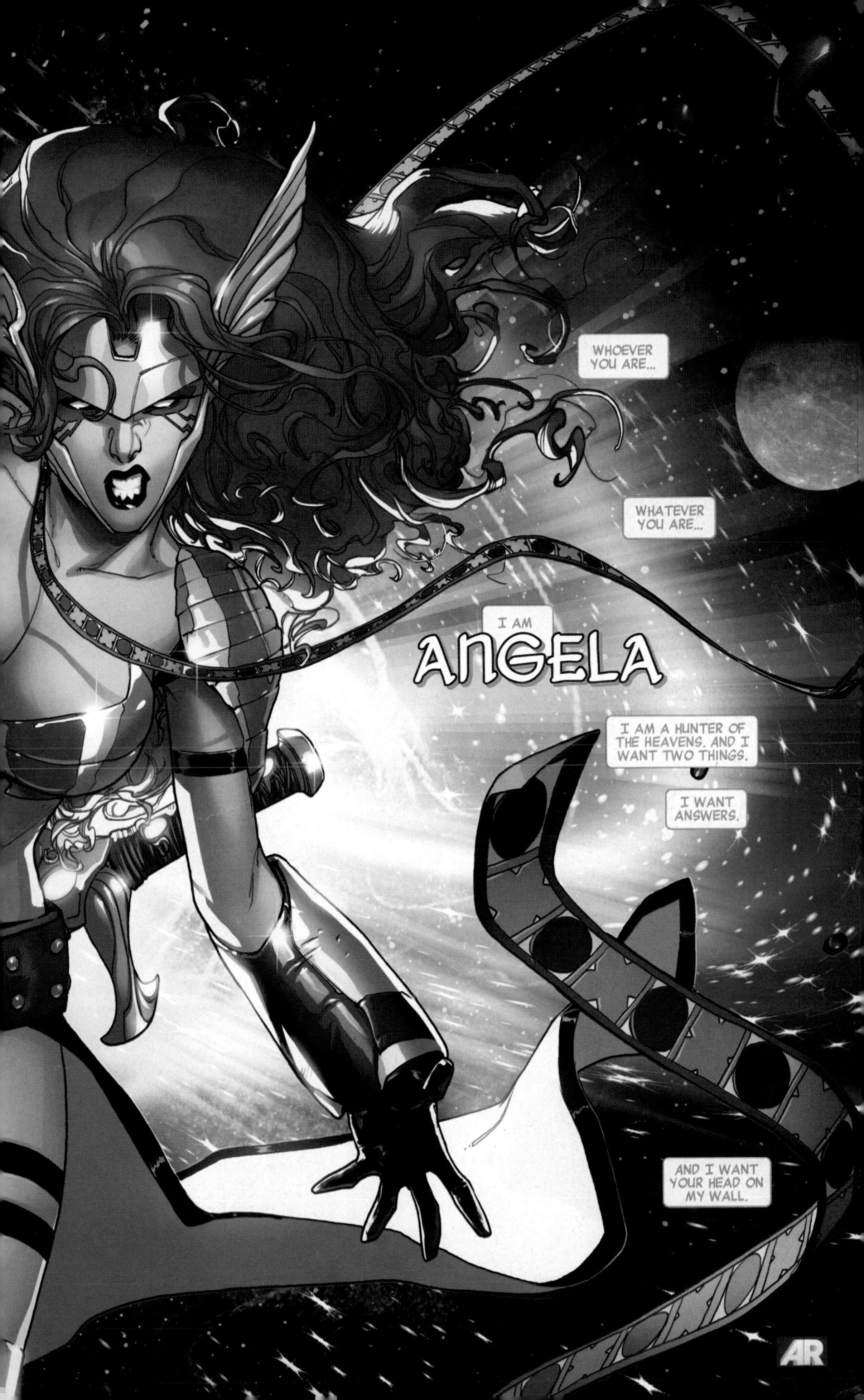
WHOEVER YOU ARE...
WHATEVER YOU ARE...
I AM
ANGELA
I AM A HUNTER OF THE HEAVENS. AND I WANT TWO THINGS.
I WANT ANSWERS.
AND I WANT YOUR HEAD ON MY WALL.
AR

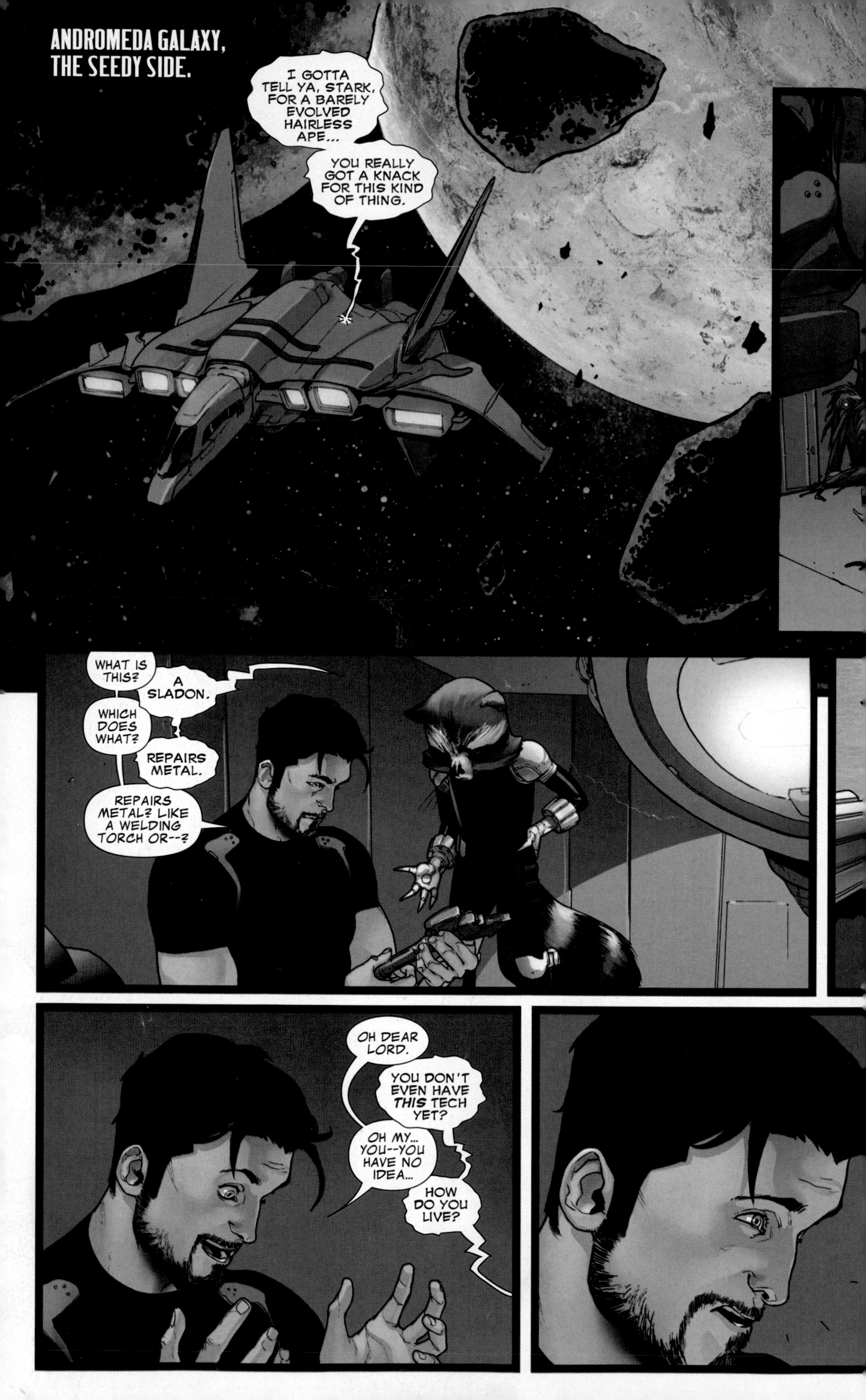
ANDROMEDA GALAXY, THE SEEDY SIDE.
I GOTTA TELL YA, STARK, FOR A BARELY EVOLVED HAIRLESS APE...
YOU REALLY GOT A KNACK FOR THIS KIND OF THING.
WHAT IS THIS?
A SLADON.
WHICH DOES WHAT?
REPAIRS METAL.
REPAIRS METAL? LIKE A WELDING TORCH OR--?
OH DEAR LORD.
YOU DON'T EVEN HAVE THIS TECH YET?
OH MY... YOU--YOU HAVE NO IDEA...
HOW DO YOU LIVE?

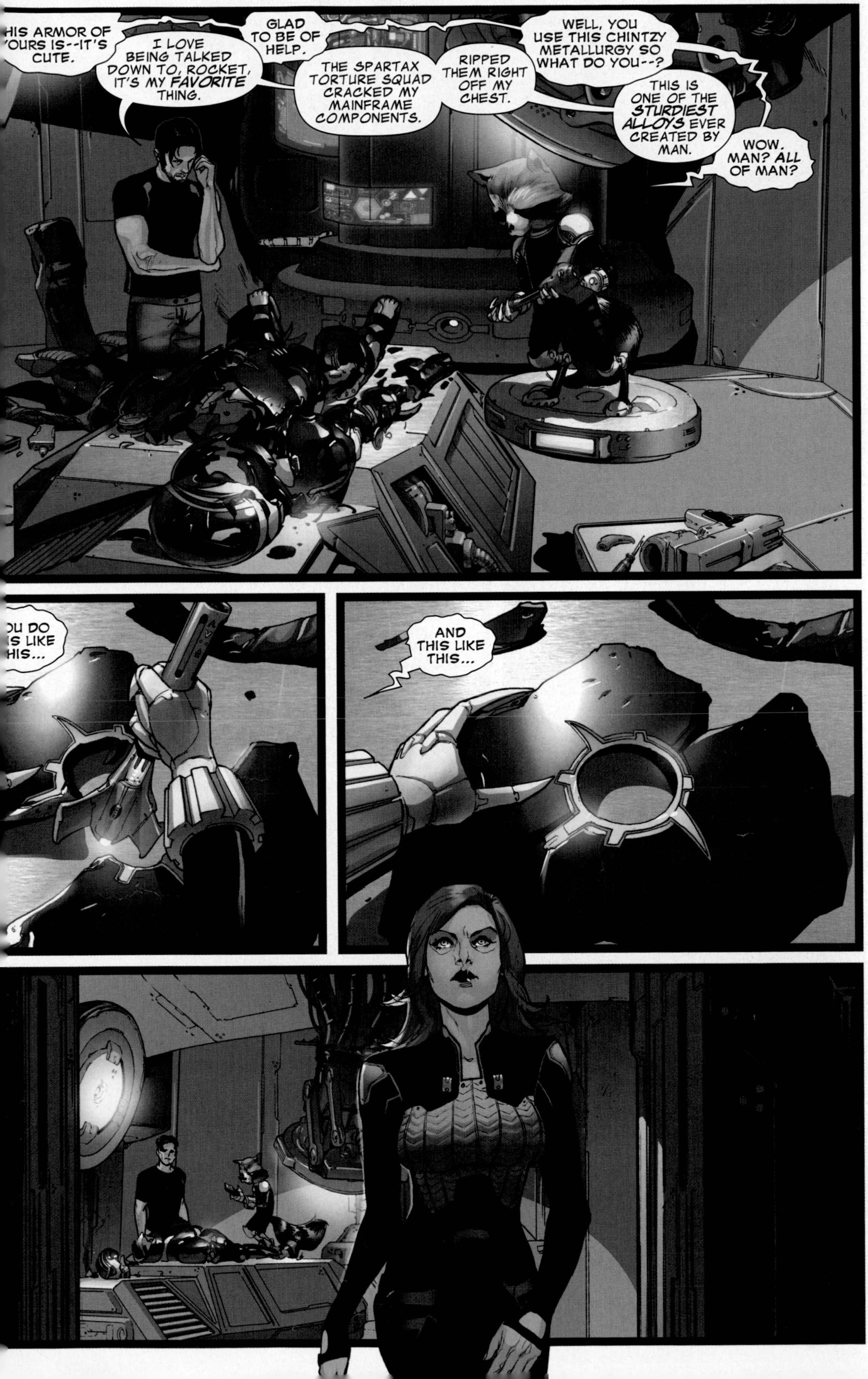
HIS ARMOR OF YOURS IS--IT'S CUTE.
I LOVE BEING TALKED DOWN TO, ROCKET, IT'S MY FAVORITE THING.
GLAD TO BE OF HELP.
THE SPARTAX TORTURE SQUAD CRACKED MY MAINFRAME COMPONENTS.
RIPPED THEM RIGHT OFF MY CHEST.
WELL, YOU USE THIS CHINTZY METALLURGY SO WHAT DO YOU--?
THIS IS ONE OF THE STURDIEST ALLOYS EVER CREATED BY MAN.
WOW. MAN? ALL OF MAN?
OU DO IS LIKE HIS...
AND THIS LIKE THIS...

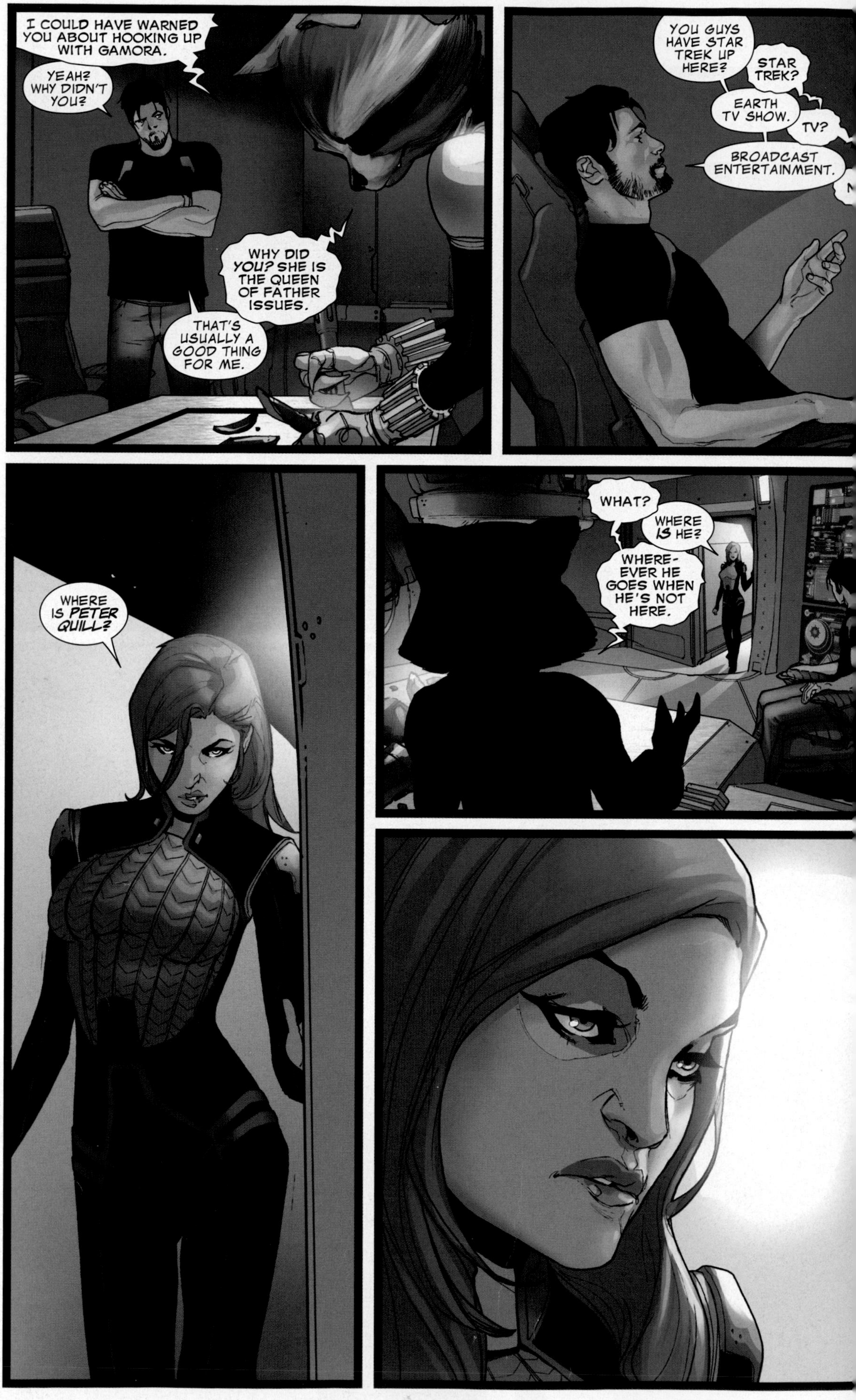
I COULD HAVE WARNED YOU ABOUT HOOKING UP WITH GAMORA.
YEAH? WHY DIDN'T YOU?
WHY DID *YOU?* SHE IS THE QUEEN OF FATHER ISSUES.
THAT'S USUALLY A GOOD THING FOR ME.
YOU GUYS HAVE STAR TREK UP HERE?
STAR TREK?
EARTH TV SHOW.
TV?
BROADCAST ENTERTAINMENT.
WHERE IS *PETER QUILL?*
WHAT?
WHERE *IS* HE?
WHERE-EVER HE GOES WHEN HE'S NOT HERE.

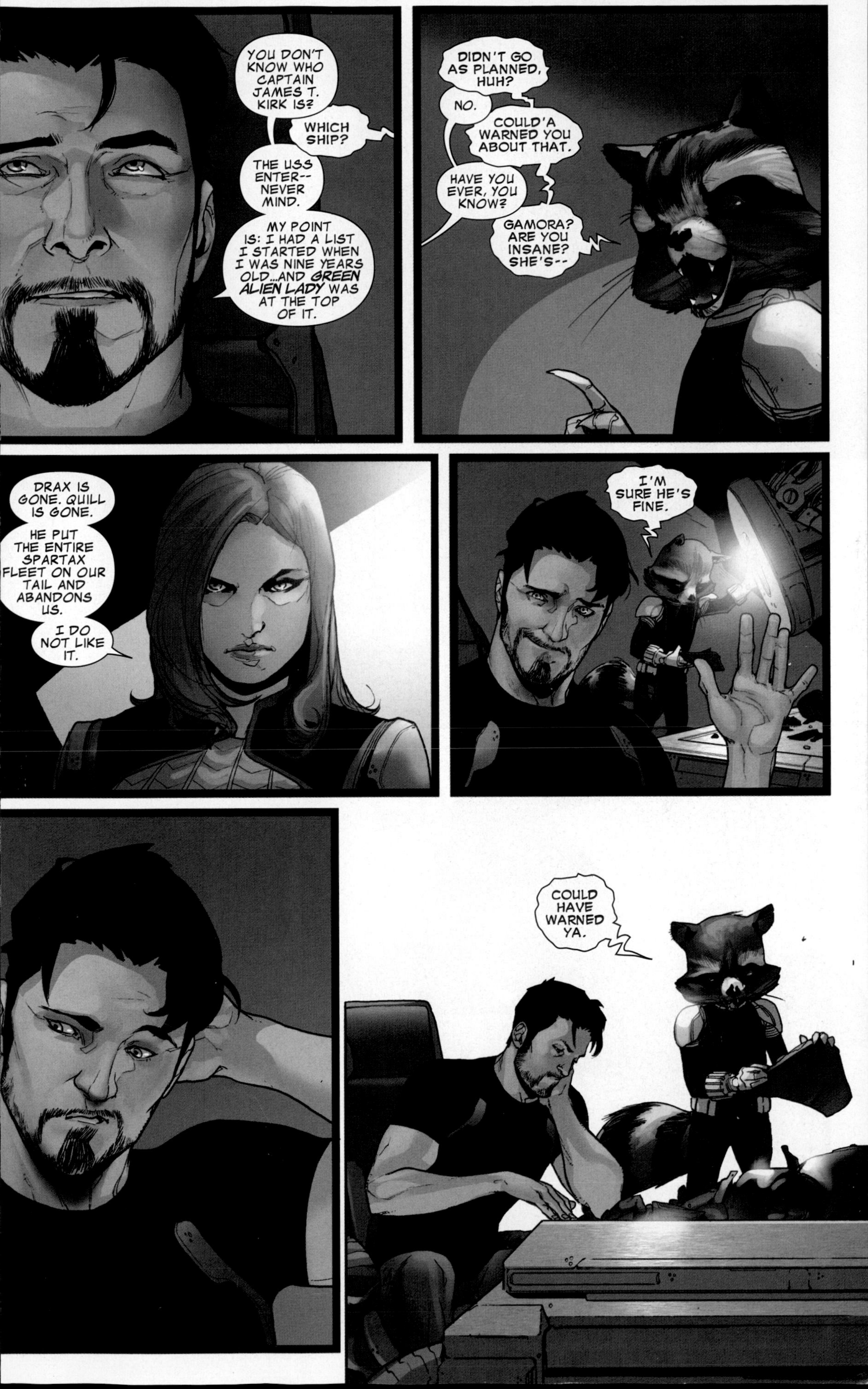
YOU DON'T KNOW WHO CAPTAIN JAMES T. KIRK IS?
WHICH SHIP?
THE USS ENTER-- NEVER MIND.
MY POINT IS: I HAD A LIST I STARTED WHEN I WAS NINE YEARS OLD...AND GREEN ALIEN LADY WAS AT THE TOP OF IT.
DIDN'T GO AS PLANNED, HUH?
NO.
COULD'A WARNED YOU ABOUT THAT.
HAVE YOU EVER, YOU KNOW?
GAMORA? ARE YOU INSANE? SHE'S--
DRAX IS GONE. QUILL IS GONE.
HE PUT THE ENTIRE SPARTAX FLEET ON OUR TAIL AND ABANDONS US.
I DO NOT LIKE IT.
I'M SURE HE'S FINE.
COULD HAVE WARNED YA.

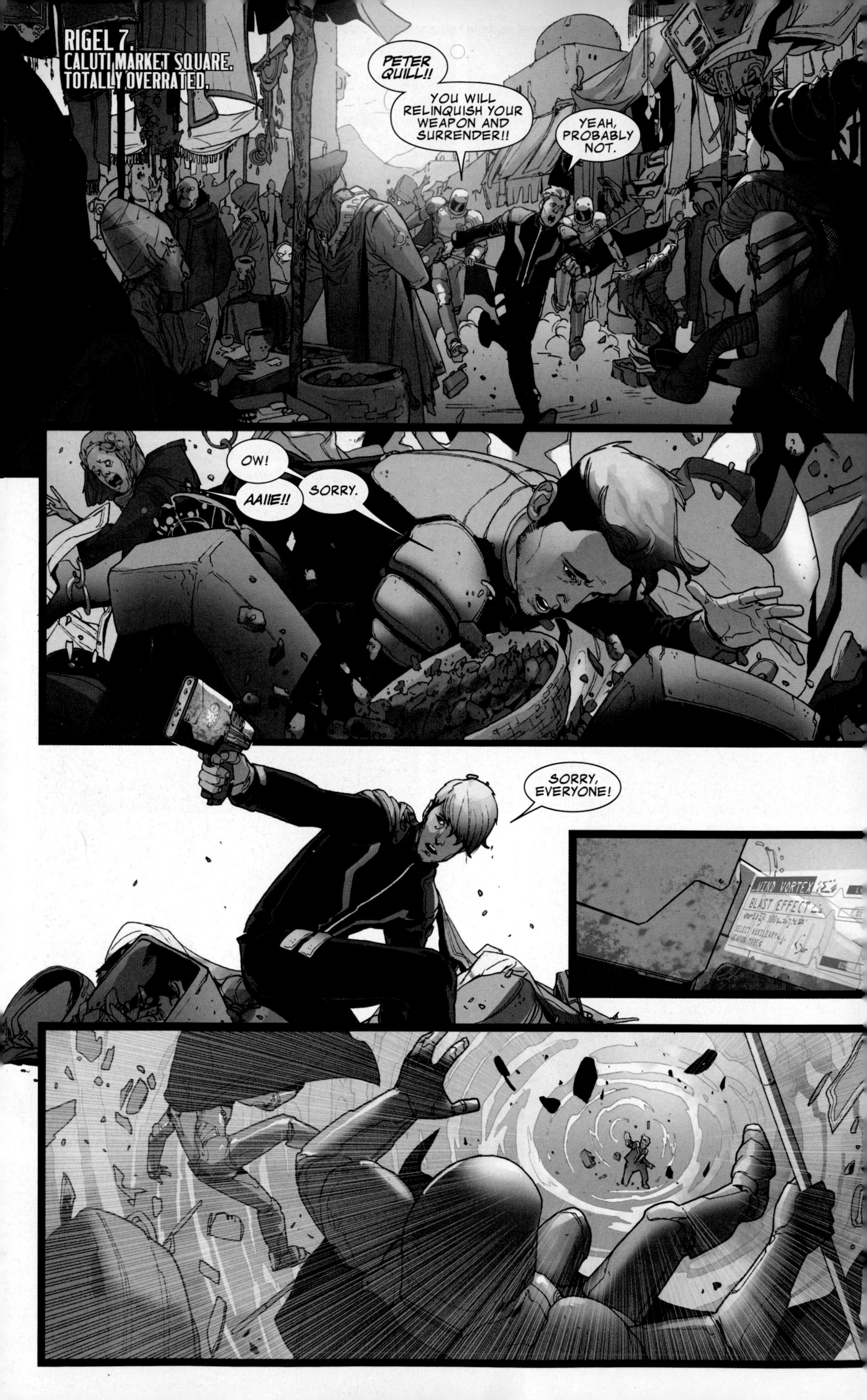
RIGEL 7.
CALUTI MARKET SQUARE.
TOTALLY OVERRATED.
PETER QUILL!!
YOU WILL RELINQUISH YOUR WEAPON AND SURRENDER!!
YEAH, PROBABLY NOT.
OW!
AAIIE!!
SORRY.
SORRY, EVERYONE!
WIND VORTEX
BLAST EFFECT

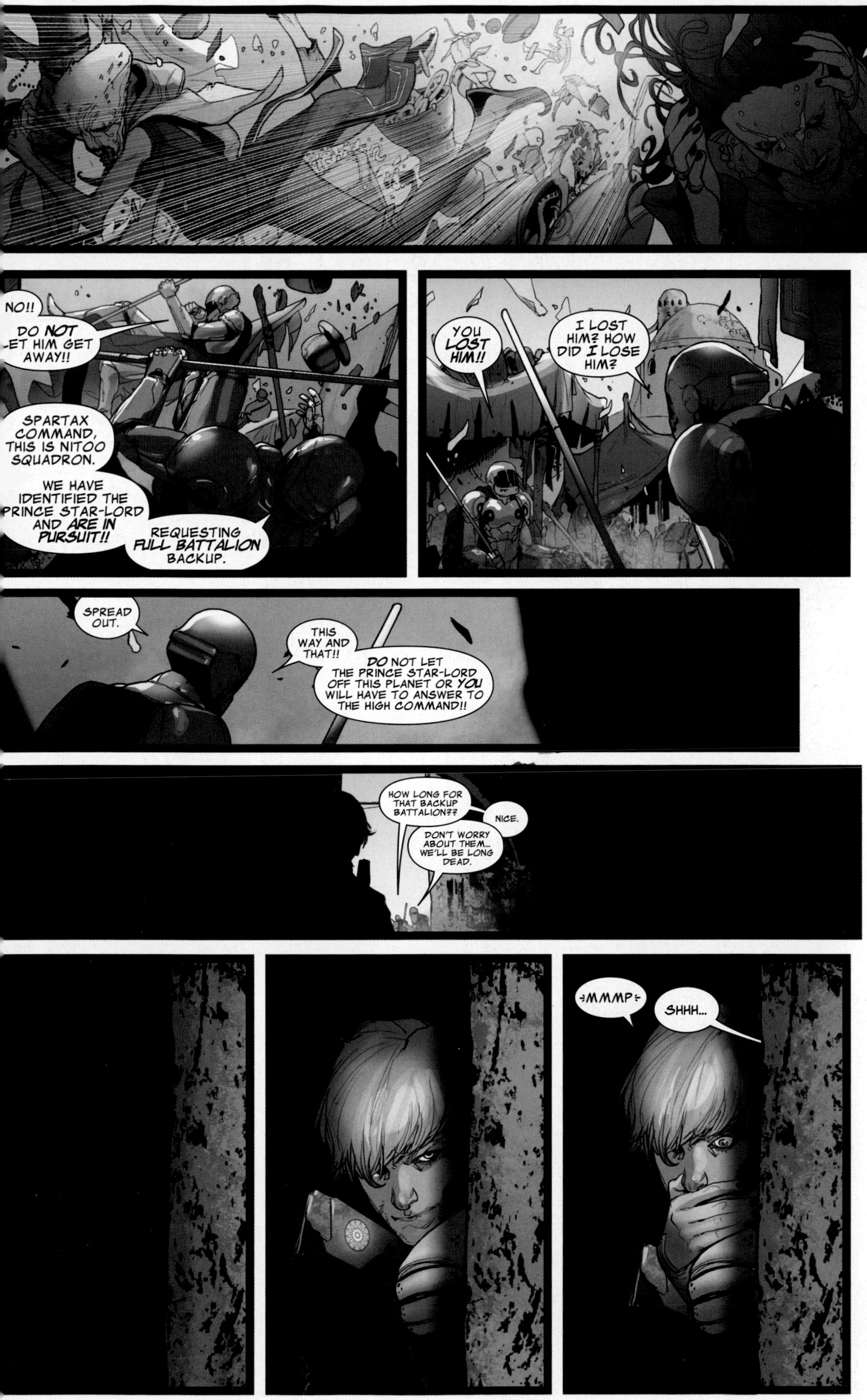
NO!!
DO NOT LET HIM GET AWAY!!
SPARTAX COMMAND, THIS IS NITOO SQUADRON.
WE HAVE IDENTIFIED THE PRINCE STAR-LORD AND ARE IN PURSUIT!!
REQUESTING FULL BATTALION BACKUP.
YOU LOST HIM!!
I LOST HIM? HOW DID I LOSE HIM?
SPREAD OUT.
THIS WAY AND THAT!!
DO NOT LET THE PRINCE STAR-LORD OFF THIS PLANET OR YOU WILL HAVE TO ANSWER TO THE HIGH COMMAND!!
HOW LONG FOR THAT BACKUP BATTALION??
NICE.
DON'T WORRY ABOUT THEM... WE'LL BE LONG DEAD.
MMMP
SHHH...

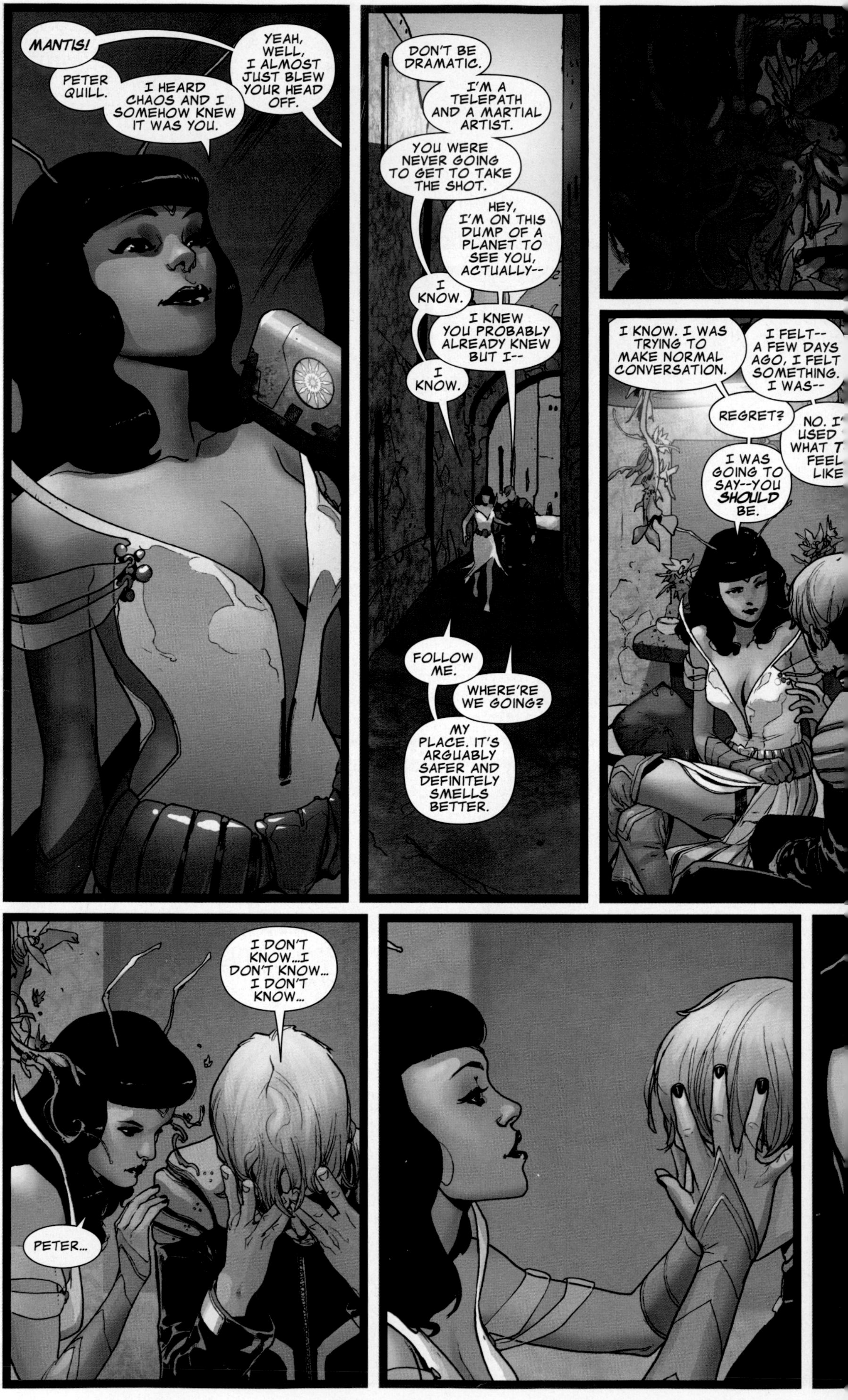
MANTIS!
PETER QUILL.
I HEARD CHAOS AND I SOMEHOW KNEW IT WAS YOU.
YEAH, WELL, I ALMOST JUST BLEW YOUR HEAD OFF.
DON'T BE DRAMATIC.
I'M A TELEPATH AND A MARTIAL ARTIST.
YOU WERE NEVER GOING TO GET TO TAKE THE SHOT.
HEY, I'M ON THIS DUMP OF A PLANET TO SEE YOU, ACTUALLY--
I KNOW.
I KNEW YOU PROBABLY ALREADY KNEW BUT I--
I KNOW.
FOLLOW ME.
WHERE'RE WE GOING?
MY PLACE. IT'S ARGUABLY SAFER AND DEFINITELY SMELLS BETTER.
I KNOW. I WAS TRYING TO MAKE NORMAL CONVERSATION.
I FELT-- A FEW DAYS AGO, I FELT SOMETHING. I WAS--
REGRET?
I WAS GOING TO SAY--YOU SHOULD BE.
I DON'T KNOW...I DON'T KNOW... I DON'T KNOW...
PETER...

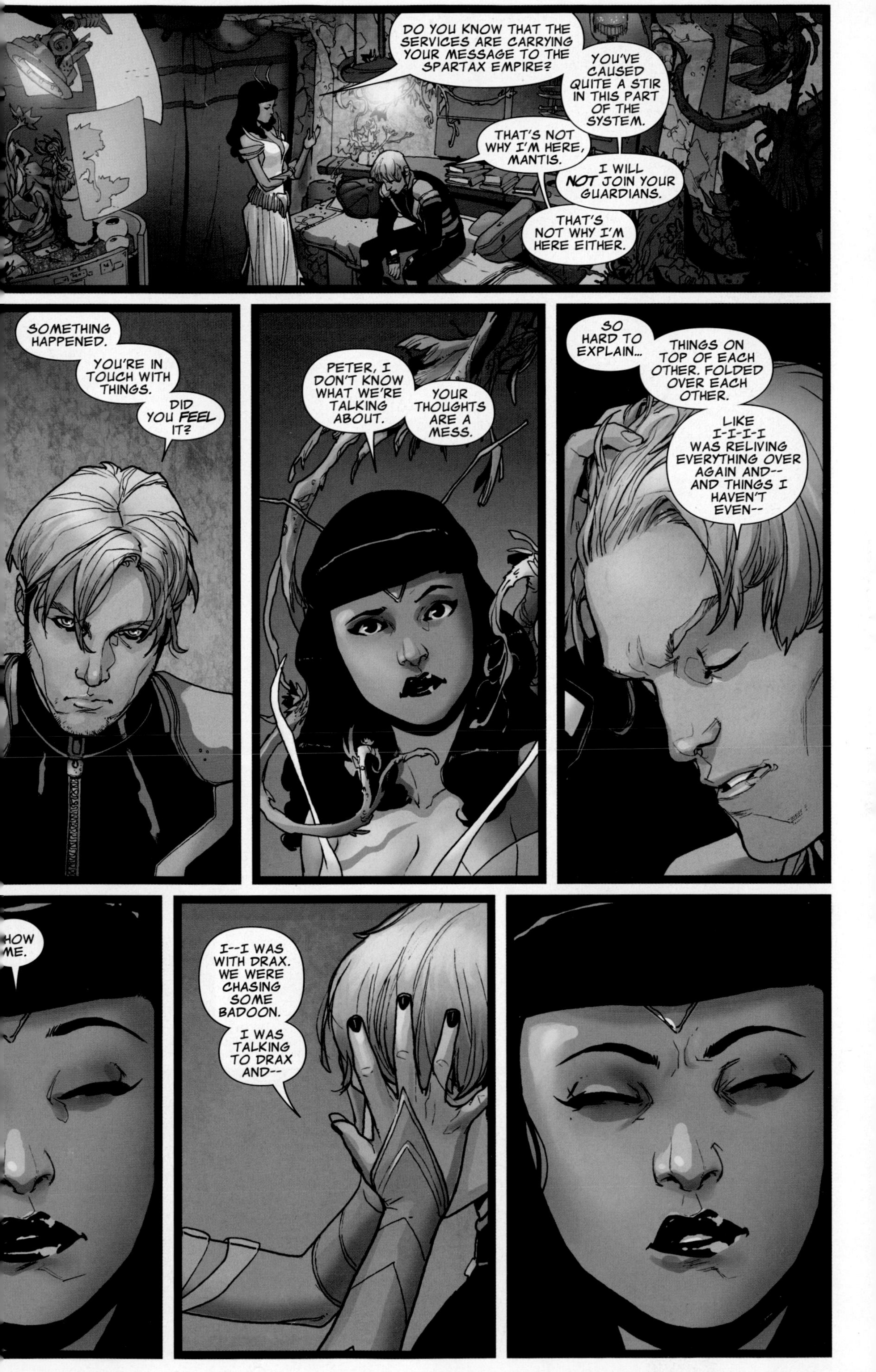

DO YOU KNOW THAT THE SERVICES ARE CARRYING YOUR MESSAGE TO THE SPARTAX EMPIRE?
YOU'VE CAUSED QUITE A STIR IN THIS PART OF THE SYSTEM.
THAT'S NOT WHY I'M HERE, MANTIS.
I WILL *NOT* JOIN YOUR GUARDIANS.
THAT'S NOT WHY I'M HERE EITHER.
SOMETHING HAPPENED.
YOU'RE IN TOUCH WITH THINGS.
DID YOU *FEEL* IT?
PETER, I DON'T KNOW WHAT WE'RE TALKING ABOUT.
YOUR THOUGHTS ARE A MESS.
SO HARD TO EXPLAIN...
THINGS ON TOP OF EACH OTHER. FOLDED OVER EACH OTHER.
LIKE I-I-I-I WAS RELIVING EVERYTHING OVER AGAIN AND-- AND THINGS I HAVEN'T EVEN--
HOW ME.
I--I WAS WITH DRAX. WE WERE CHASING SOME BADOON.
I WAS TALKING TO DRAX AND--

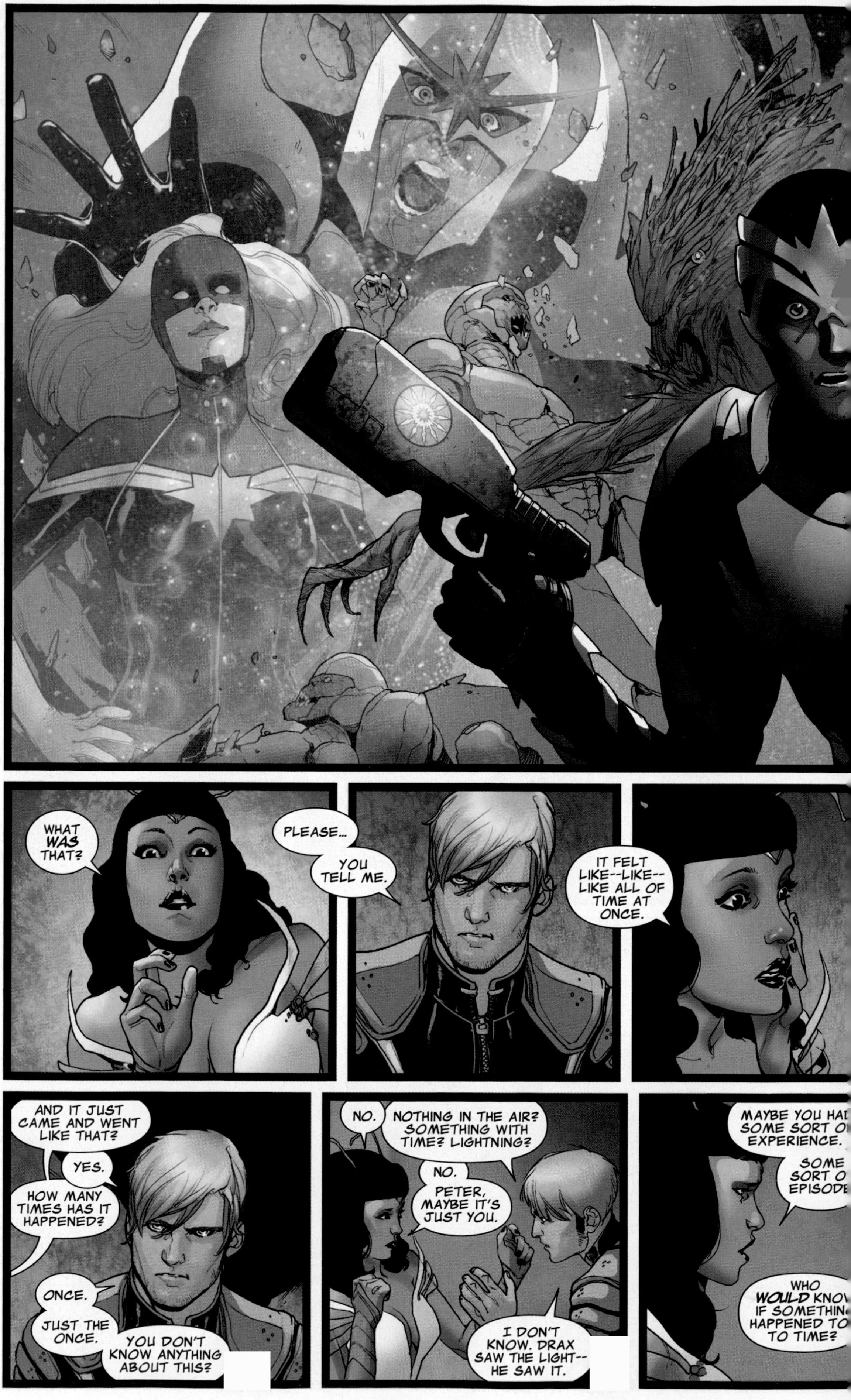
WHAT WAS THAT?
PLEASE...
YOU TELL ME.
IT FELT LIKE--LIKE--LIKE ALL OF TIME AT ONCE.
AND IT JUST CAME AND WENT LIKE THAT?
YES.
HOW MANY TIMES HAS IT HAPPENED?
ONCE.
JUST THE ONCE.
YOU DON'T KNOW ANYTHING ABOUT THIS?
NO.
NOTHING IN THE AIR? SOMETHING WITH TIME? LIGHTNING?
NO.
PETER, MAYBE IT'S JUST YOU.
I DON'T KNOW. DRAX SAW THE LIGHT-- HE SAW IT.
MAYBE YOU HAD SOME SORT OF EXPERIENCE.
SOME SORT OF EPISODE.
WHO WOULD KNOW IF SOMETHING HAPPENED TO-- TO TIME?

WHEN--**WHEN** DID THIS HAPPEN?

JUST, JUST A COUPLE OF DAYS AGO.

THERE WAS THIS--LIKE THIS LIGHTNING AND THEN--

THAT WAS THE ODDEST THING.

ALL TIME-- YES.

ODD??!! IT'S FREAKING ME OUT.

AND--AND IT DIDN'T HAPPEN TO ANYONE **BUT** ME!!

DRAX SAW THE--THE LIGHTNING BUT-- HE'S FINE.

WELL, FOR DRAX HE'S FINE.

WHO CAN I...?

OH.

IF YOU WANT TO OPEN THAT DOOR.

IF IT'S BOTHERING YOU **THAT** MUCH.

YOU KNOW EXACTLY WHO WOULD KNOW.

IF THE SPACE-TIME CONTINUUM HAD A HICCUP OR--OR IF SOMETHING WAS OFF.

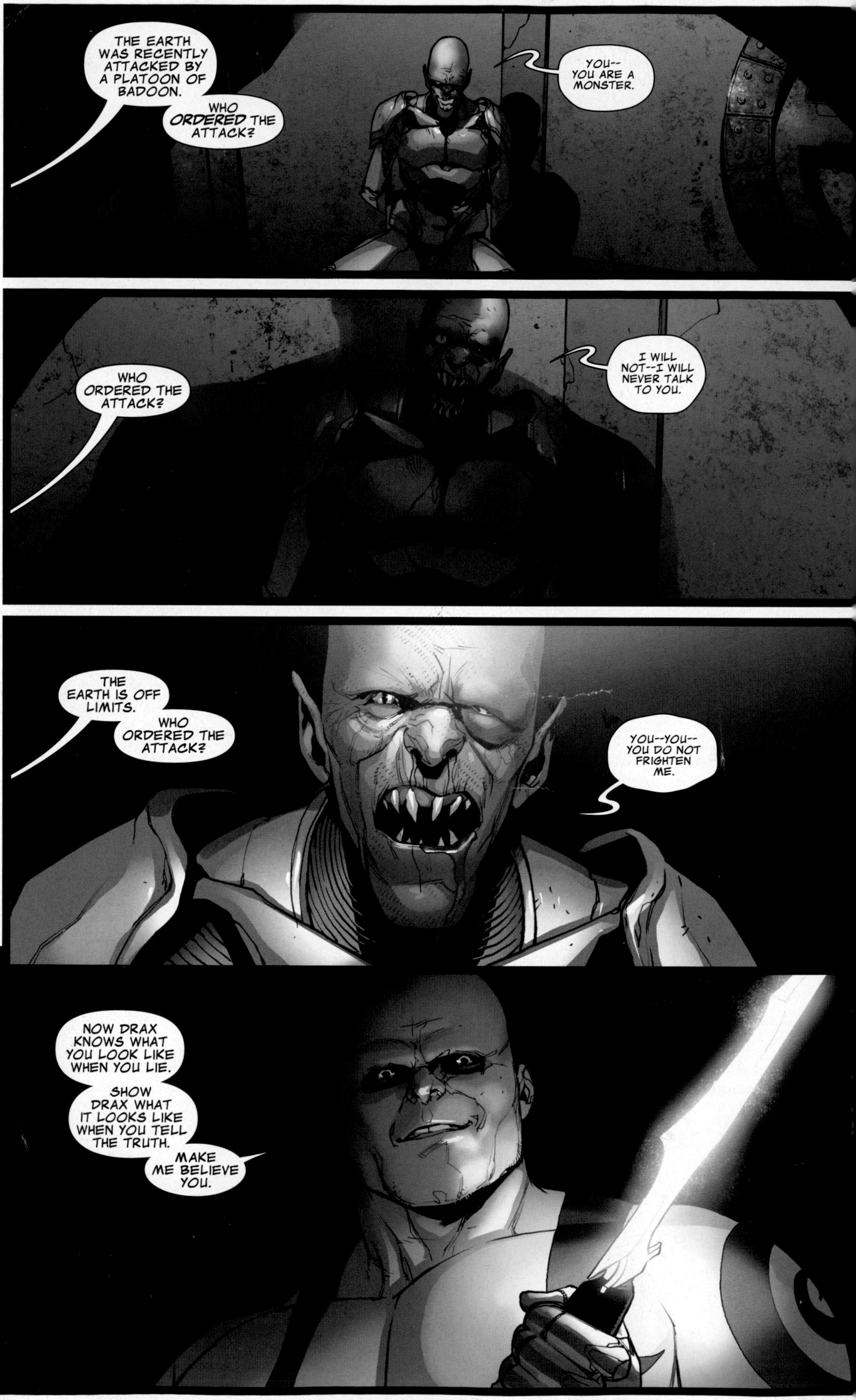
THE EARTH WAS RECENTLY ATTACKED BY A PLATOON OF BADOON.
WHO ORDERED THE ATTACK?
YOU-- YOU ARE A MONSTER.
WHO ORDERED THE ATTACK?
I WILL NOT--I WILL NEVER TALK TO YOU.
THE EARTH IS OFF LIMITS.
WHO ORDERED THE ATTACK?
YOU--YOU-- YOU DO NOT FRIGHTEN ME.
NOW DRAX KNOWS WHAT YOU LOOK LIKE WHEN YOU LIE.
SHOW DRAX WHAT IT LOOKS LIKE WHEN YOU TELL THE TRUTH.
MAKE ME BELIEVE YOU.

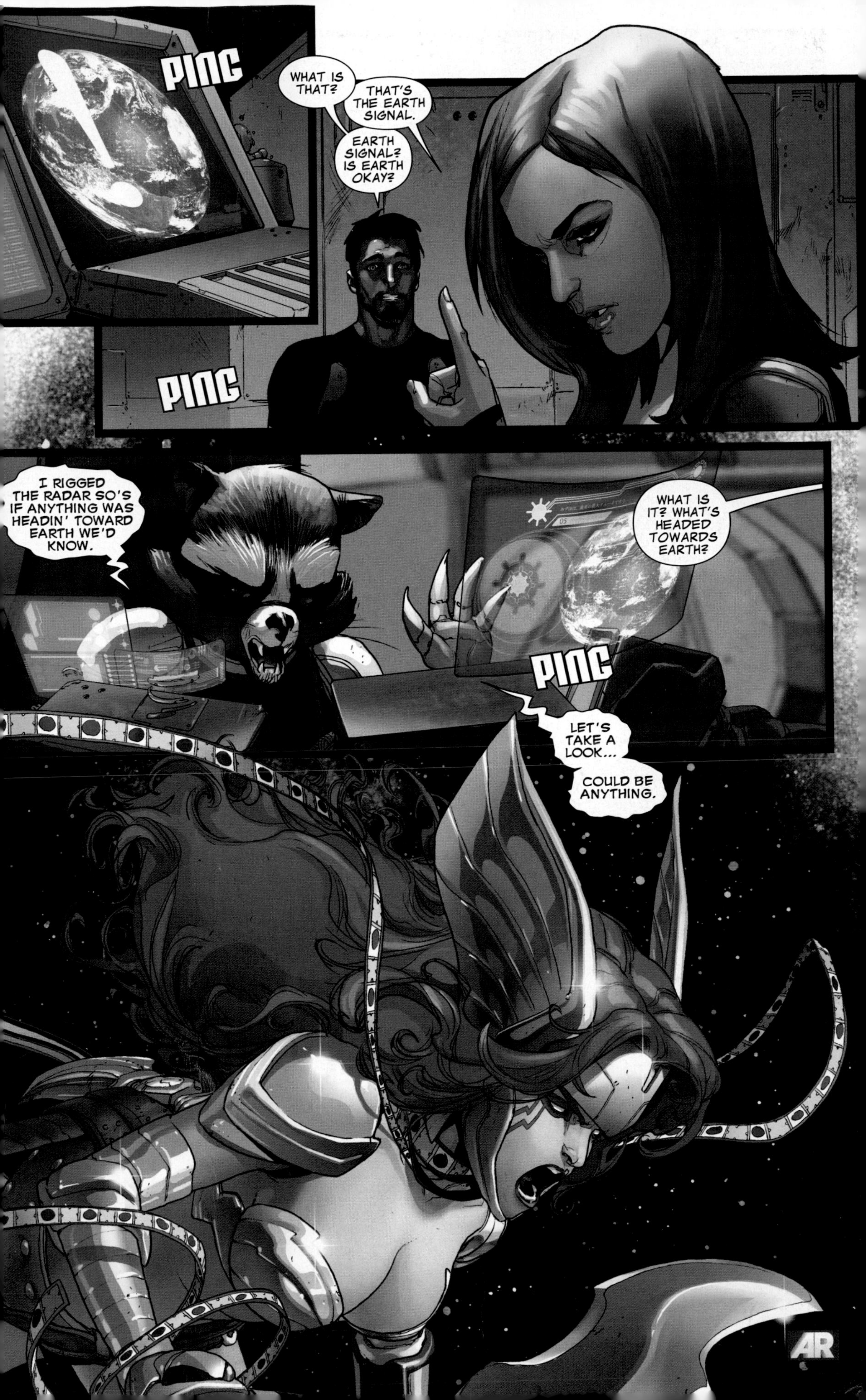
PING
WHAT IS THAT?
THAT'S THE EARTH SIGNAL.
EARTH SIGNAL? IS EARTH OKAY?
PING
I RIGGED THE RADAR SO'S IF ANYTHING WAS HEADIN' TOWARD EARTH WE'D KNOW.
WHAT IS IT? WHAT'S HEADED TOWARDS EARTH?
PING
LET'S TAKE A LOOK...
COULD BE ANYTHING.

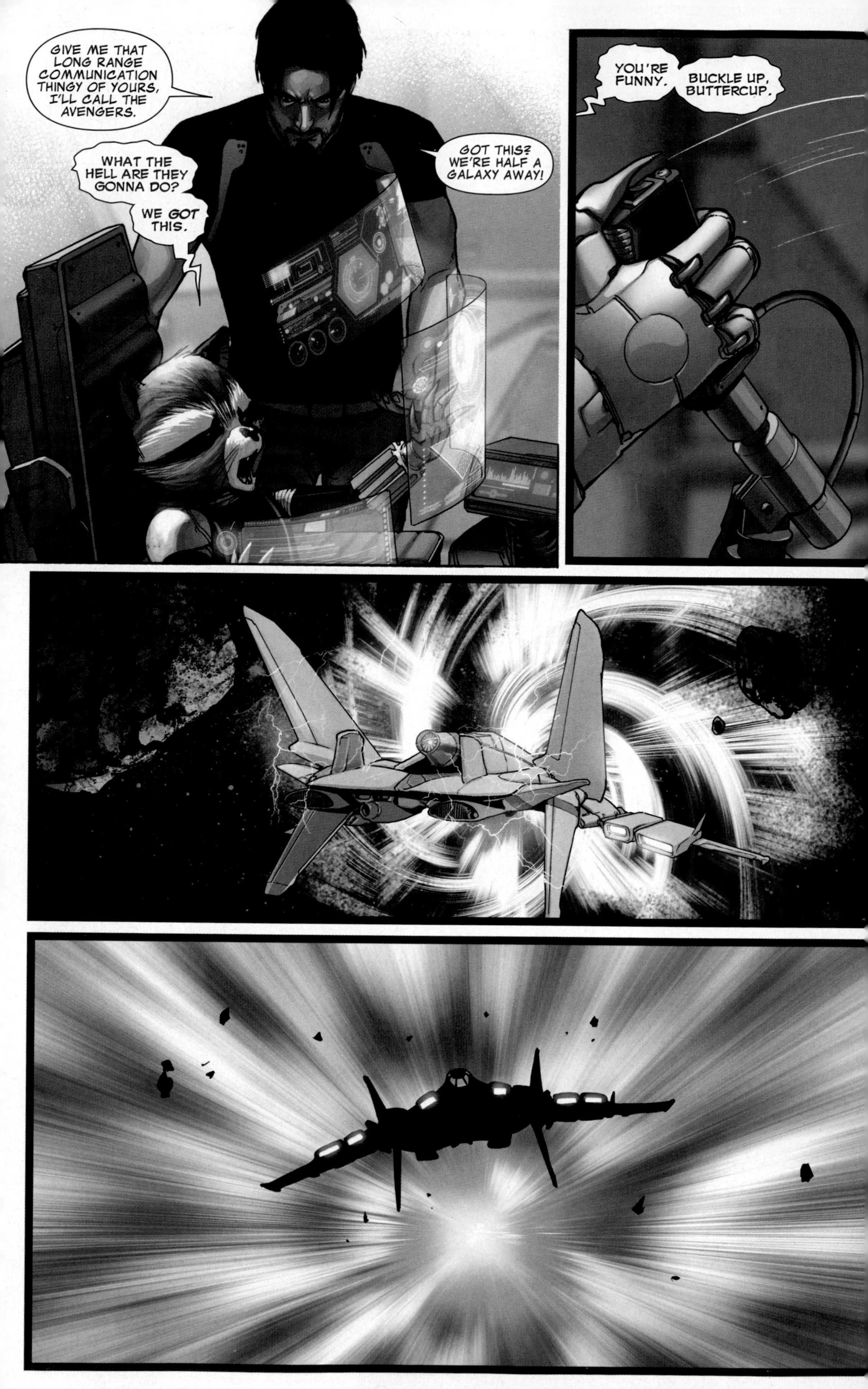
GIVE ME THAT LONG RANGE COMMUNICATION THINGY OF YOURS, I'LL CALL THE AVENGERS.
WHAT THE HELL ARE THEY GONNA DO?
WE GOT THIS.
GOT THIS? WE'RE HALF A GALAXY AWAY!
YOU'RE FUNNY.
BUCKLE UP, BUTTERCUP.

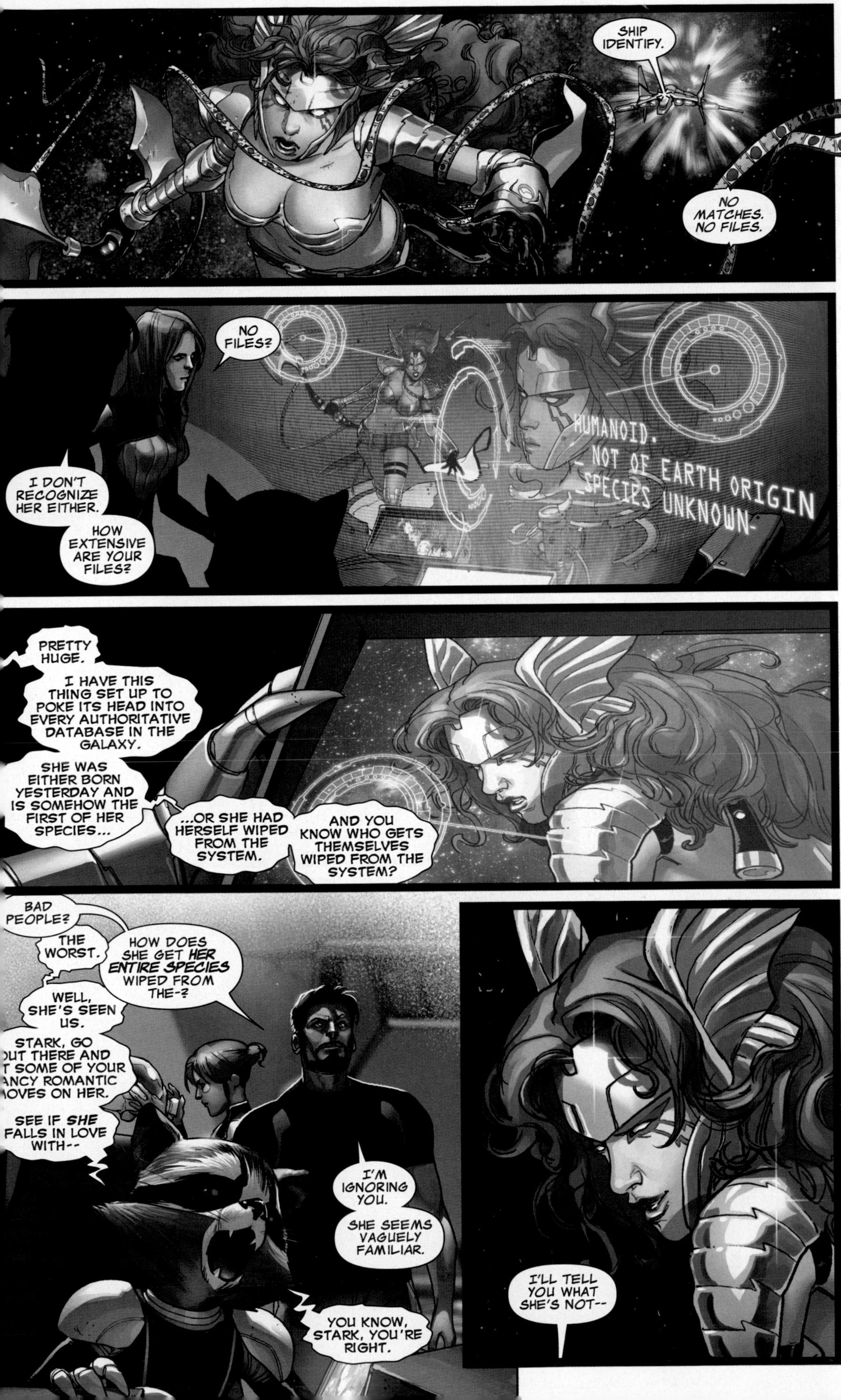
SHIP IDENTIFY.
NO MATCHES. NO FILES.
NO FILES?
HUMANOID.
- NOT OF EARTH ORIGIN
- SPECIES UNKNOWN-
I DON'T RECOGNIZE HER EITHER.
HOW EXTENSIVE ARE YOUR FILES?
PRETTY HUGE.
I HAVE THIS THING SET UP TO POKE ITS HEAD INTO EVERY AUTHORITATIVE DATABASE IN THE GALAXY.
SHE WAS EITHER BORN YESTERDAY AND IS SOMEHOW THE FIRST OF HER SPECIES...
...OR SHE HAD HERSELF WIPED FROM THE SYSTEM.
AND YOU KNOW WHO GETS THEMSELVES WIPED FROM THE SYSTEM?
BAD PEOPLE?
THE WORST.
HOW DOES SHE GET HER ENTIRE SPECIES WIPED FROM THE-?
WELL, SHE'S SEEN US.
SEE IF SHE FALLS IN LOVE WITH--
I'M IGNORING YOU.
SHE SEEMS VAGUELY FAMILIAR.
YOU KNOW, STARK, YOU'RE RIGHT.
I'LL TELL YOU WHAT SHE'S NOT--

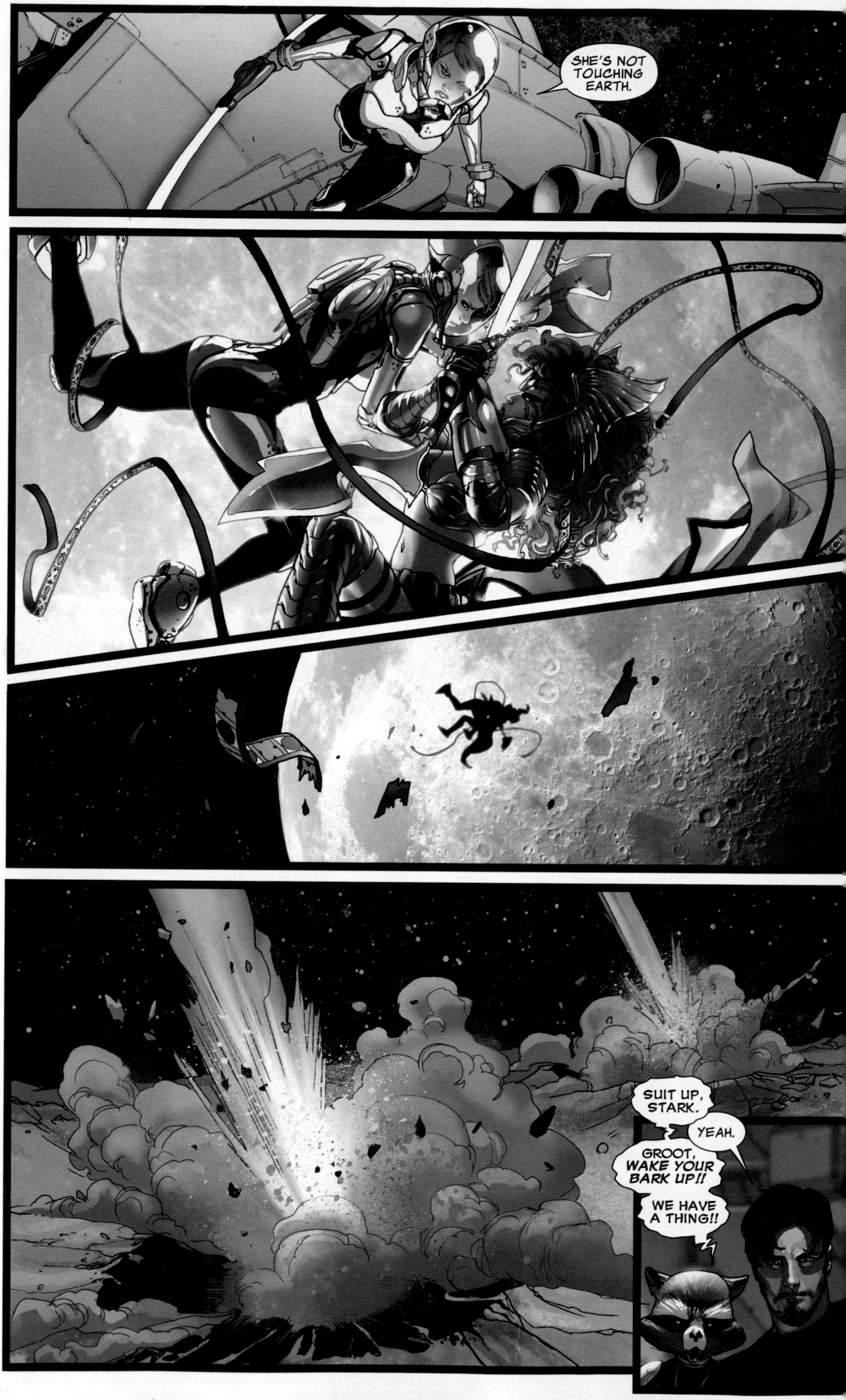
SHE'S NOT TOUCHING EARTH.
SUIT UP, STARK.
YEAH.
GROOT, *WAKE YOUR BARK UP!!*
WE HAVE A THING!!

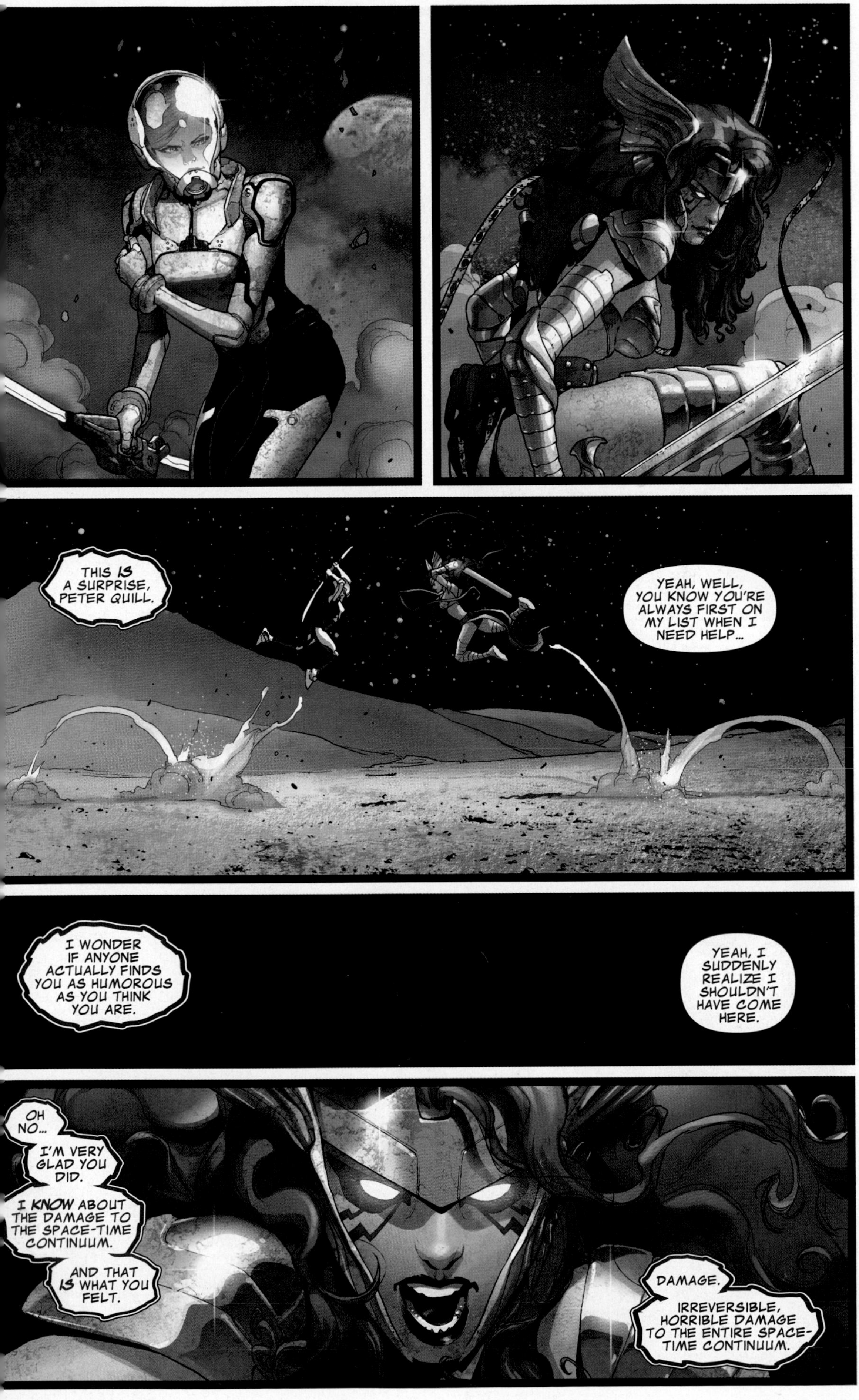
THIS IS A SURPRISE, PETER QUILL.
YEAH, WELL, YOU KNOW YOU'RE ALWAYS FIRST ON MY LIST WHEN I NEED HELP...
I WONDER IF ANYONE ACTUALLY FINDS YOU AS HUMOROUS AS YOU THINK YOU ARE.
YEAH, I SUDDENLY REALIZE I SHOULDN'T HAVE COME HERE.
OH NO...
I'M VERY GLAD YOU DID.
I KNOW ABOUT THE DAMAGE TO THE SPACE-TIME CONTINUUM.
AND THAT IS WHAT YOU FELT.
DAMAGE.
IRREVERSIBLE, HORRIBLE DAMAGE TO THE ENTIRE SPACE-TIME CONTINUUM.

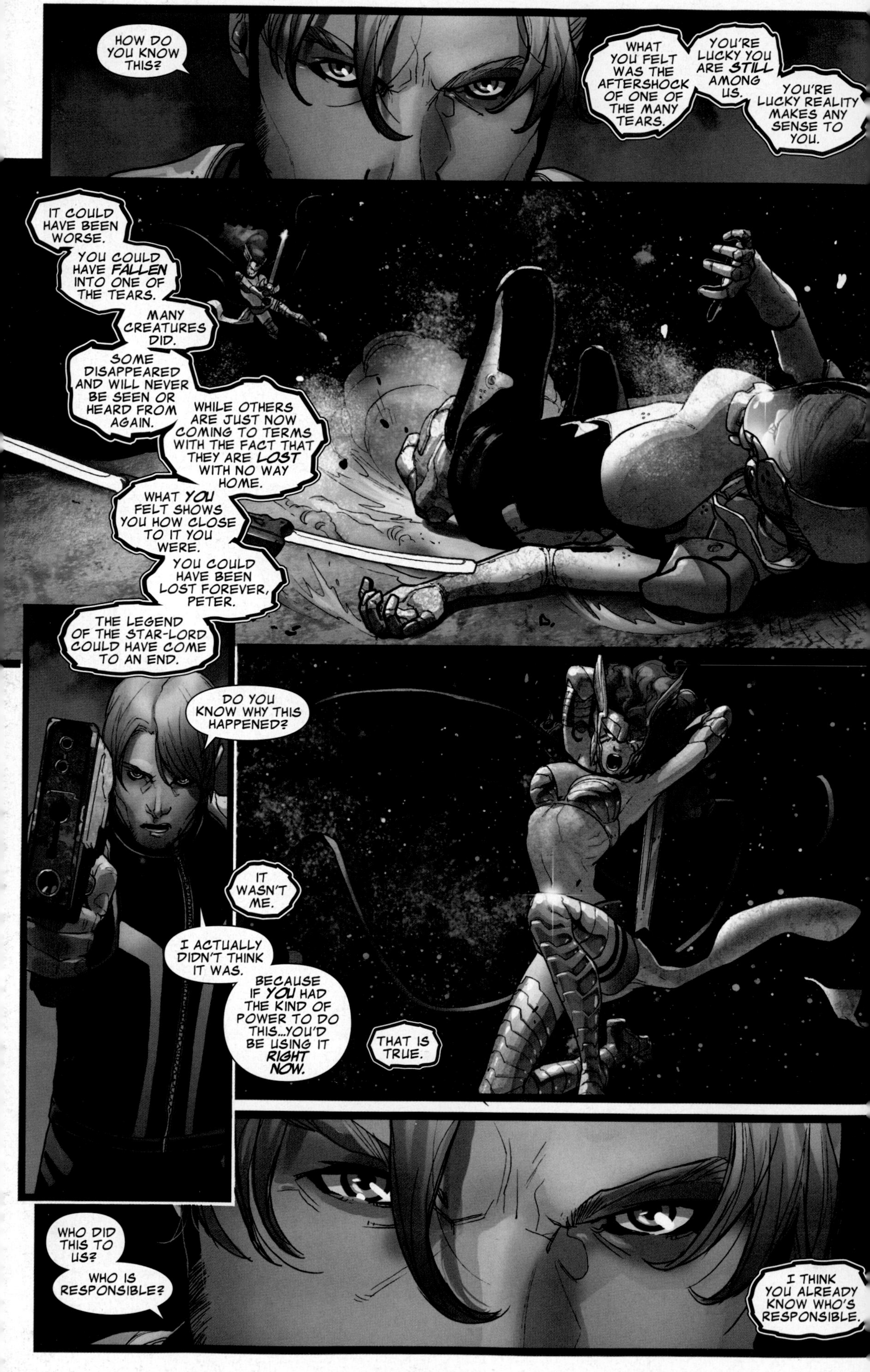
HOW DO YOU KNOW THIS?
WHAT YOU FELT WAS THE AFTERSHOCK OF ONE OF THE MANY TEARS.
YOU'RE LUCKY YOU ARE STILL AMONG US.
YOU'RE LUCKY REALITY MAKES ANY SENSE TO YOU.
IT COULD HAVE BEEN WORSE.
YOU COULD HAVE FALLEN INTO ONE OF THE TEARS.
MANY CREATURES DID.
SOME DISAPPEARED AND WILL NEVER BE SEEN OR HEARD FROM AGAIN.
WHILE OTHERS ARE JUST NOW COMING TO TERMS WITH THE FACT THAT THEY ARE LOST WITH NO WAY HOME.
WHAT YOU FELT SHOWS YOU HOW CLOSE TO IT YOU WERE.
YOU COULD HAVE BEEN LOST FOREVER, PETER.
THE LEGEND OF THE STAR-LORD COULD HAVE COME TO AN END.
DO YOU KNOW WHY THIS HAPPENED?
IT WASN'T ME.
I ACTUALLY DIDN'T THINK IT WAS.
BECAUSE IF YOU HAD THE KIND OF POWER TO DO THIS...YOU'D BE USING IT RIGHT NOW.
THAT IS TRUE.
WHO DID THIS TO US?
WHO IS RESPONSIBLE?
I THINK YOU ALREADY KNOW WHO'S RESPONSIBLE.

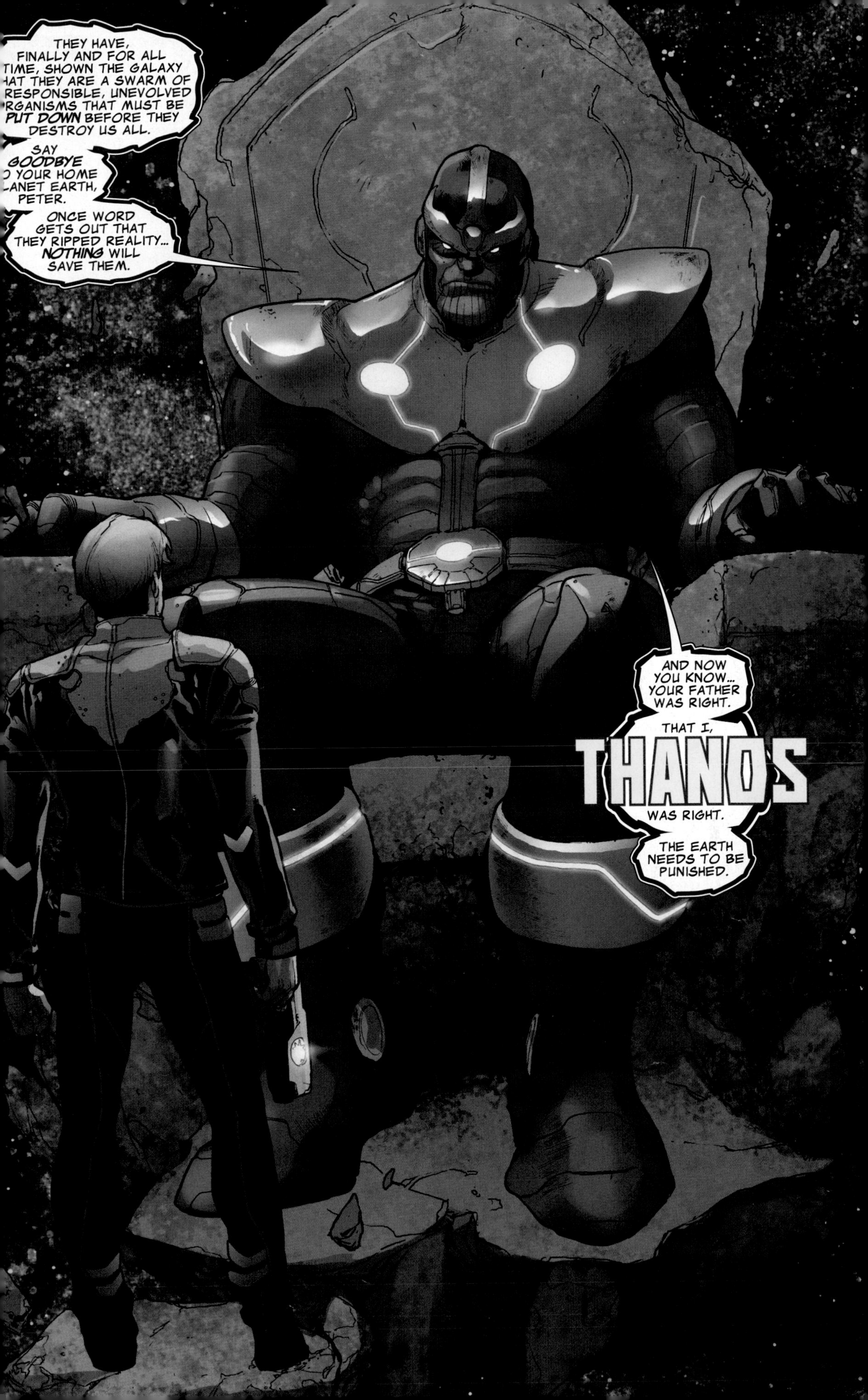

THEY HAVE, FINALLY AND FOR ALL TIME, SHOWN THE GALAXY HAT THEY ARE A SWARM OF RESPONSIBLE, UNEVOLVED RGANISMS THAT MUST BE PUT DOWN BEFORE THEY DESTROY US ALL.
SAY GOODBYE O YOUR HOME LANET EARTH, PETER.
ONCE WORD GETS OUT THAT THEY RIPPED REALITY... NOTHING WILL SAVE THEM.
AND NOW YOU KNOW... YOUR FATHER WAS RIGHT.
THAT I, THANOS WAS RIGHT.
THE EARTH NEEDS TO BE PUNISHED.

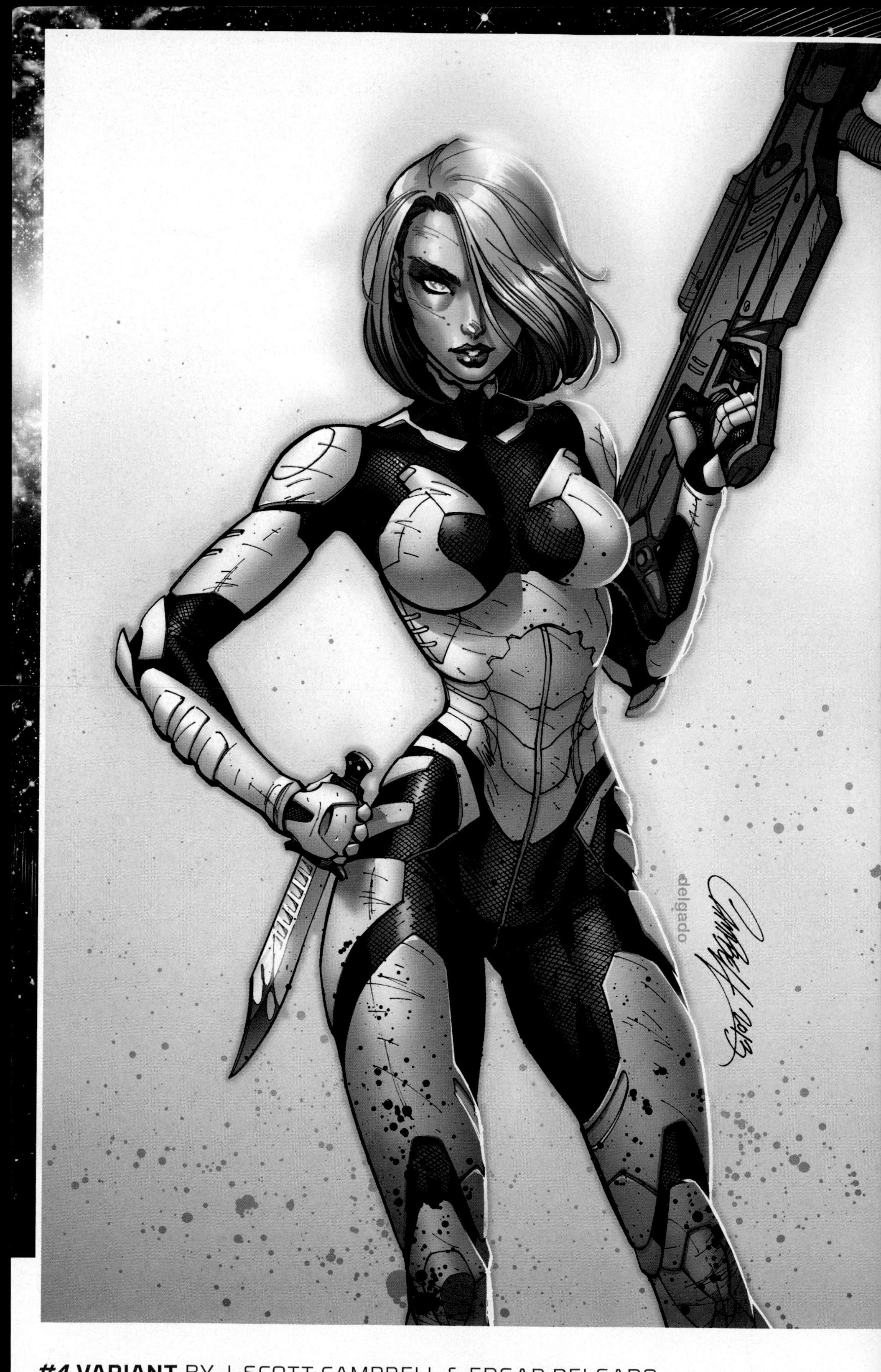
delgado

#4 VARIANT BY J. SCOTT CAMPBELL & EDGAR DELGADO

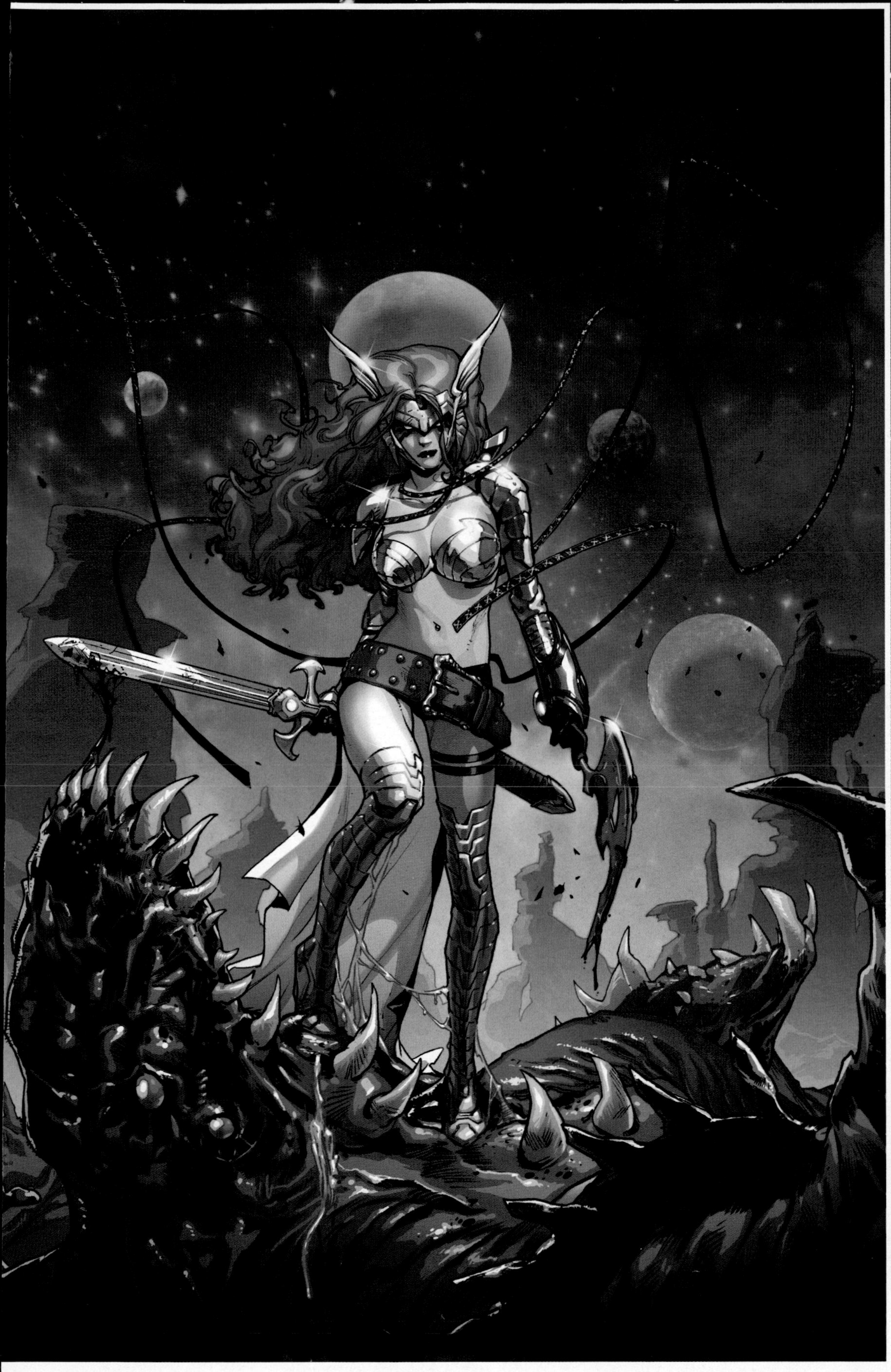

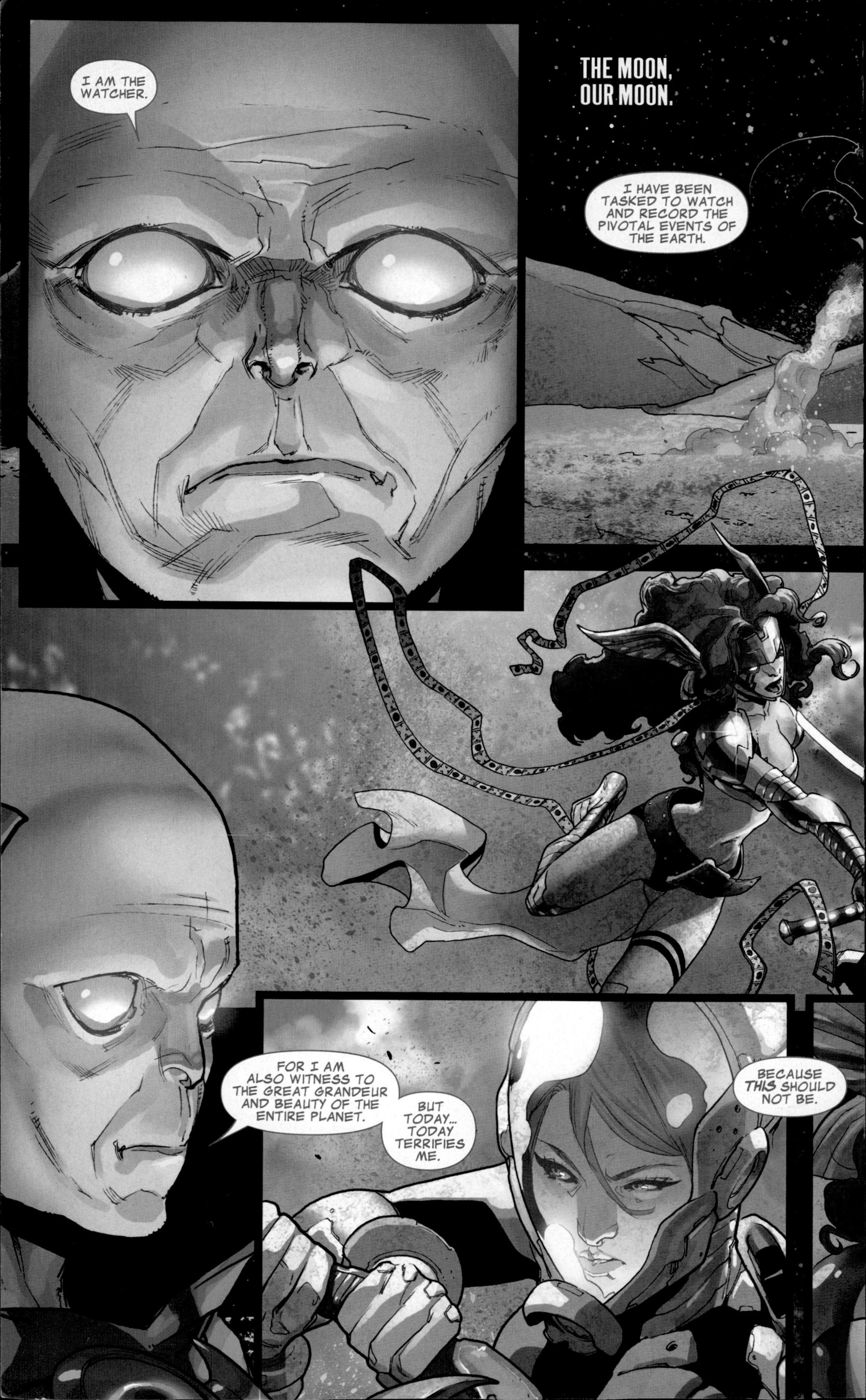
I AM THE WATCHER.
THE MOON, OUR MOON.
I HAVE BEEN TASKED TO WATCH AND RECORD THE PIVOTAL EVENTS OF THE EARTH.
FOR I AM ALSO WITNESS TO THE GREAT GRANDEUR AND BEAUTY OF THE ENTIRE PLANET.
BUT TODAY... TODAY TERRIFIES ME.
BECAUSE THIS SHOULD NOT BE.

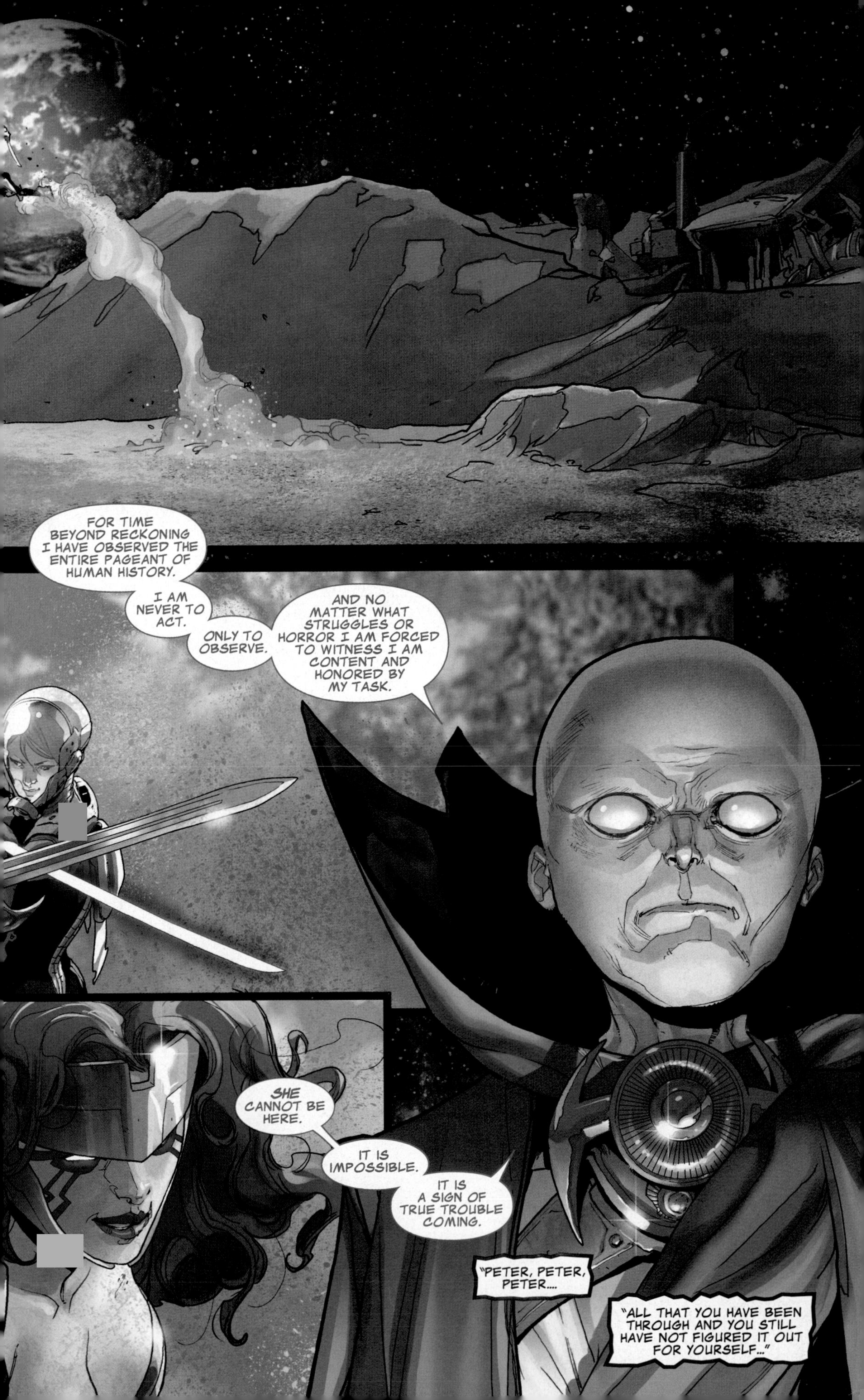
FOR TIME BEYOND RECKONING I HAVE OBSERVED THE ENTIRE PAGEANT OF HUMAN HISTORY.
I AM NEVER TO ACT.
ONLY TO OBSERVE.
AND NO MATTER WHAT STRUGGLES OR HORROR I AM FORCED TO WITNESS I AM CONTENT AND HONORED BY MY TASK.
SHE CANNOT BE HERE.
IT IS IMPOSSIBLE.
IT IS A SIGN OF TRUE TROUBLE COMING.
"PETER, PETER, PETER....
"ALL THAT YOU HAVE BEEN THROUGH AND YOU STILL HAVE NOT FIGURED IT OUT FOR YOURSELF..."

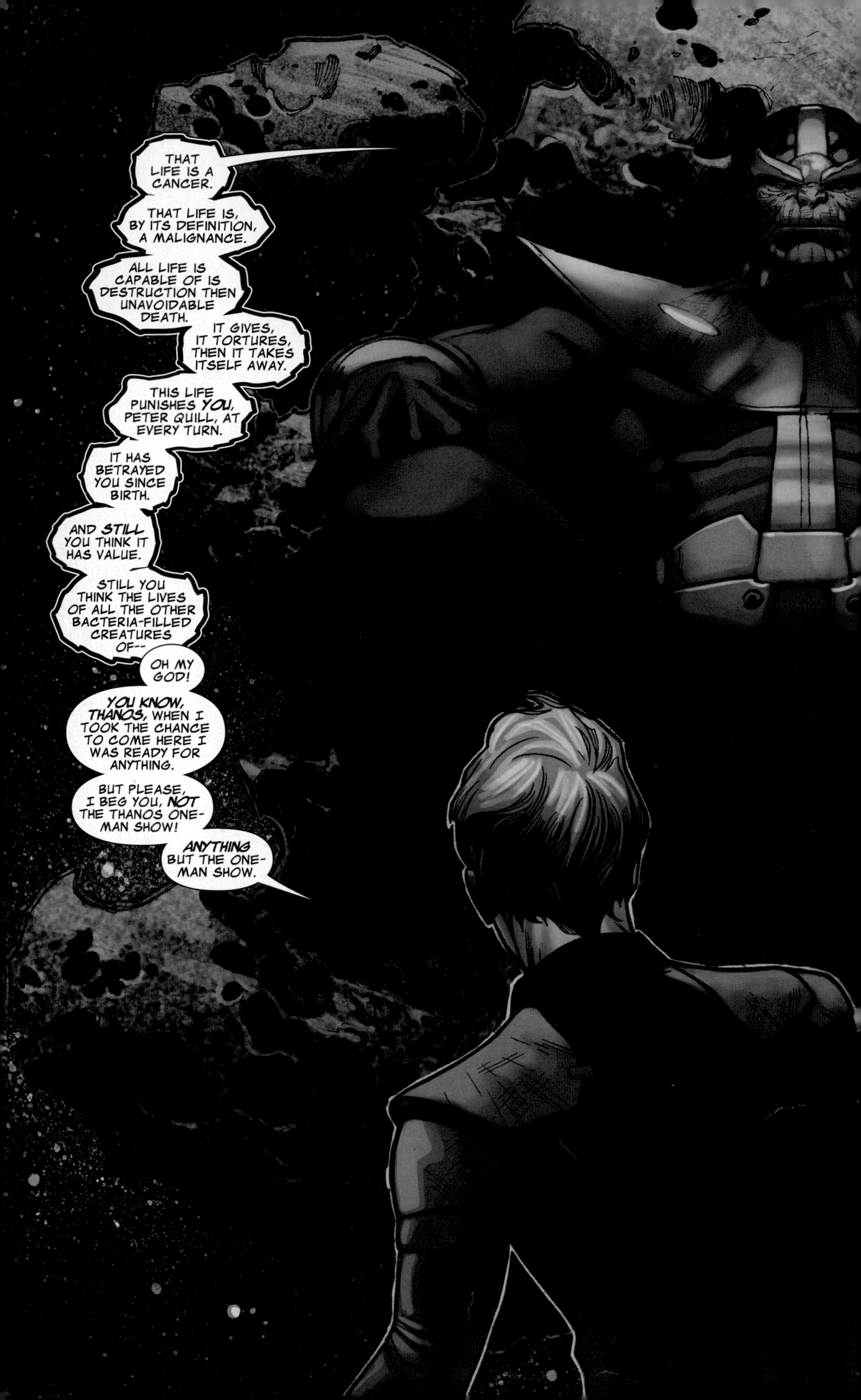
THAT LIFE IS A CANCER.
THAT LIFE IS, BY ITS DEFINITION, A MALIGNANCE.
ALL LIFE IS CAPABLE OF IS DESTRUCTION THEN UNAVOIDABLE DEATH.
IT GIVES, IT TORTURES, THEN IT TAKES ITSELF AWAY.
THIS LIFE PUNISHES YOU, PETER QUILL, AT EVERY TURN.
IT HAS BETRAYED YOU SINCE BIRTH.
AND STILL YOU THINK IT HAS VALUE.
STILL YOU THINK THE LIVES OF ALL THE OTHER BACTERIA-FILLED CREATURES OF--
OH MY GOD!
YOU KNOW, THANOS, WHEN I TOOK THE CHANCE TO COME HERE I WAS READY FOR ANYTHING.
BUT PLEASE, I BEG YOU, NOT THE THANOS ONE-MAN SHOW!
ANYTHING BUT THE ONE-MAN SHOW.

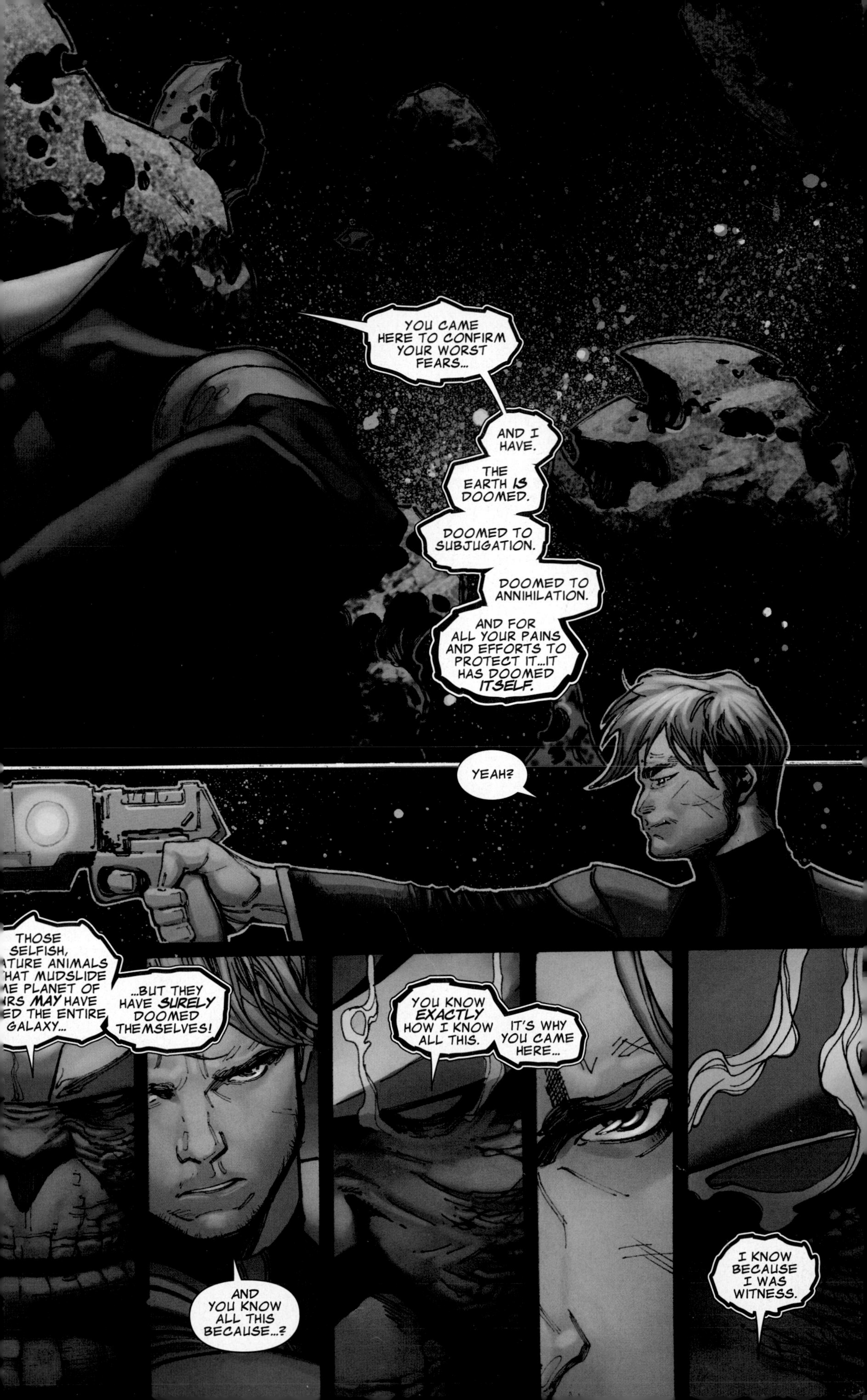
YOU CAME HERE TO CONFIRM YOUR WORST FEARS...
AND I HAVE.
THE EARTH IS DOOMED.
DOOMED TO SUBJUGATION.
DOOMED TO ANNIHILATION.
AND FOR ALL YOUR PAINS AND EFFORTS TO PROTECT IT...IT HAS DOOMED ITSELF.
YEAH?
THOSE SELFISH, ATURE ANIMALS HAT MUDSLIDE ME PLANET OF RS MAY HAVE ED THE ENTIRE GALAXY...
...BUT THEY HAVE SURELY DOOMED THEMSELVES!
AND YOU KNOW ALL THIS BECAUSE...?
YOU KNOW EXACTLY HOW I KNOW ALL THIS.
IT'S WHY YOU CAME HERE...
I KNOW BECAUSE I WAS WITNESS.

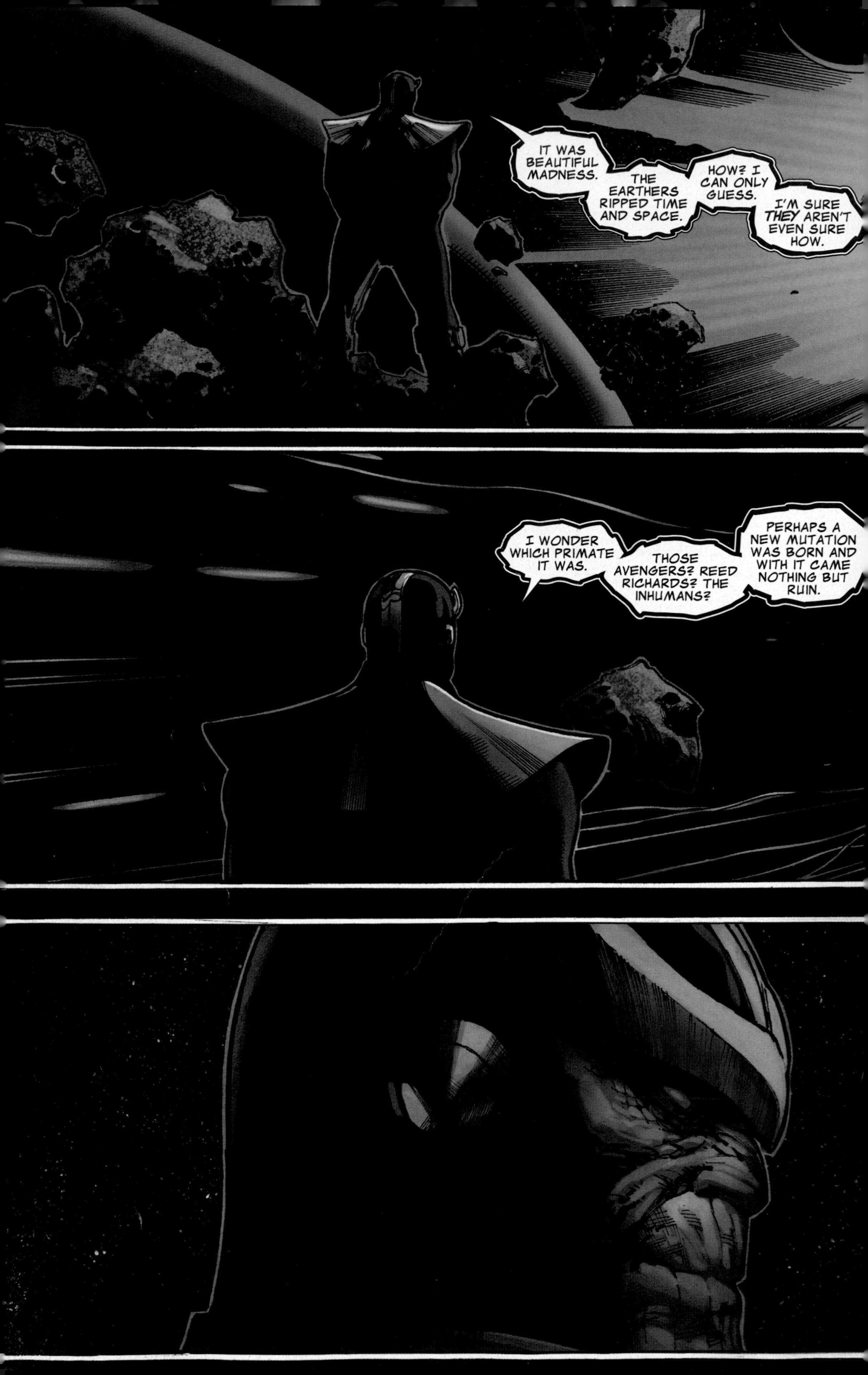
IT WAS BEAUTIFUL MADNESS.
THE EARTHERS RIPPED TIME AND SPACE.
HOW? I CAN ONLY GUESS.
I'M SURE THEY AREN'T EVEN SURE HOW.
I WONDER WHICH PRIMATE IT WAS.
THOSE AVENGERS? REED RICHARDS? THE INHUMANS?
PERHAPS A NEW MUTATION WAS BORN AND WITH IT CAME NOTHING BUT RUIN.

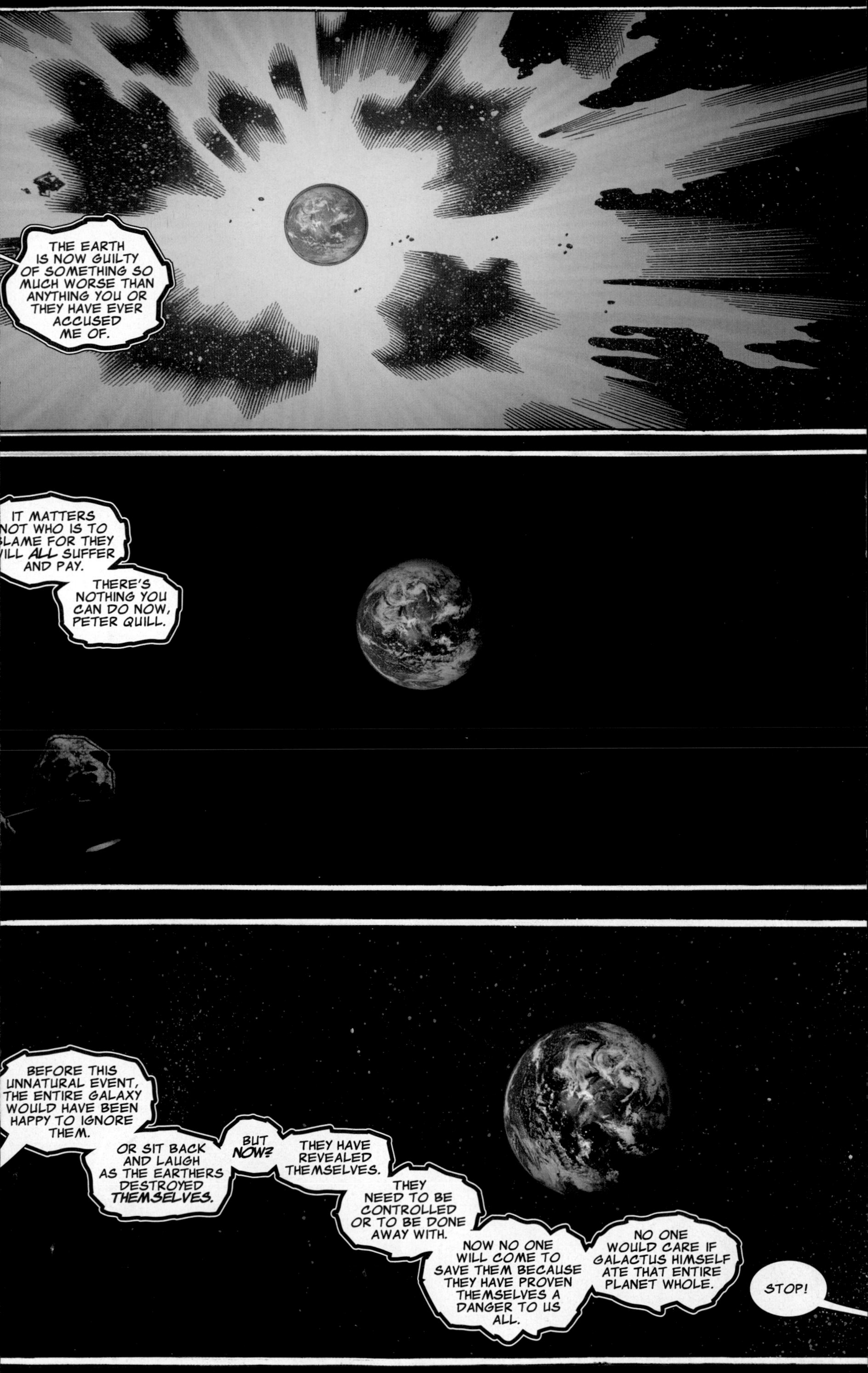
THE EARTH IS NOW GUILTY OF SOMETHING SO MUCH WORSE THAN ANYTHING YOU OR THEY HAVE EVER ACCUSED ME OF.
IT MATTERS NOT WHO IS TO BLAME FOR THEY WILL ALL SUFFER AND PAY.
THERE'S NOTHING YOU CAN DO NOW, PETER QUILL.
BEFORE THIS UNNATURAL EVENT, THE ENTIRE GALAXY WOULD HAVE BEEN HAPPY TO IGNORE THEM.
OR SIT BACK AND LAUGH AS THE EARTHERS DESTROYED THEMSELVES.
BUT NOW?
THEY HAVE REVEALED THEMSELVES.
THEY NEED TO BE CONTROLLED OR TO BE DONE AWAY WITH.
NOW NO ONE WILL COME TO SAVE THEM BECAUSE THEY HAVE PROVEN THEMSELVES A DANGER TO US ALL.
NO ONE WOULD CARE IF GALACTUS HIMSELF ATE THAT ENTIRE PLANET WHOLE.
STOP!

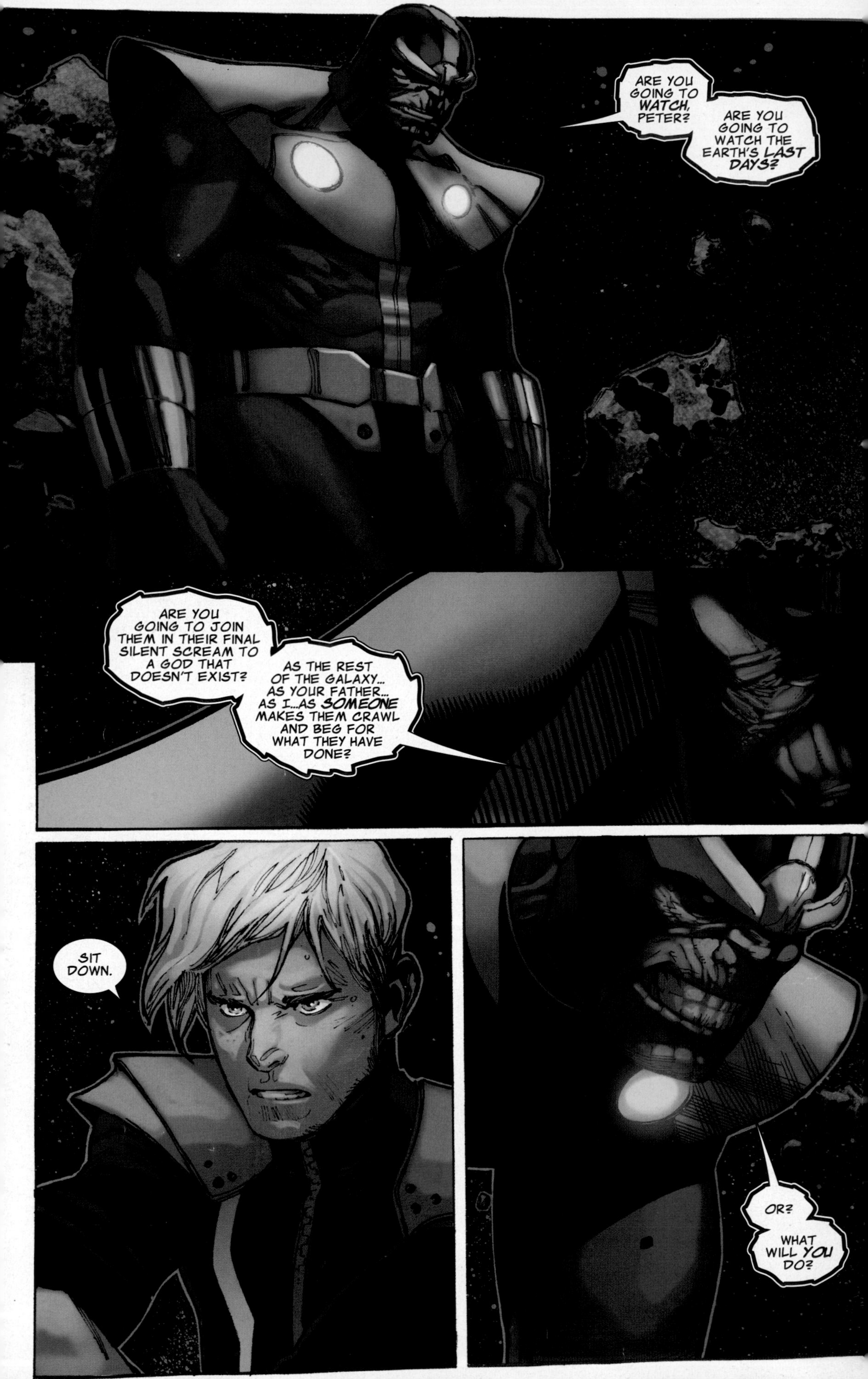
ARE YOU GOING TO WATCH, PETER?
ARE YOU GOING TO WATCH THE EARTH'S LAST DAYS?
ARE YOU GOING TO JOIN THEM IN THEIR FINAL SILENT SCREAM TO A GOD THAT DOESN'T EXIST?
AS THE REST OF THE GALAXY... AS YOUR FATHER... AS I...AS SOMEONE MAKES THEM CRAWL AND BEG FOR WHAT THEY HAVE DONE?
SIT DOWN.
OR?
WHAT WILL YOU DO?

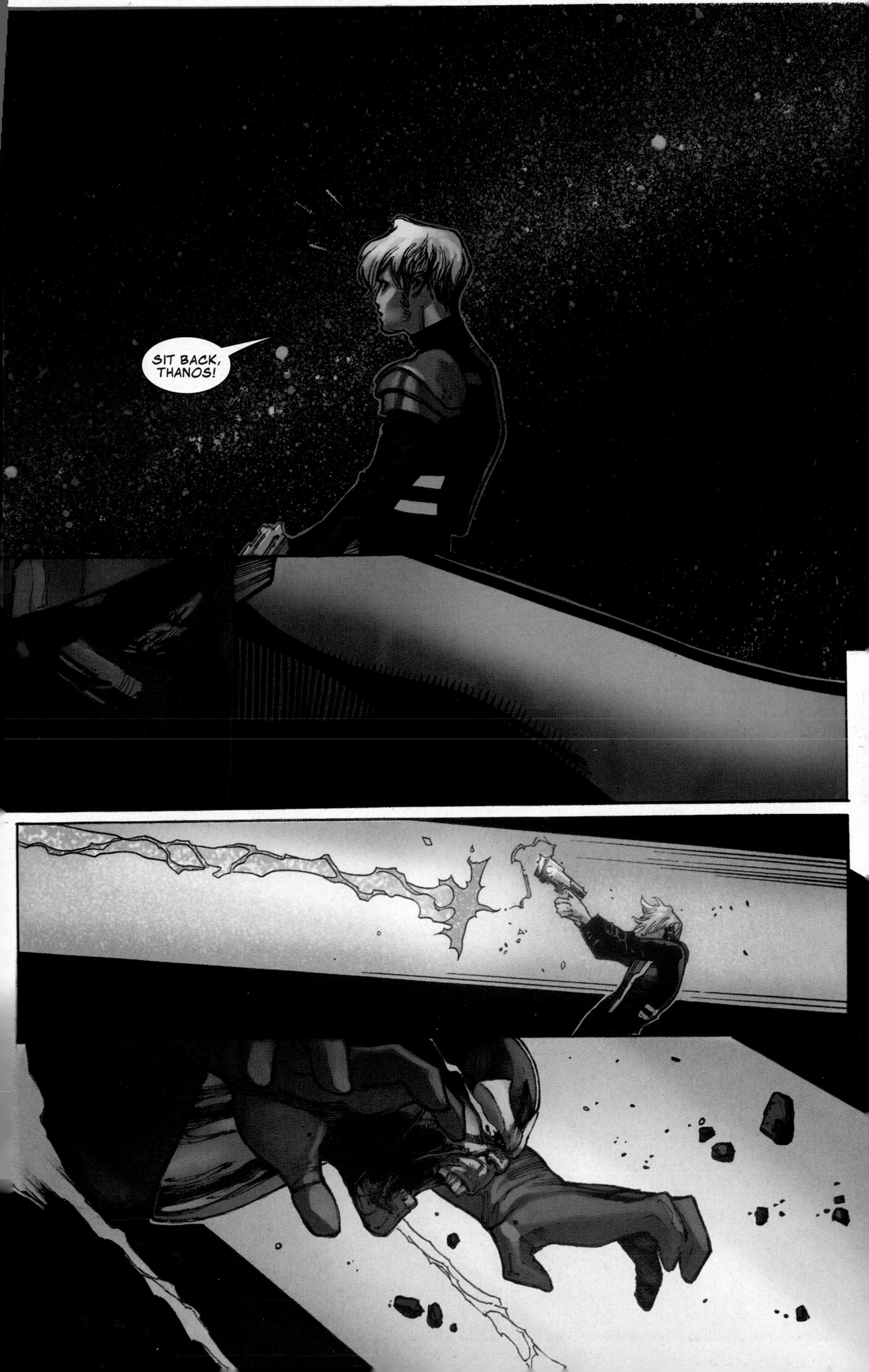
SIT BACK, THANOS!

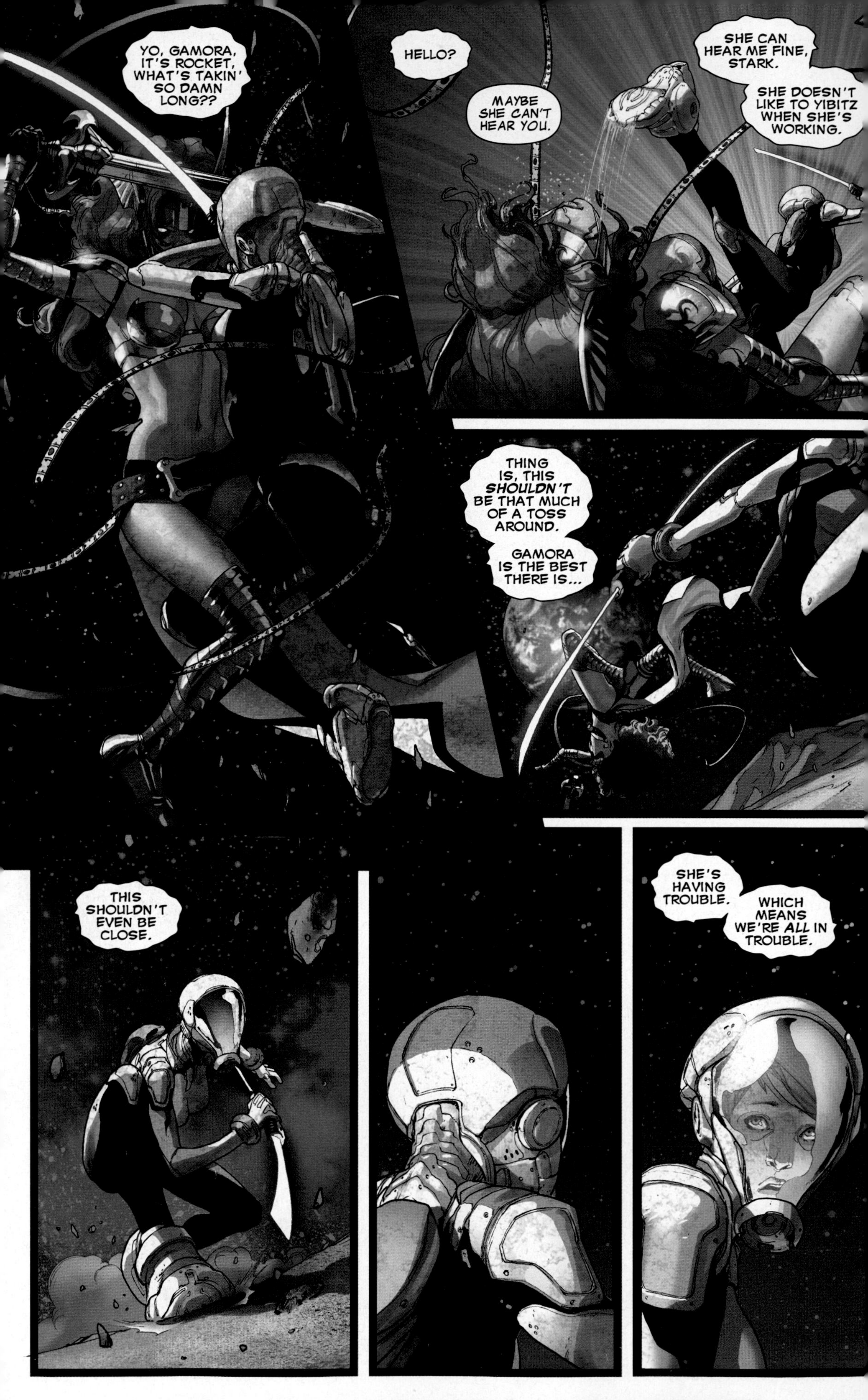
YO, GAMORA, IT'S ROCKET, WHAT'S TAKIN' SO DAMN LONG??
HELLO?
MAYBE SHE CAN'T HEAR YOU.
SHE CAN HEAR ME FINE, STARK.
SHE DOESN'T LIKE TO YIBITZ WHEN SHE'S WORKING.
THING IS, THIS *SHOULDN'T* BE THAT MUCH OF A TOSS AROUND.
GAMORA IS THE BEST THERE IS...
THIS SHOULDN'T EVEN BE CLOSE.
SHE'S HAVING TROUBLE.
WHICH MEANS WE'RE *ALL* IN TROUBLE.

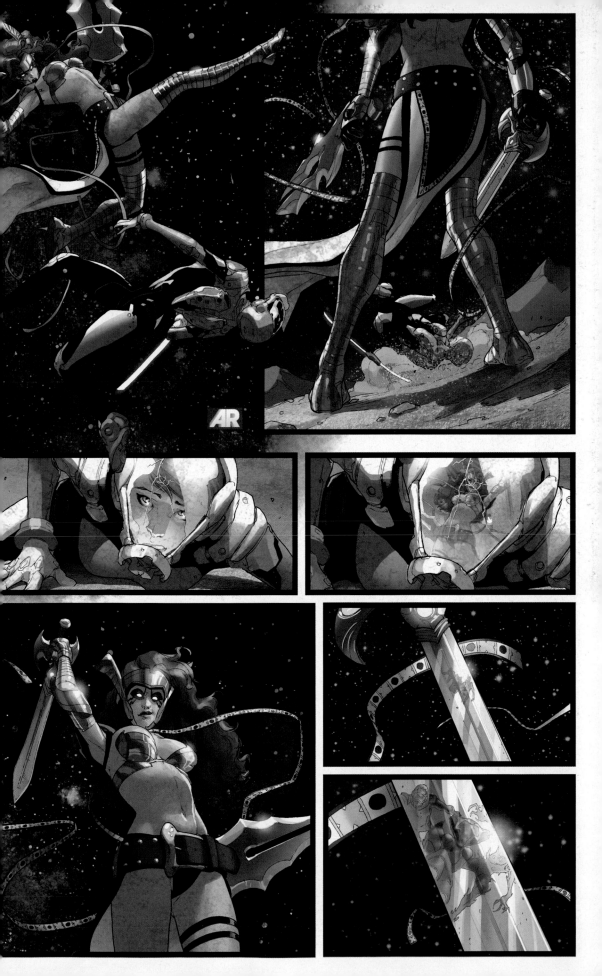

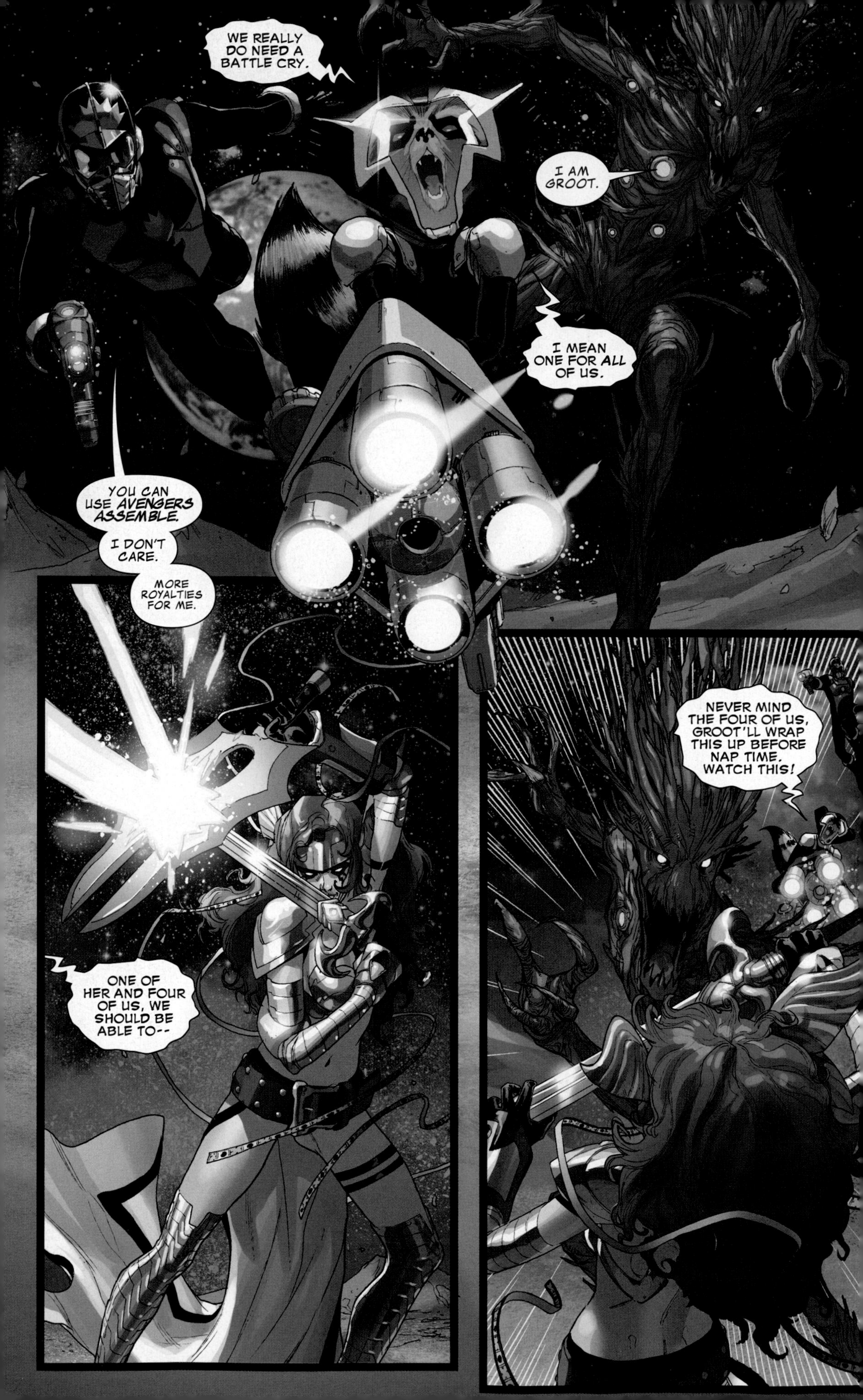
WE REALLY DO NEED A BATTLE CRY.
I AM GROOT.
I MEAN ONE FOR ALL OF US.
YOU CAN USE AVENGERS ASSEMBLE.
I DON'T CARE.
MORE ROYALTIES FOR ME.
ONE OF HER AND FOUR OF US, WE SHOULD BE ABLE TO--
NEVER MIND THE FOUR OF US, GROOT'LL WRAP THIS UP BEFORE NAP TIME. WATCH THIS!

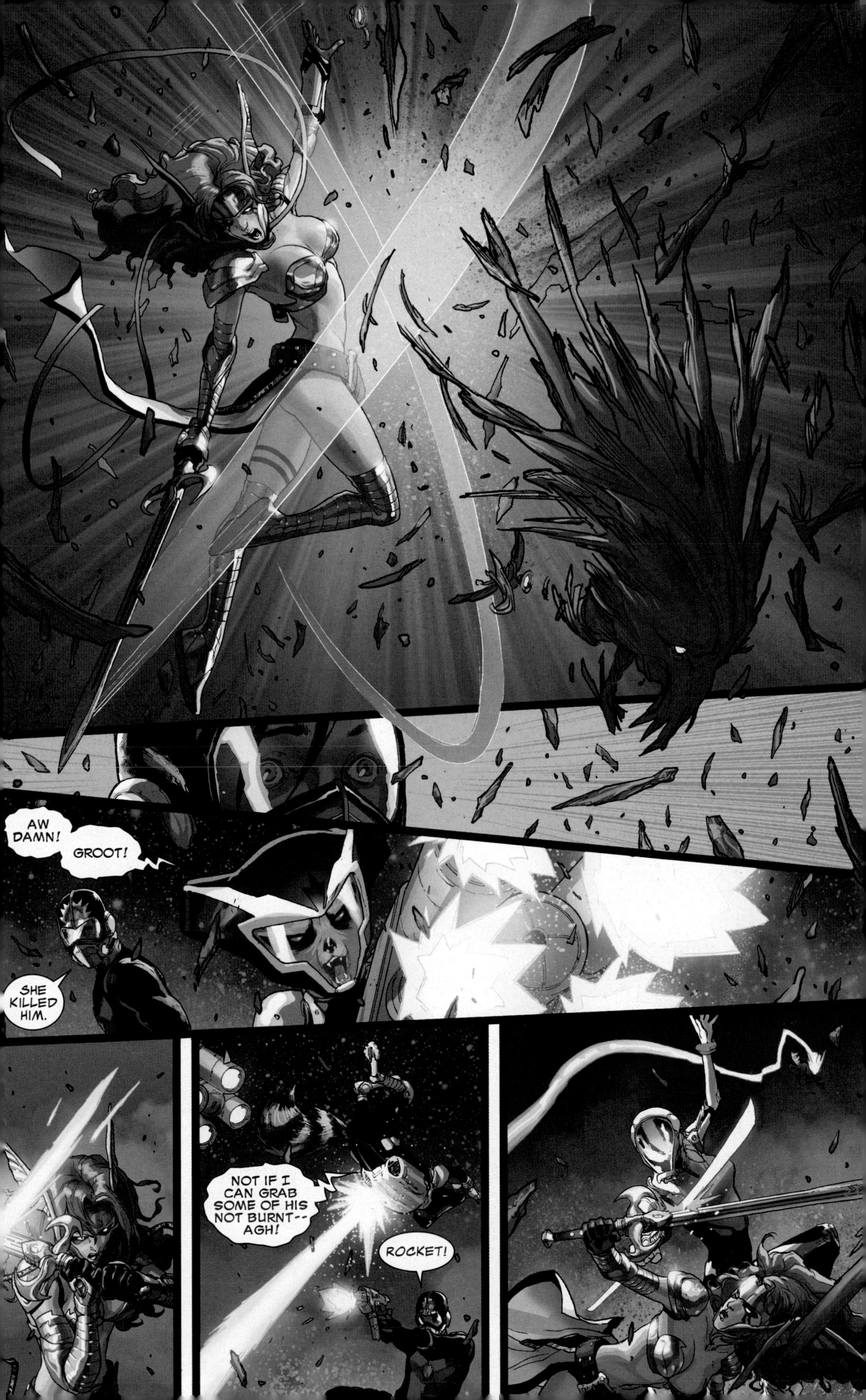
AW DAMN!
GROOT!
SHE KILLED HIM.
NOT IF I CAN GRAB SOME OF HIS NOT BURNT-- AGH!
ROCKET!

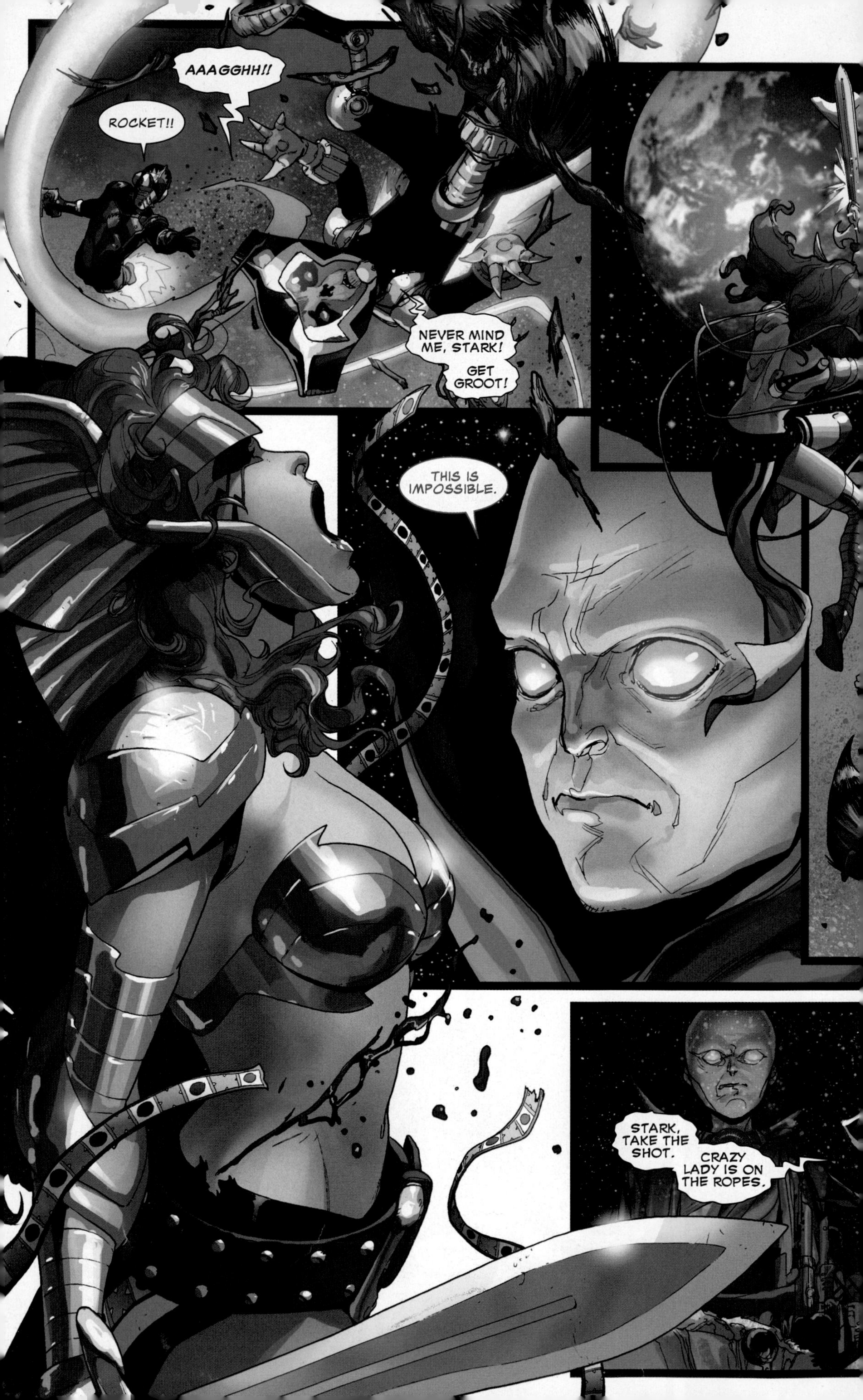
AAAGGHH!!
ROCKET!!
NEVER MIND ME, STARK!
GET GROOT!
THIS IS IMPOSSIBLE.
STARK, TAKE THE SHOT.
CRAZY LADY IS ON THE ROPES.

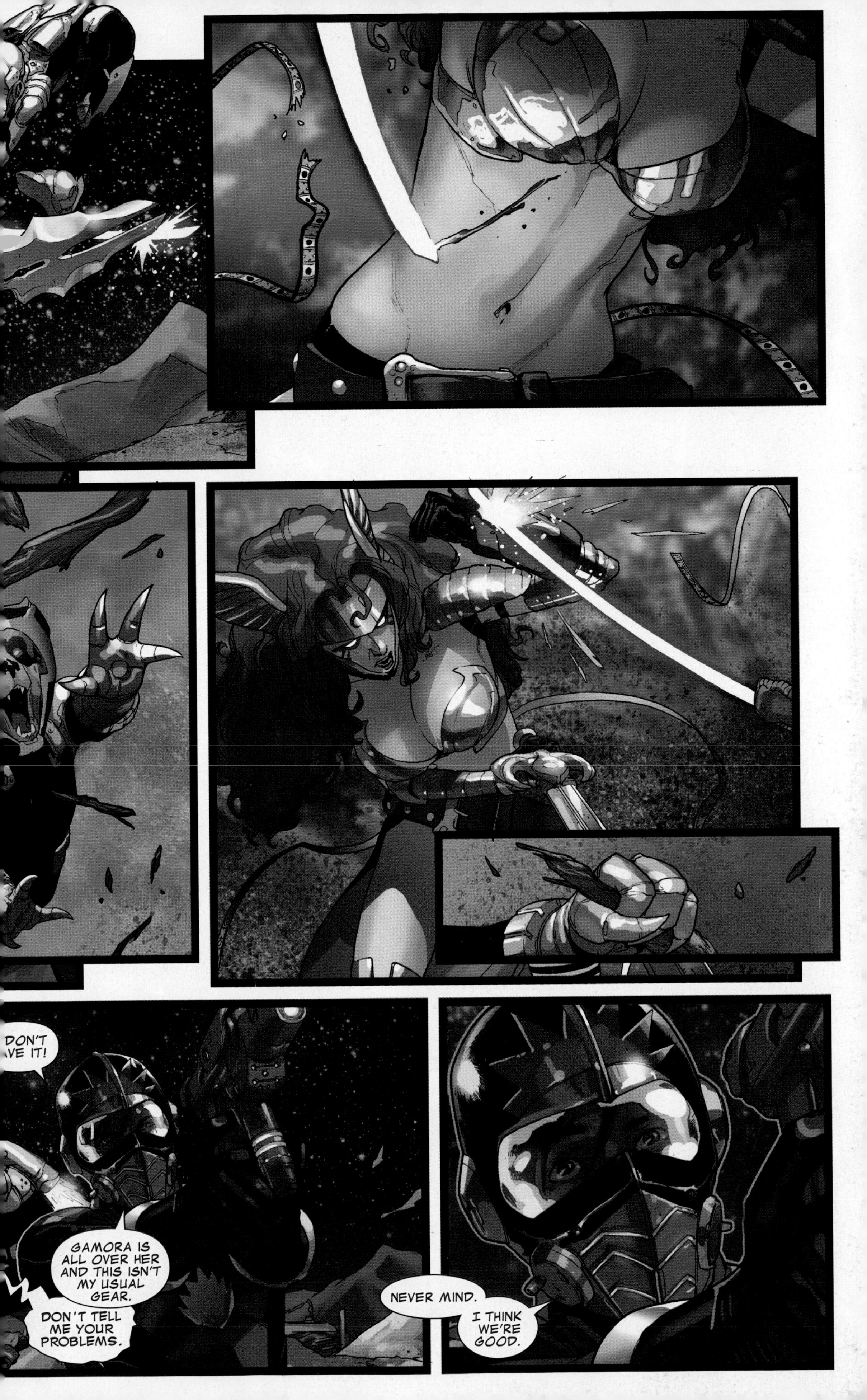
DON'T
VE IT!
GAMORA IS ALL OVER HER AND THIS ISN'T MY USUAL GEAR.
DON'T TELL ME YOUR PROBLEMS.
NEVER MIND.
I THINK WE'RE GOOD.

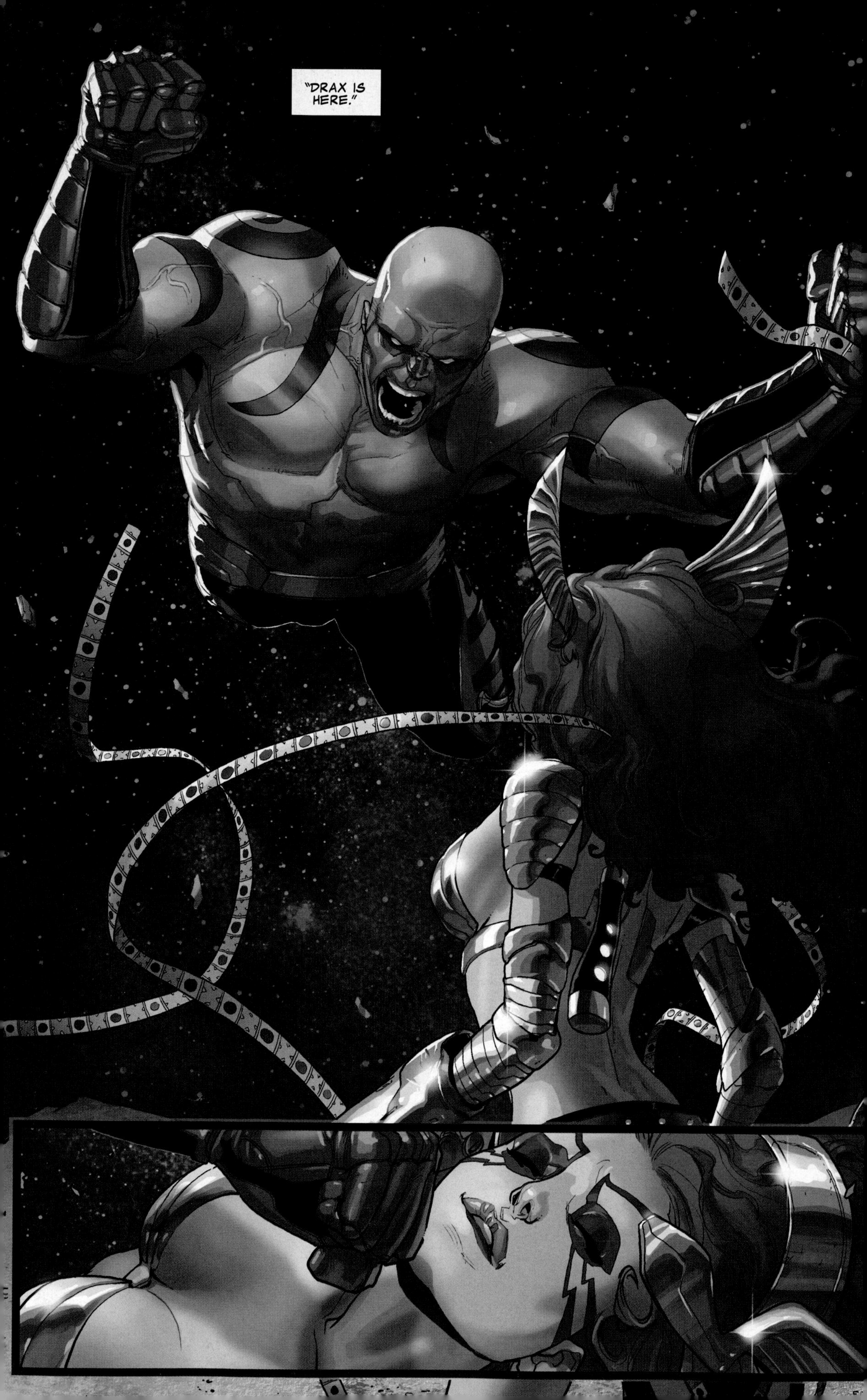
"DRAX IS HERE."

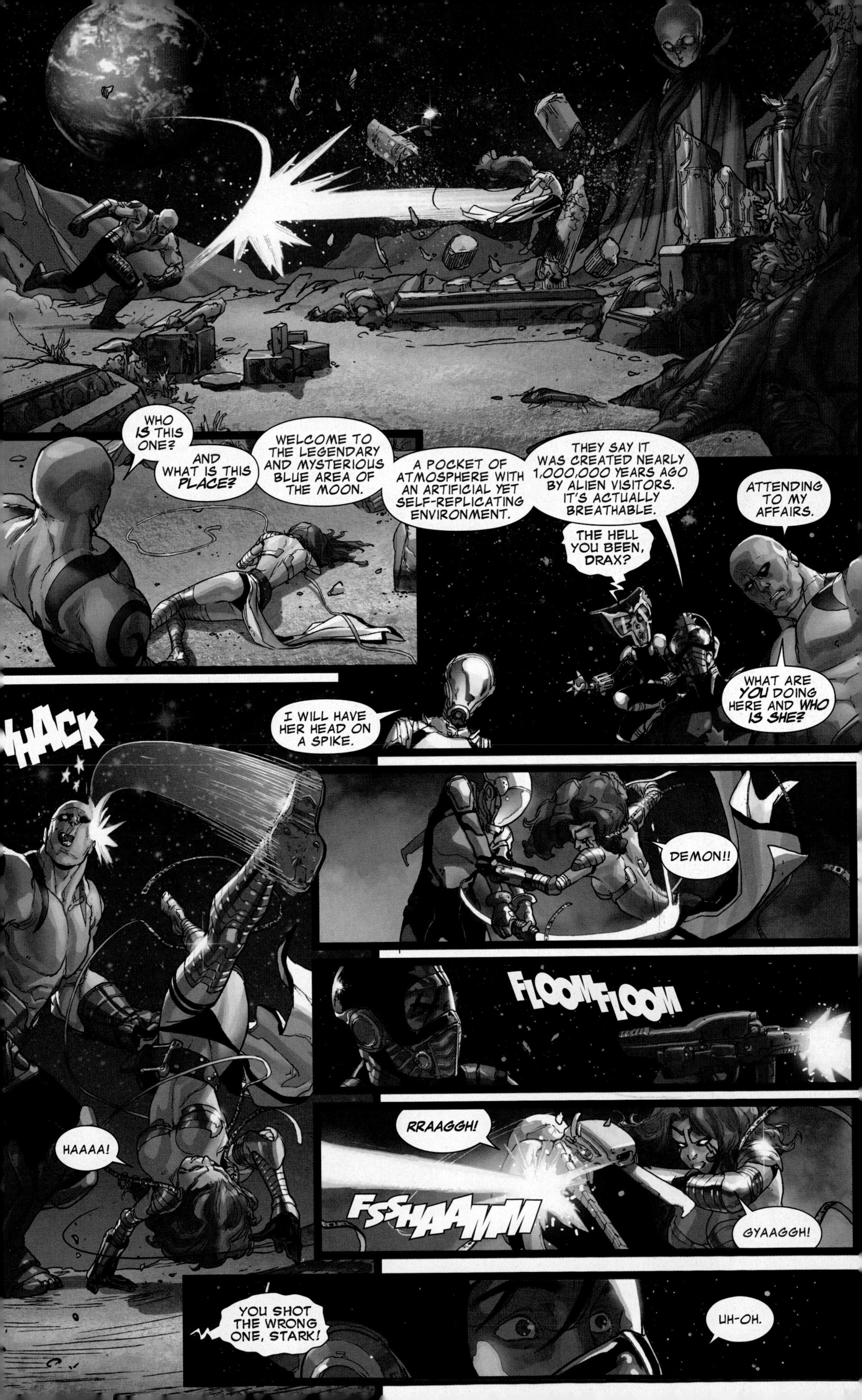
WHO IS THIS ONE?
AND WHAT IS THIS PLACE?
WELCOME TO THE LEGENDARY AND MYSTERIOUS BLUE AREA OF THE MOON.
A POCKET OF ATMOSPHERE WITH AN ARTIFICIAL YET SELF-REPLICATING ENVIRONMENT.
THEY SAY IT WAS CREATED NEARLY 1,000,000 YEARS AGO BY ALIEN VISITORS. IT'S ACTUALLY BREATHABLE.
THE HELL YOU BEEN, DRAX?
ATTENDING TO MY AFFAIRS.
WHAT ARE YOU DOING HERE AND WHO IS SHE?
I WILL HAVE HER HEAD ON A SPIKE.
HACK
DEMON!!
FLOOMFLOOM
HAAAA!
RRAAGGH!
FSSHAAMM
GYAAGGH!
YOU SHOT THE WRONG ONE, STARK!
UH-OH.

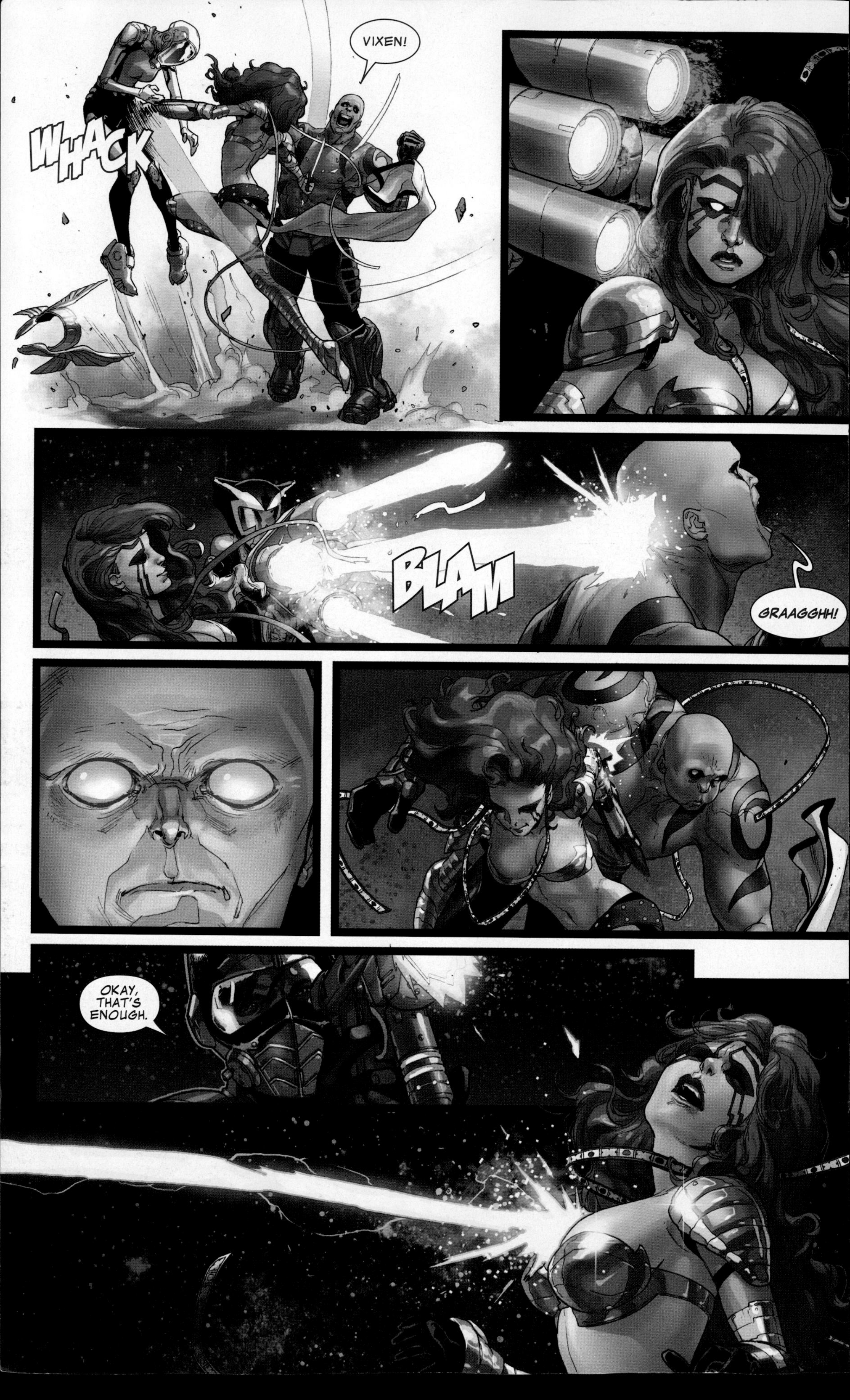
VIXEN!
WHACK
BLAM
GRAAGGHH!
OKAY, THAT'S ENOUGH.

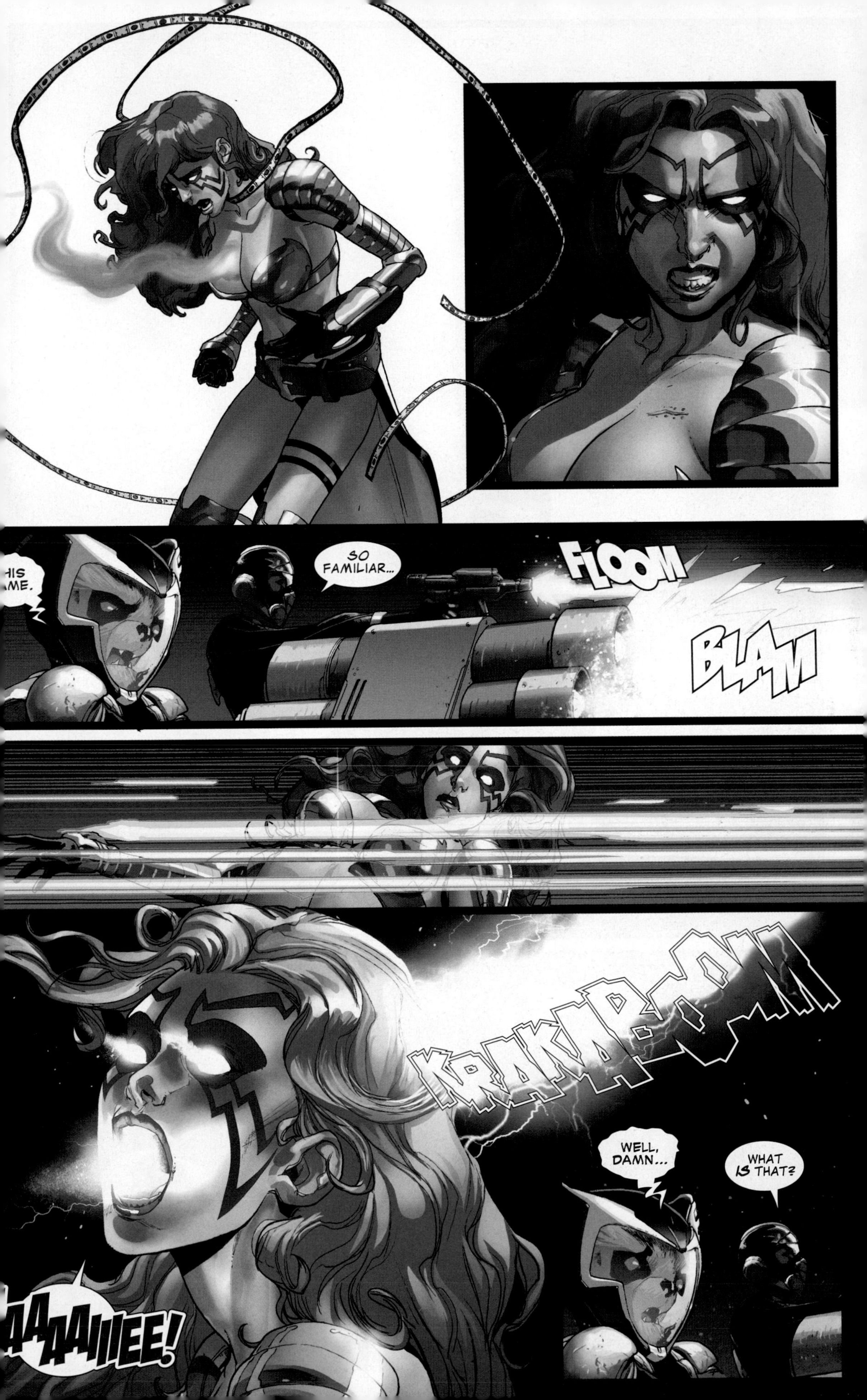

SO FAMILIAR...
FLOOM
BLAM
KRAKA-BOOM
AAAAIIIEE!
WELL, DAMN...
WHAT IS THAT?

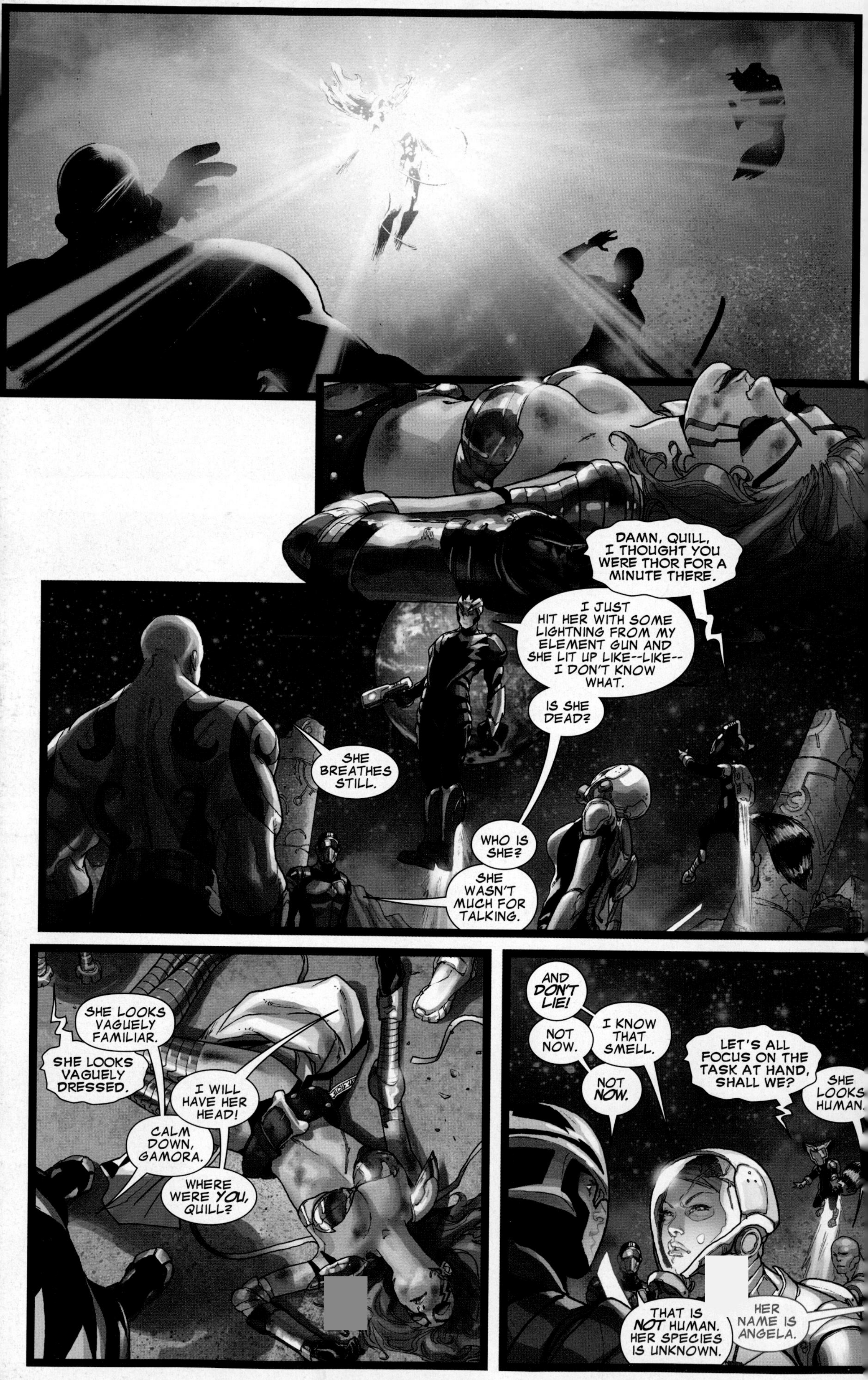
DAMN, QUILL, I THOUGHT YOU WERE THOR FOR A MINUTE THERE.
I JUST HIT HER WITH SOME LIGHTNING FROM MY ELEMENT GUN AND SHE LIT UP LIKE--LIKE-- I DON'T KNOW WHAT.
IS SHE DEAD?
SHE BREATHES STILL.
WHO IS SHE?
SHE WASN'T MUCH FOR TALKING.
SHE LOOKS VAGUELY FAMILIAR.
SHE LOOKS VAGUELY DRESSED.
I WILL HAVE HER HEAD!
CALM DOWN, GAMORA.
WHERE WERE *YOU*, QUILL?
AND *DON'T LIE!*
I KNOW THAT SMELL.
NOT NOW.
NOT *NOW.*
LET'S ALL FOCUS ON THE TASK AT HAND, SHALL WE?
SHE LOOKS HUMAN.
THAT IS *NOT* HUMAN. HER SPECIES IS UNKNOWN.
HER NAME IS ANGELA.

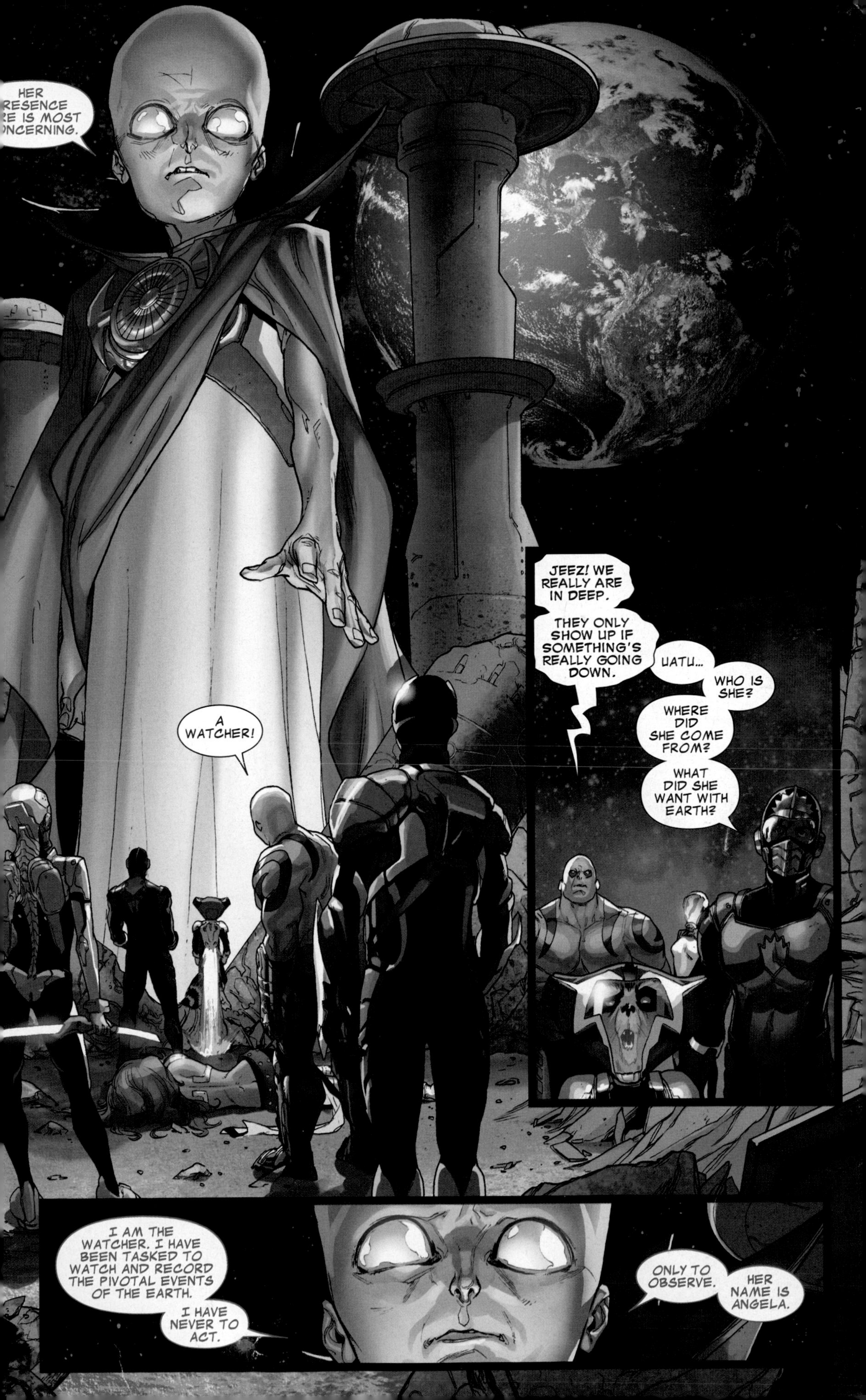
HER RESENCE RE IS MOST NCERNING.
A WATCHER!
JEEZ! WE REALLY ARE IN DEEP.
THEY ONLY SHOW UP IF SOMETHING'S REALLY GOING DOWN.
UATU...
WHO IS SHE?
WHERE DID SHE COME FROM?
WHAT DID SHE WANT WITH EARTH?
I AM THE WATCHER. I HAVE BEEN TASKED TO WATCH AND RECORD THE PIVOTAL EVENTS OF THE EARTH.
I HAVE NEVER TO ACT.
ONLY TO OBSERVE.
HER NAME IS ANGELA.

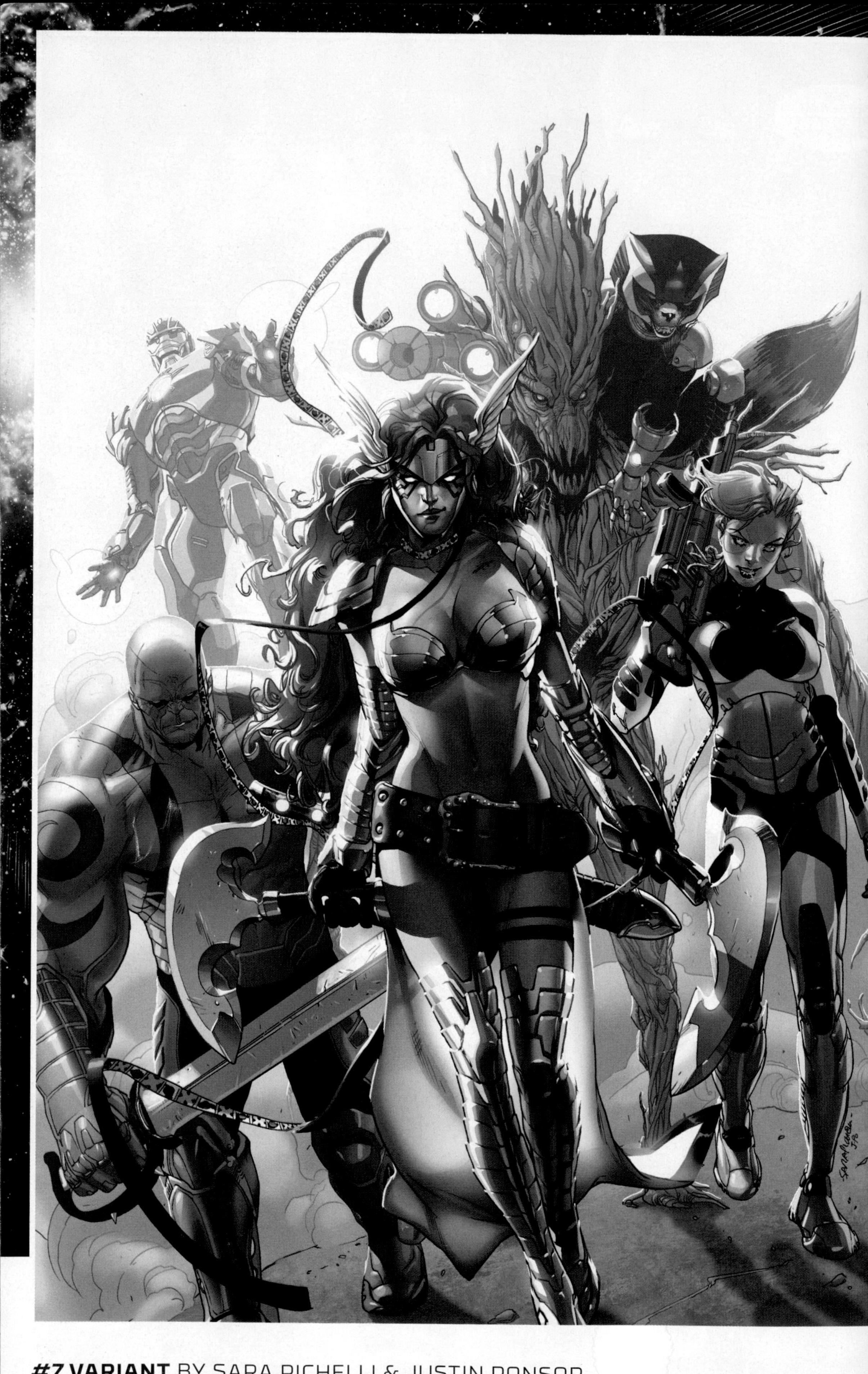

#7 VARIANT BY SARA PICHELLI & JUSTIN PONSOR

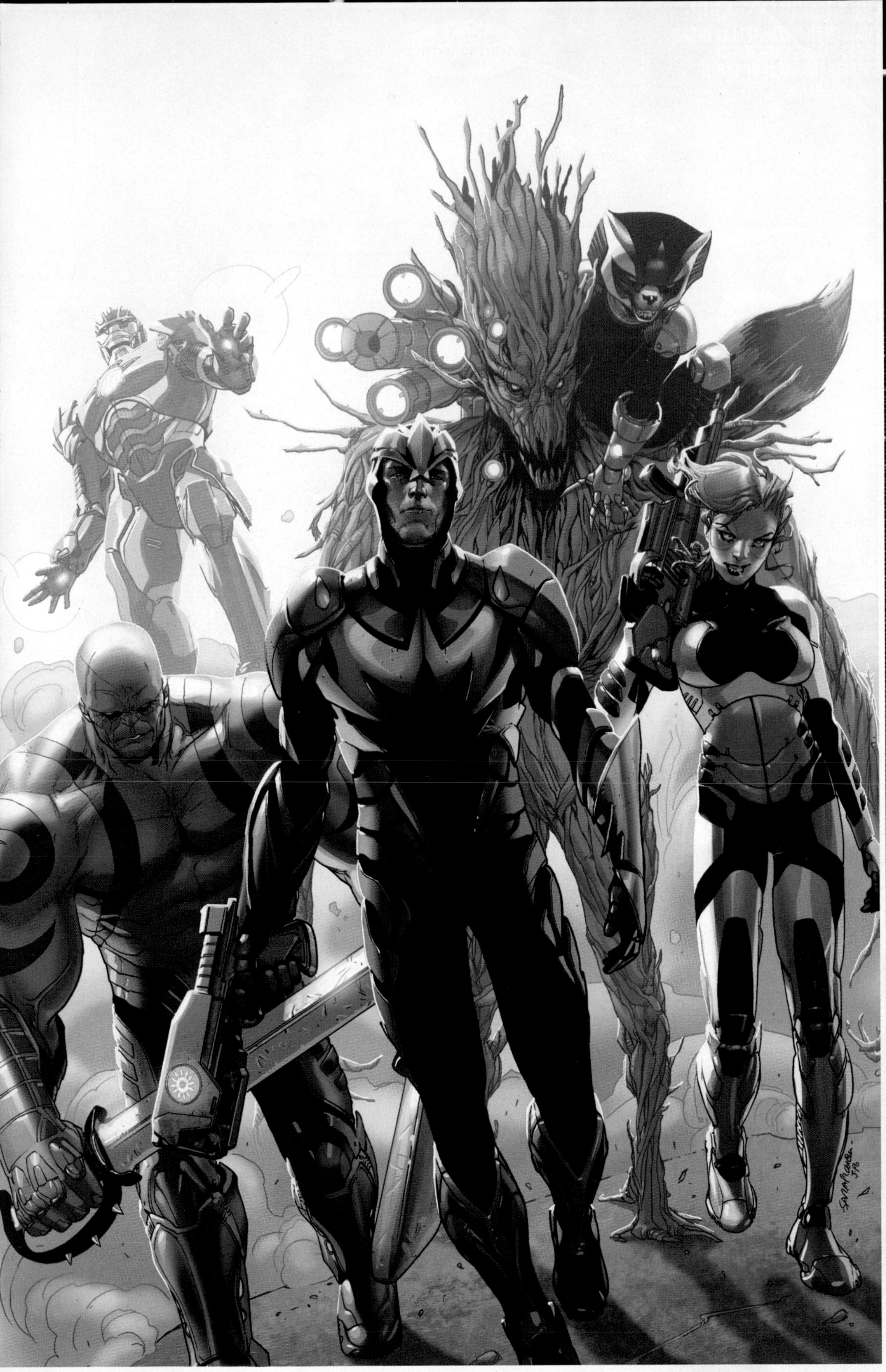

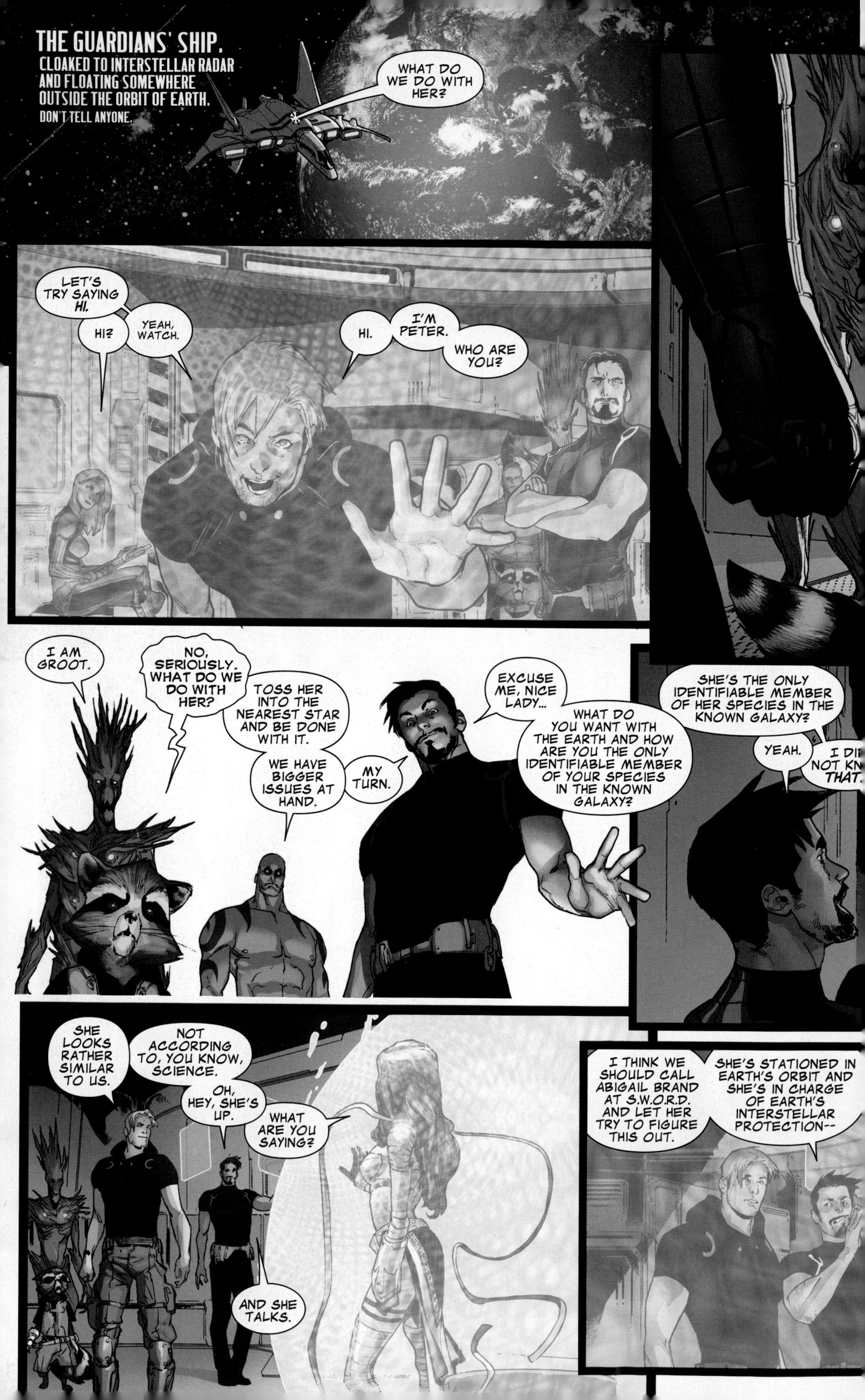
THE GUARDIANS' SHIP.
CLOAKED TO INTERSTELLAR RADAR AND FLOATING SOMEWHERE OUTSIDE THE ORBIT OF EARTH.
DON'T TELL ANYONE.
WHAT DO WE DO WITH HER?
LET'S TRY SAYING *HI.*
HI?
YEAH, WATCH.
HI.
I'M PETER.
WHO ARE YOU?
I AM GROOT.
NO, SERIOUSLY. WHAT DO WE DO WITH HER?
TOSS HER INTO THE NEAREST STAR AND BE DONE WITH IT.
WE HAVE BIGGER ISSUES AT HAND.
MY TURN.
EXCUSE ME, NICE LADY...
WHAT DO YOU WANT WITH THE EARTH AND HOW ARE YOU THE ONLY IDENTIFIABLE MEMBER OF YOUR SPECIES IN THE KNOWN GALAXY?
SHE'S THE ONLY IDENTIFIABLE MEMBER OF HER SPECIES IN THE KNOWN GALAXY?
YEAH.
SHE LOOKS RATHER SIMILAR TO US.
NOT ACCORDING TO, YOU KNOW, SCIENCE.
OH, HEY, SHE'S UP.
WHAT ARE YOU SAYING?
AND SHE TALKS.
I THINK WE SHOULD CALL ABIGAIL BRAND AT S.W.O.R.D. AND LET HER TRY TO FIGURE THIS OUT.
SHE'S STATIONED IN EARTH'S ORBIT AND SHE'S IN CHARGE OF EARTH'S INTERSTELLAR PROTECTION--

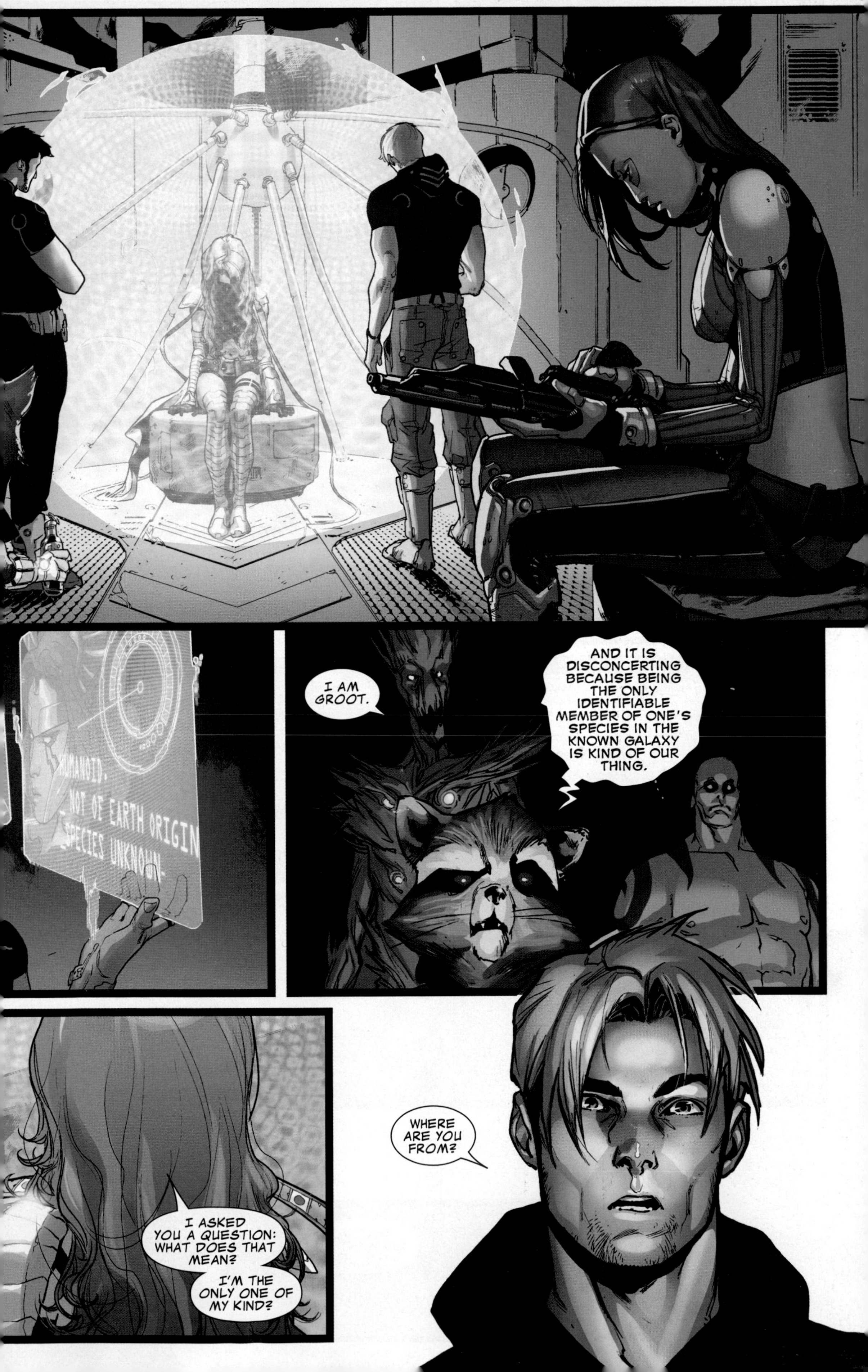
HUMANOID.
NOT OF EARTH ORIGIN
-SPECIES UNKNOWN-
I AM GROOT.
AND IT IS DISCONCERTING BECAUSE BEING THE ONLY IDENTIFIABLE MEMBER OF ONE'S SPECIES IN THE KNOWN GALAXY IS KIND OF OUR THING.
I ASKED YOU A QUESTION: WHAT DOES THAT MEAN?
I'M THE ONLY ONE OF MY KIND?
WHERE ARE YOU FROM?

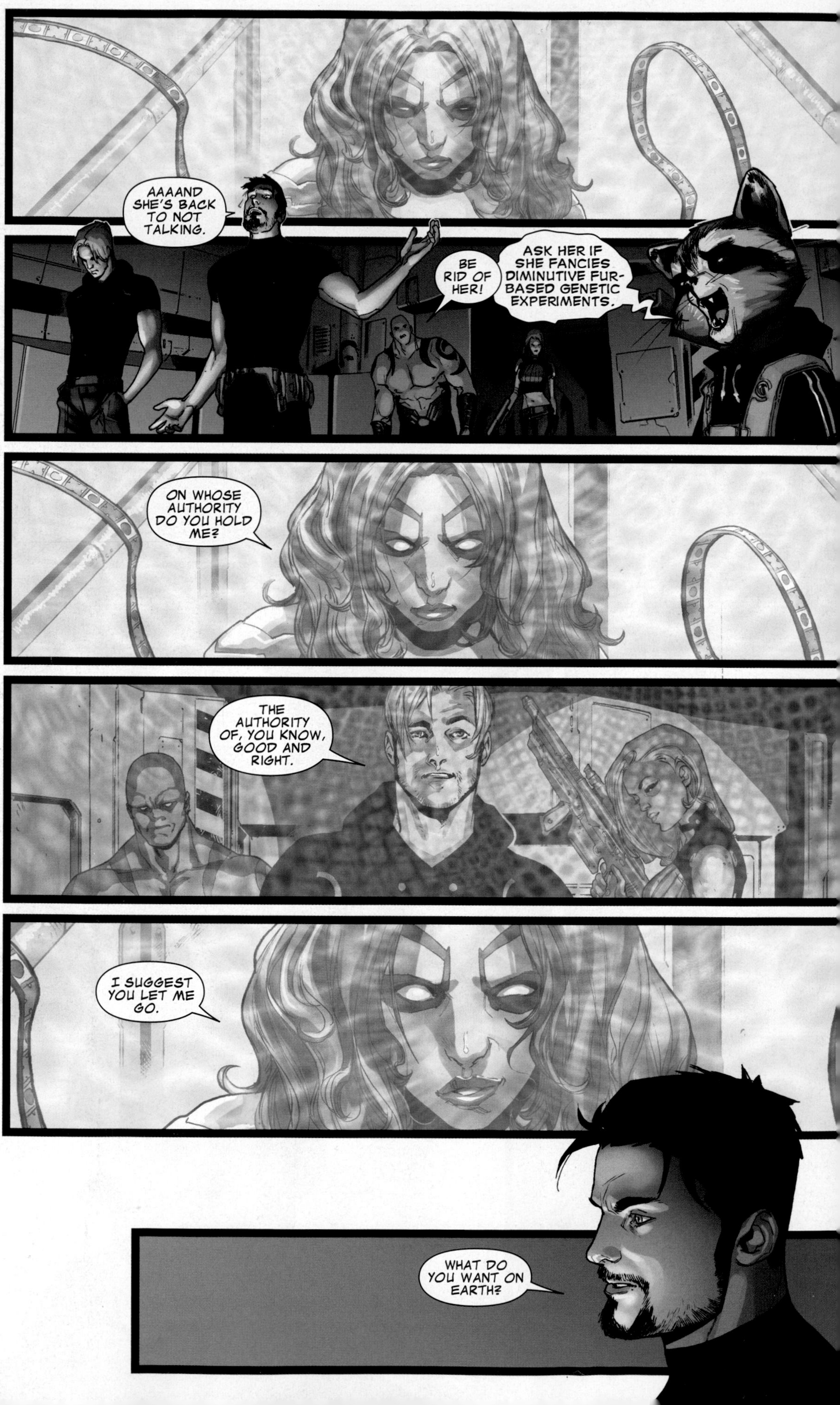
AAAAND SHE'S BACK TO NOT TALKING.
BE RID OF HER!
ASK HER IF SHE FANCIES DIMINUTIVE FUR-BASED GENETIC EXPERIMENTS.
ON WHOSE AUTHORITY DO YOU HOLD ME?
THE AUTHORITY OF, YOU KNOW, GOOD AND RIGHT.
I SUGGEST YOU LET ME GO.
WHAT DO YOU WANT ON EARTH?

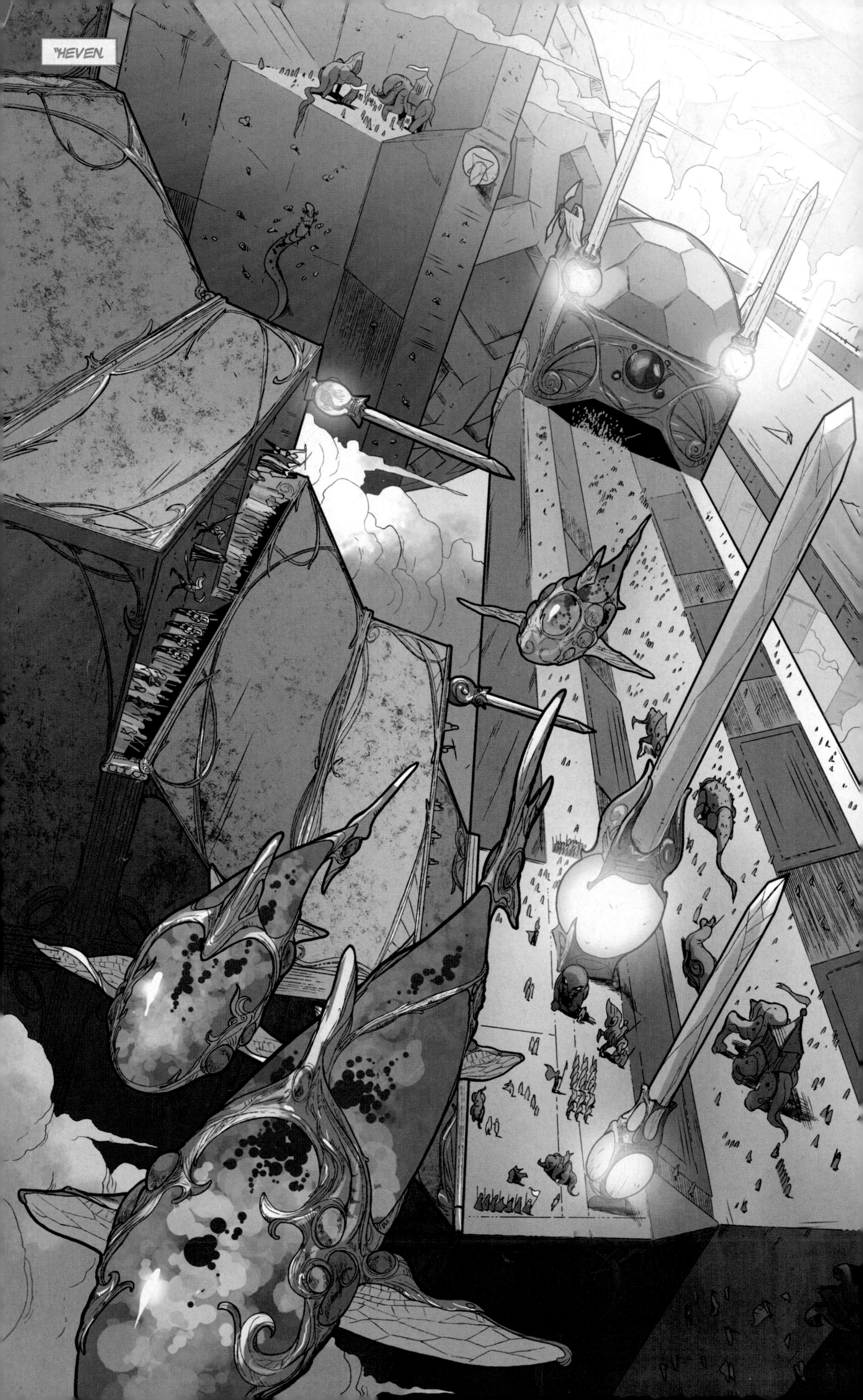
"HEVEN.

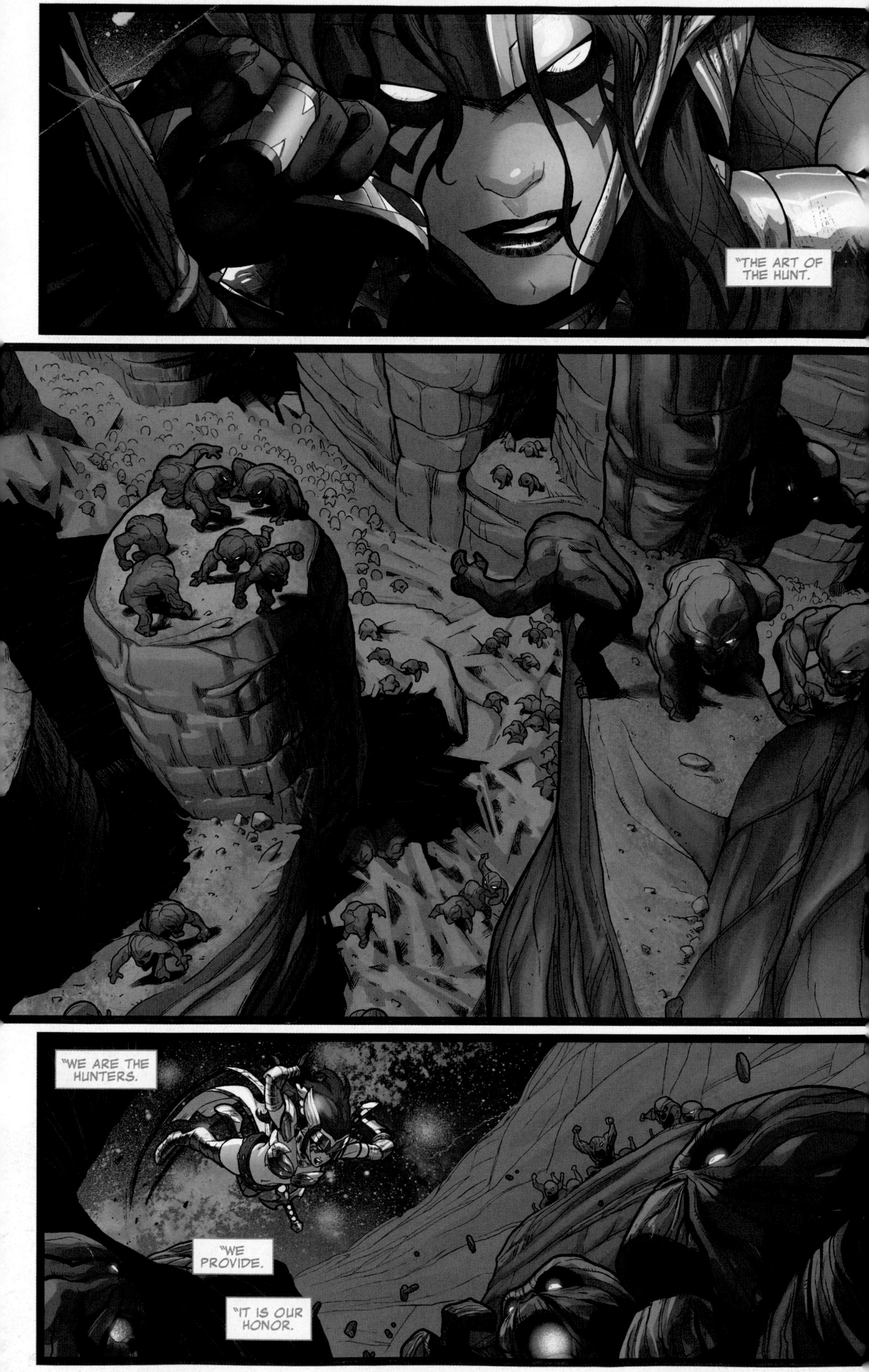
"THE ART OF THE HUNT.
"WE ARE THE HUNTERS.
"WE PROVIDE.
"IT IS OUR HONOR.

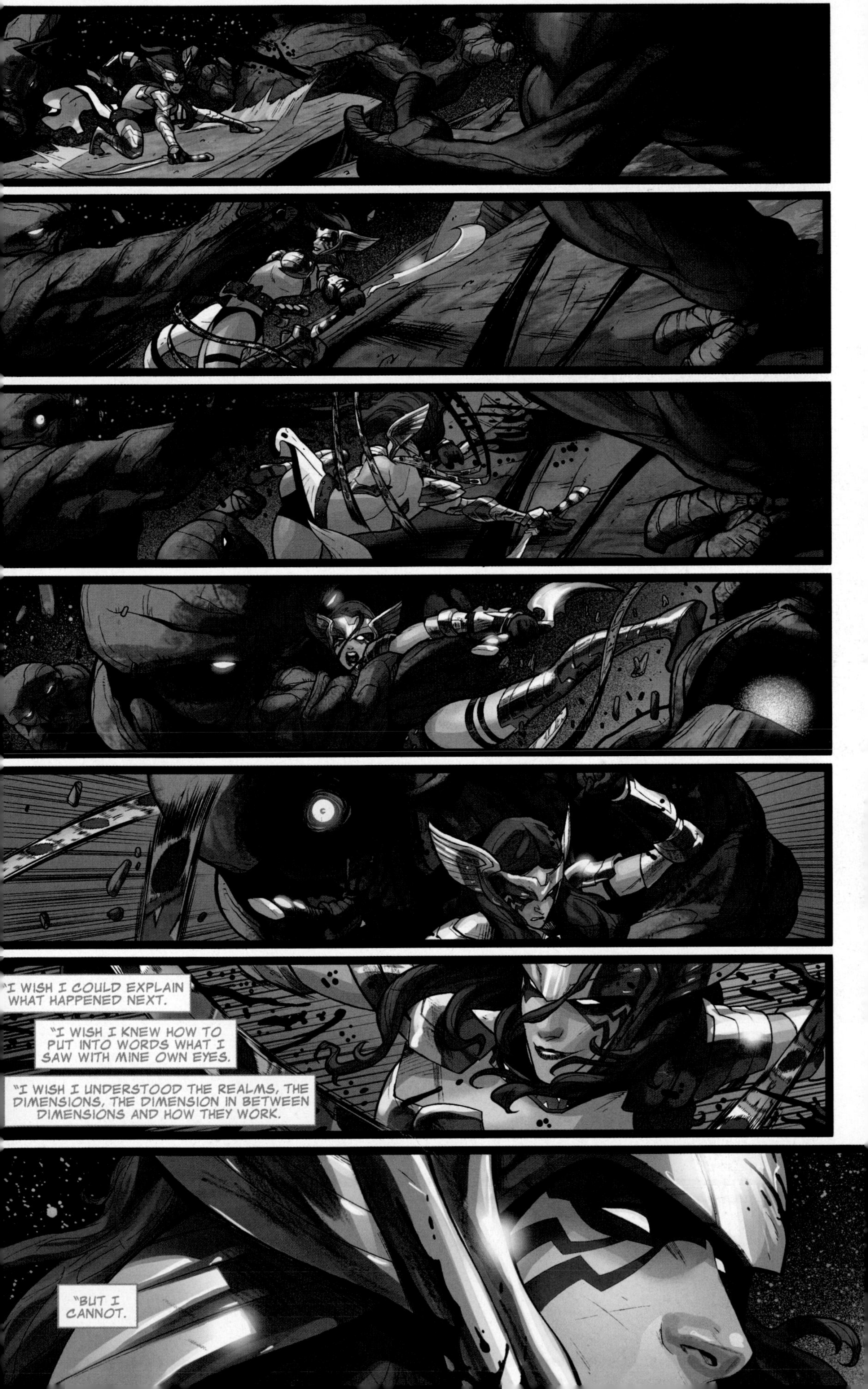

"I WISH I COULD EXPLAIN WHAT HAPPENED NEXT.
"I WISH I KNEW HOW TO PUT INTO WORDS WHAT I SAW WITH MINE OWN EYES.
"I WISH I UNDERSTOOD THE REALMS, THE DIMENSIONS, THE DIMENSION IN BETWEEN DIMENSIONS AND HOW THEY WORK.
"BUT I CANNOT.

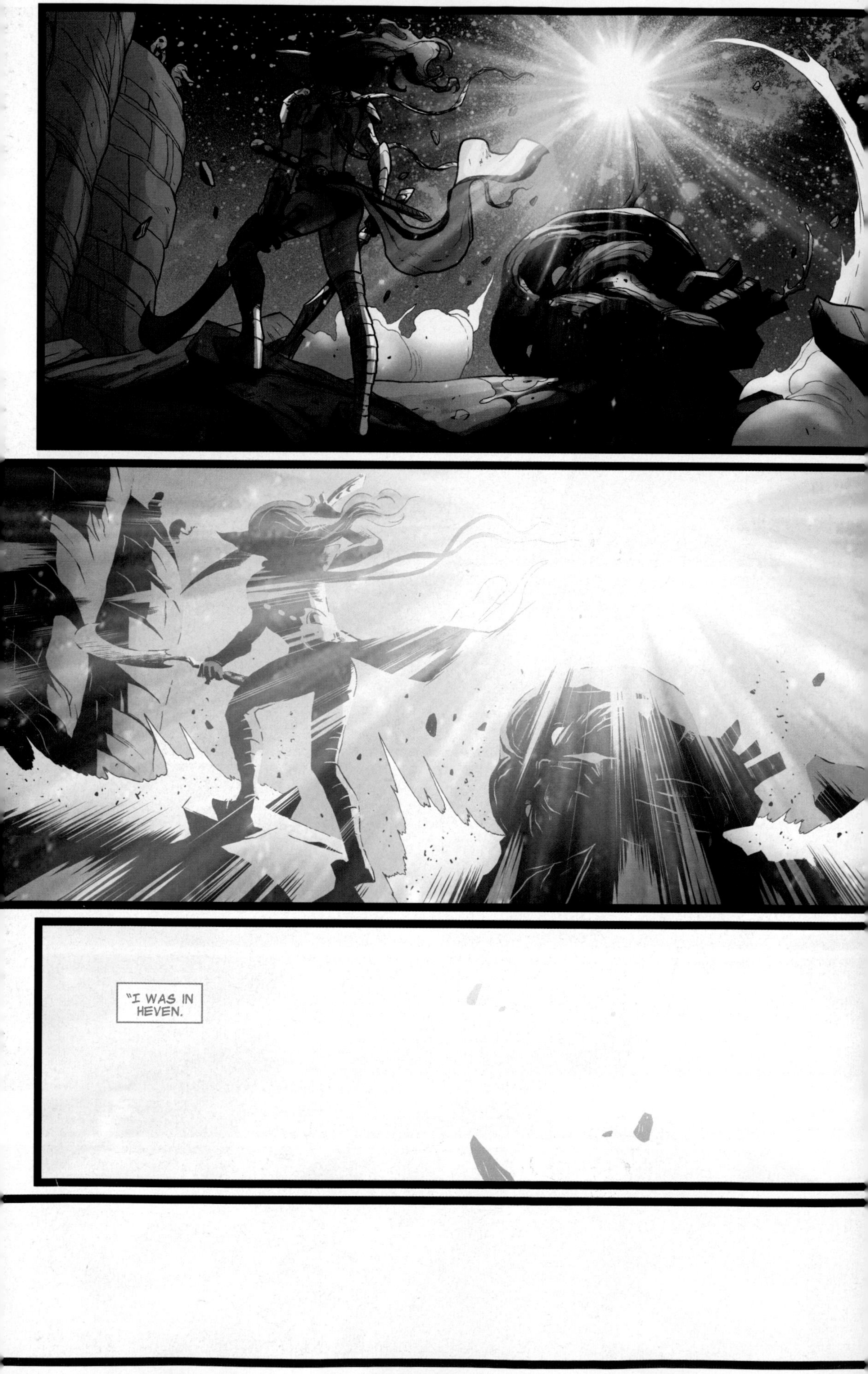
"I WAS IN HEVEN.

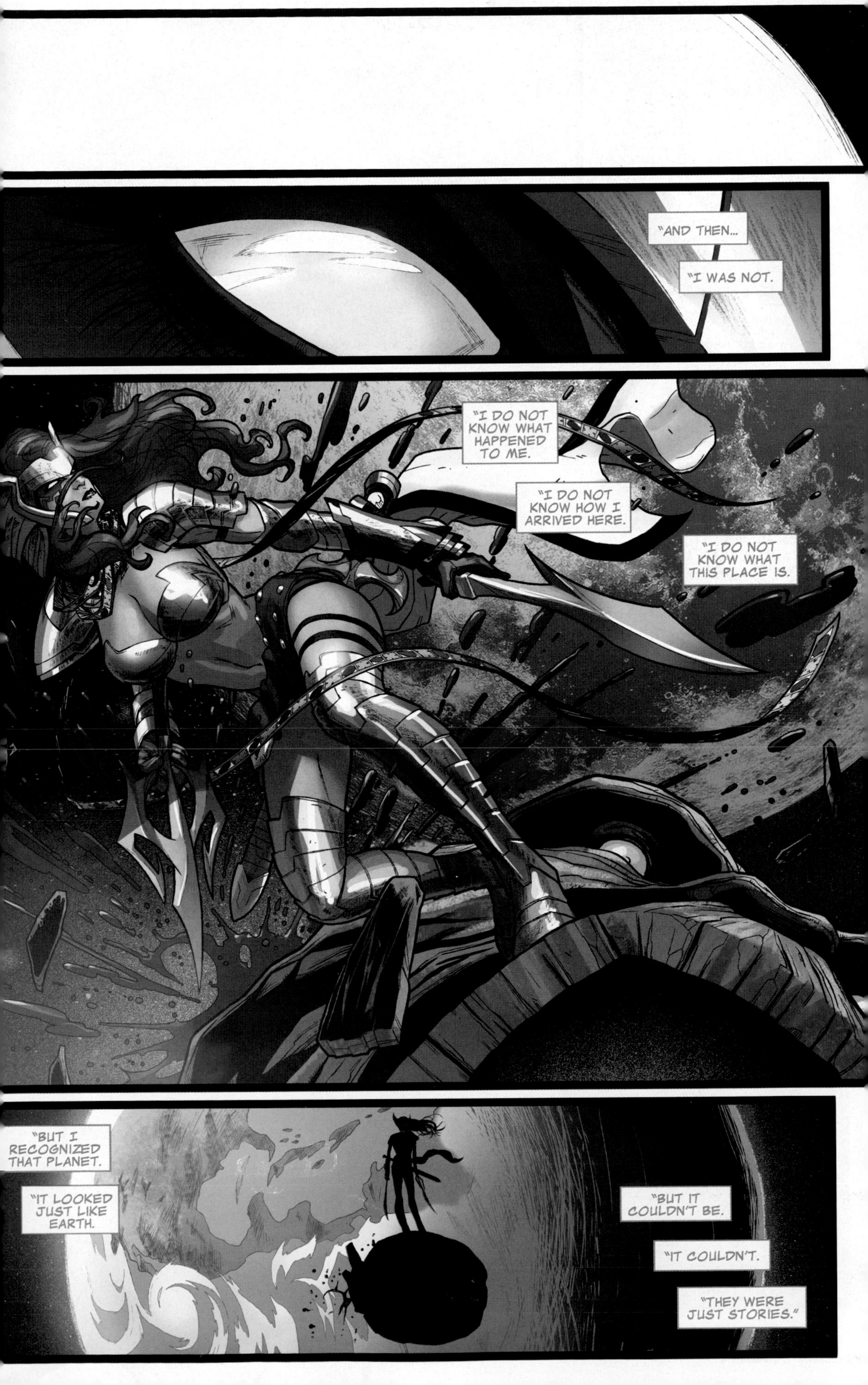
"AND THEN...
"I WAS NOT.
"I DO NOT KNOW WHAT HAPPENED TO ME.
"I DO NOT KNOW HOW I ARRIVED HERE.
"I DO NOT KNOW WHAT THIS PLACE IS.
"BUT I RECOGNIZED THAT PLANET.
"IT LOOKED JUST LIKE EARTH.
"BUT IT COULDN'T BE.
"IT COULDN'T.
"THEY WERE JUST STORIES."

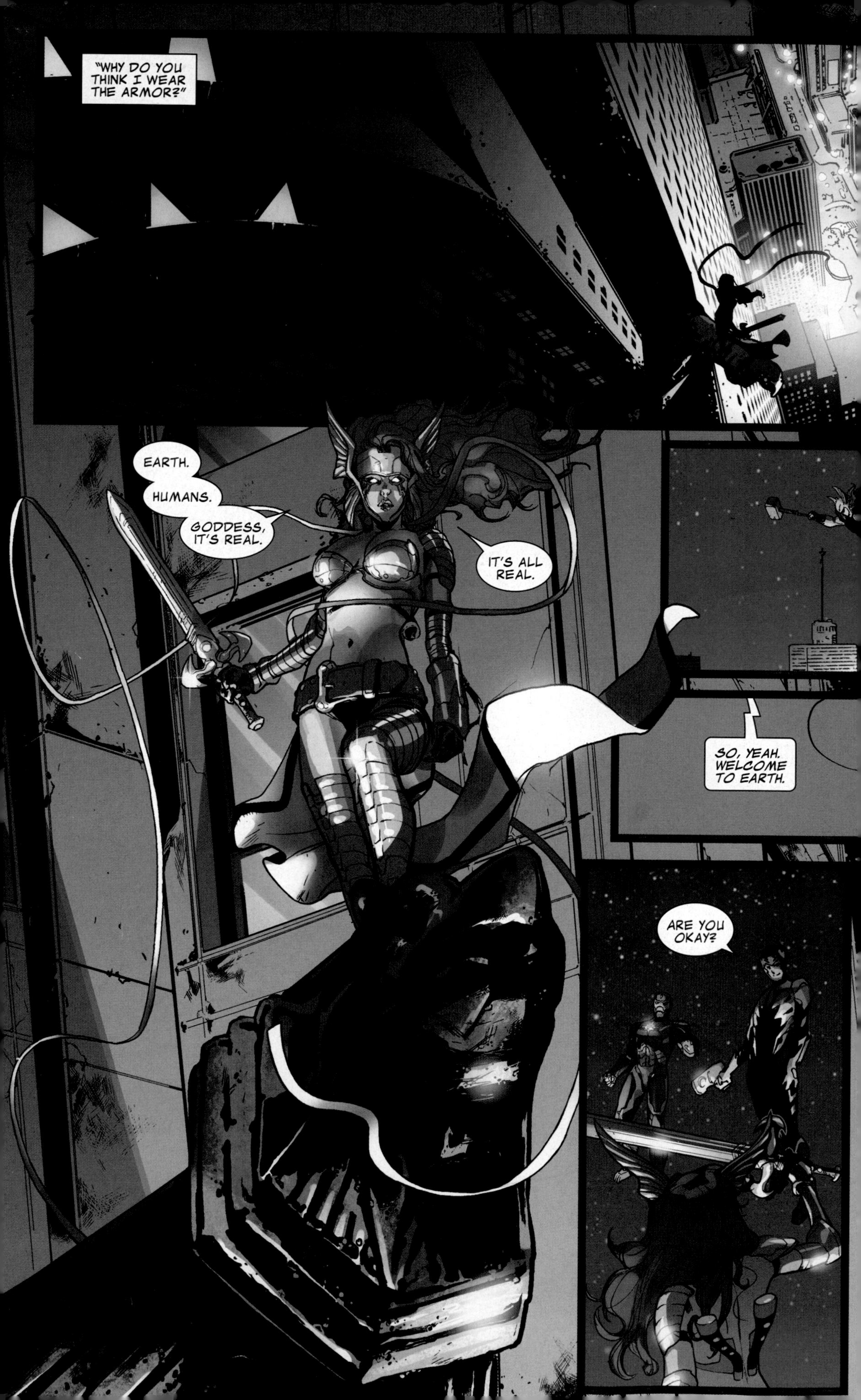
"WHY DO YOU THINK I WEAR THE ARMOR?"
EARTH.
HUMANS.
GODDESS, IT'S REAL.
IT'S ALL REAL.
SO, YEAH. WELCOME TO EARTH.
ARE YOU OKAY?

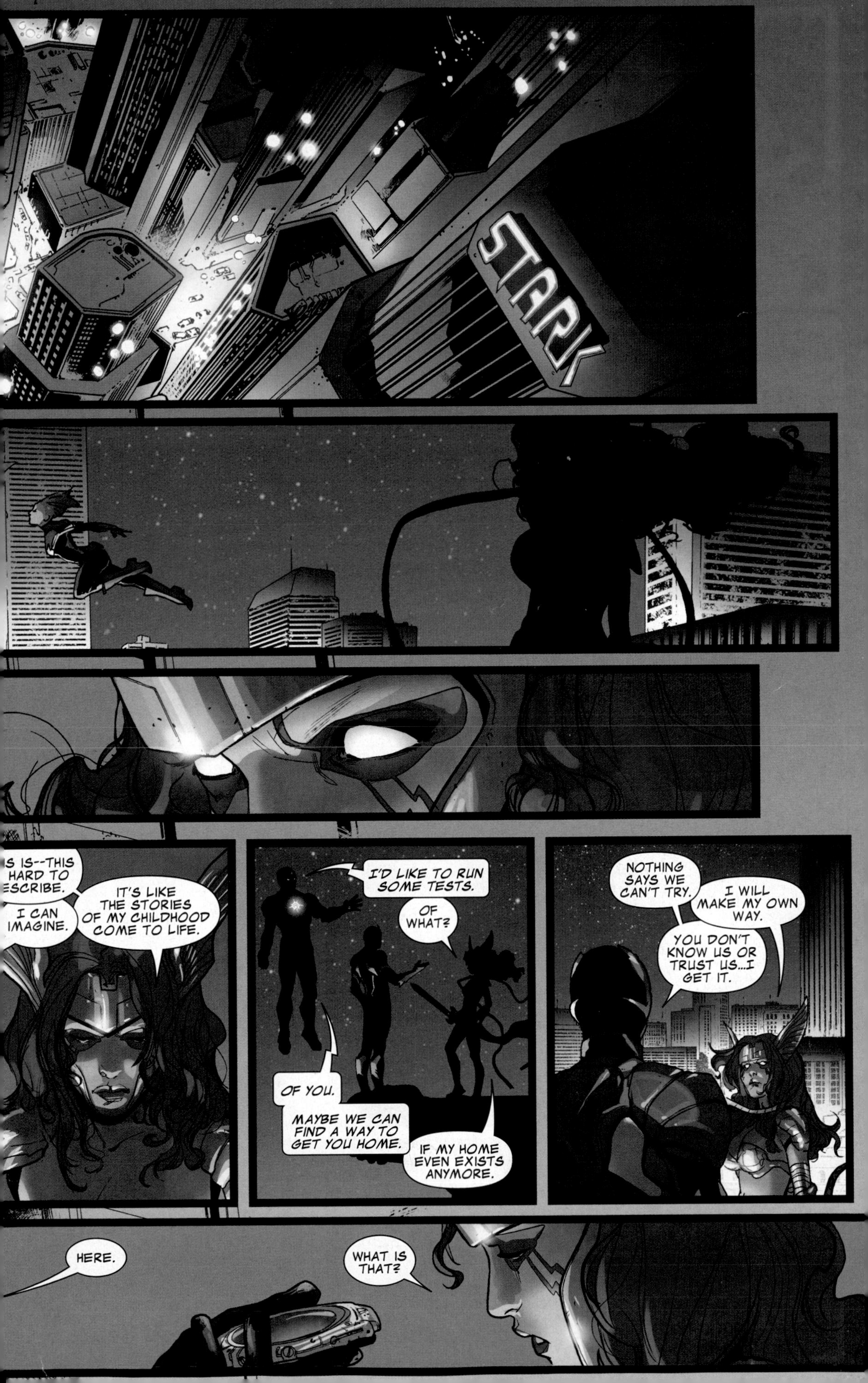
STARK
S IS--THIS HARD TO ESCRIBE.
I CAN IMAGINE.
IT'S LIKE THE STORIES OF MY CHILDHOOD COME TO LIFE.
I'D LIKE TO RUN SOME TESTS.
OF WHAT?
OF YOU.
MAYBE WE CAN FIND A WAY TO GET YOU HOME.
IF MY HOME EVEN EXISTS ANYMORE.
NOTHING SAYS WE CAN'T TRY.
YOU DON'T KNOW US OR TRUST US...I GET IT.
I WILL MAKE MY OWN WAY.
HERE.
WHAT IS THAT?

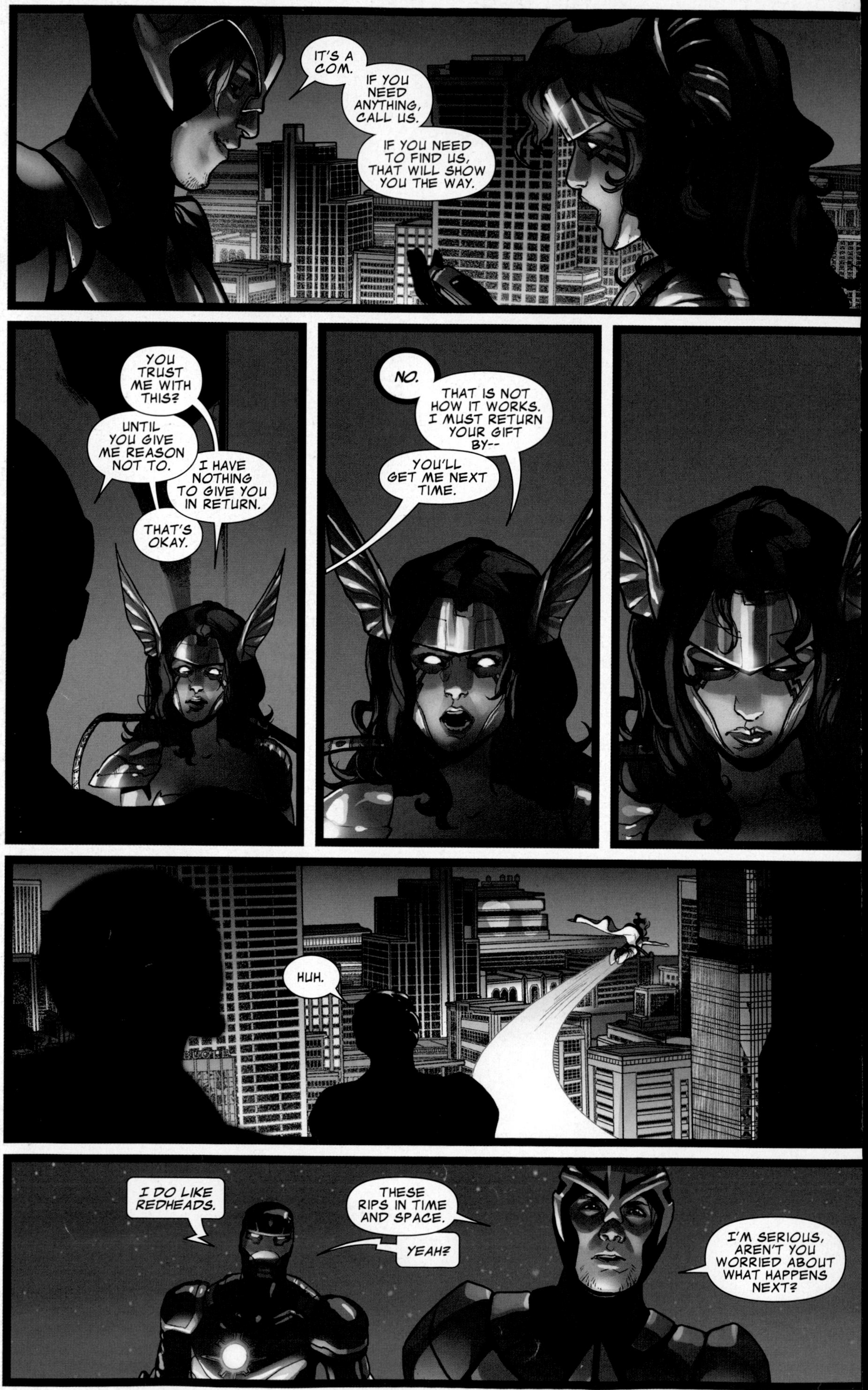
IT'S A COM.
IF YOU NEED ANYTHING, CALL US.
IF YOU NEED TO FIND US, THAT WILL SHOW YOU THE WAY.
YOU TRUST ME WITH THIS?
UNTIL YOU GIVE ME REASON NOT TO.
I HAVE NOTHING TO GIVE YOU IN RETURN.
THAT'S OKAY.
NO.
THAT IS NOT HOW IT WORKS. I MUST RETURN YOUR GIFT BY--
YOU'LL GET ME NEXT TIME.
HUH.
I DO LIKE REDHEADS.
THESE RIPS IN TIME AND SPACE.
YEAH?
I'M SERIOUS, AREN'T YOU WORRIED ABOUT WHAT HAPPENS NEXT?

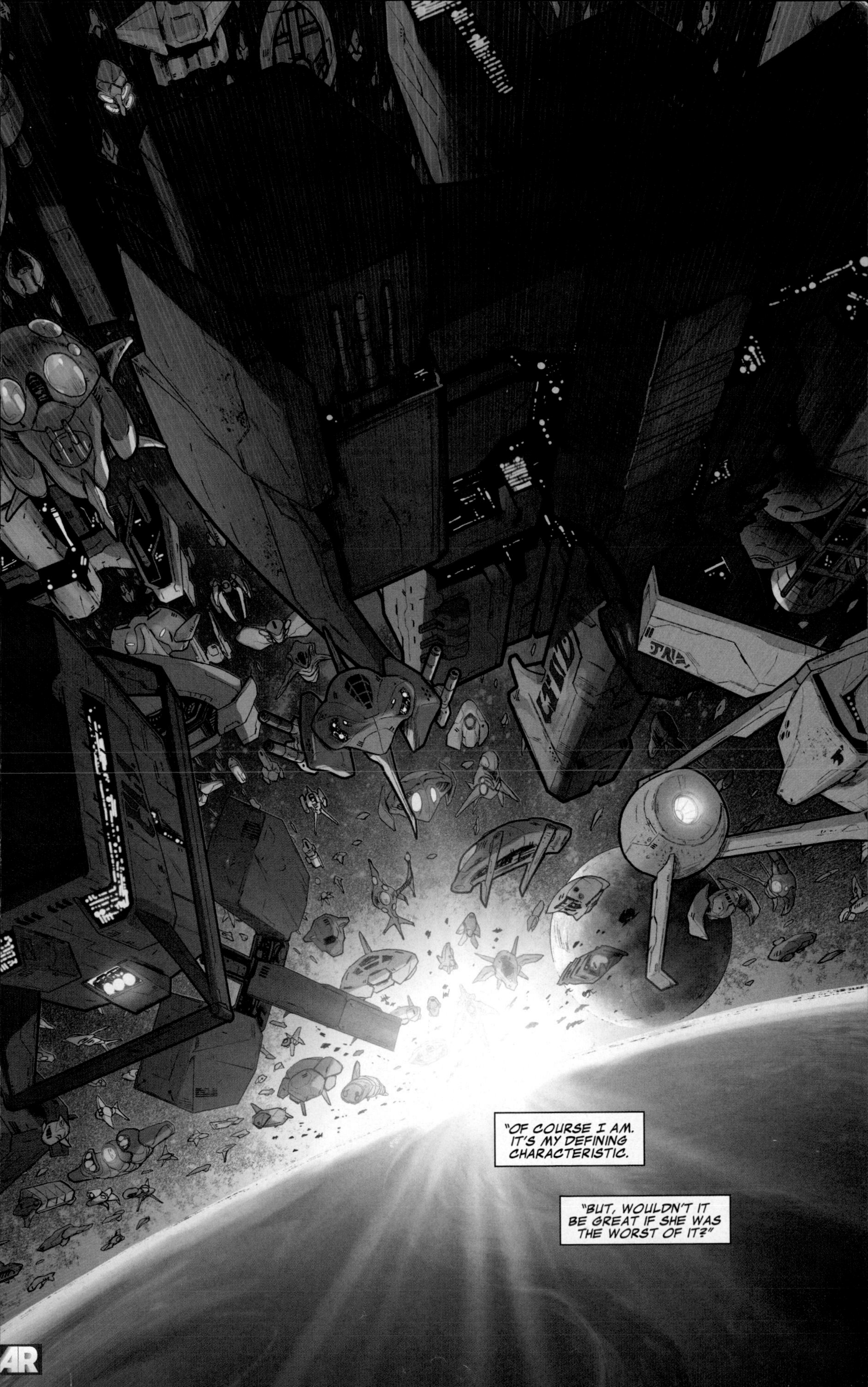
"OF COURSE I AM. IT'S MY DEFINING CHARACTERISTIC.
"BUT, WOULDN'T IT BE GREAT IF SHE WAS THE WORST OF IT?"

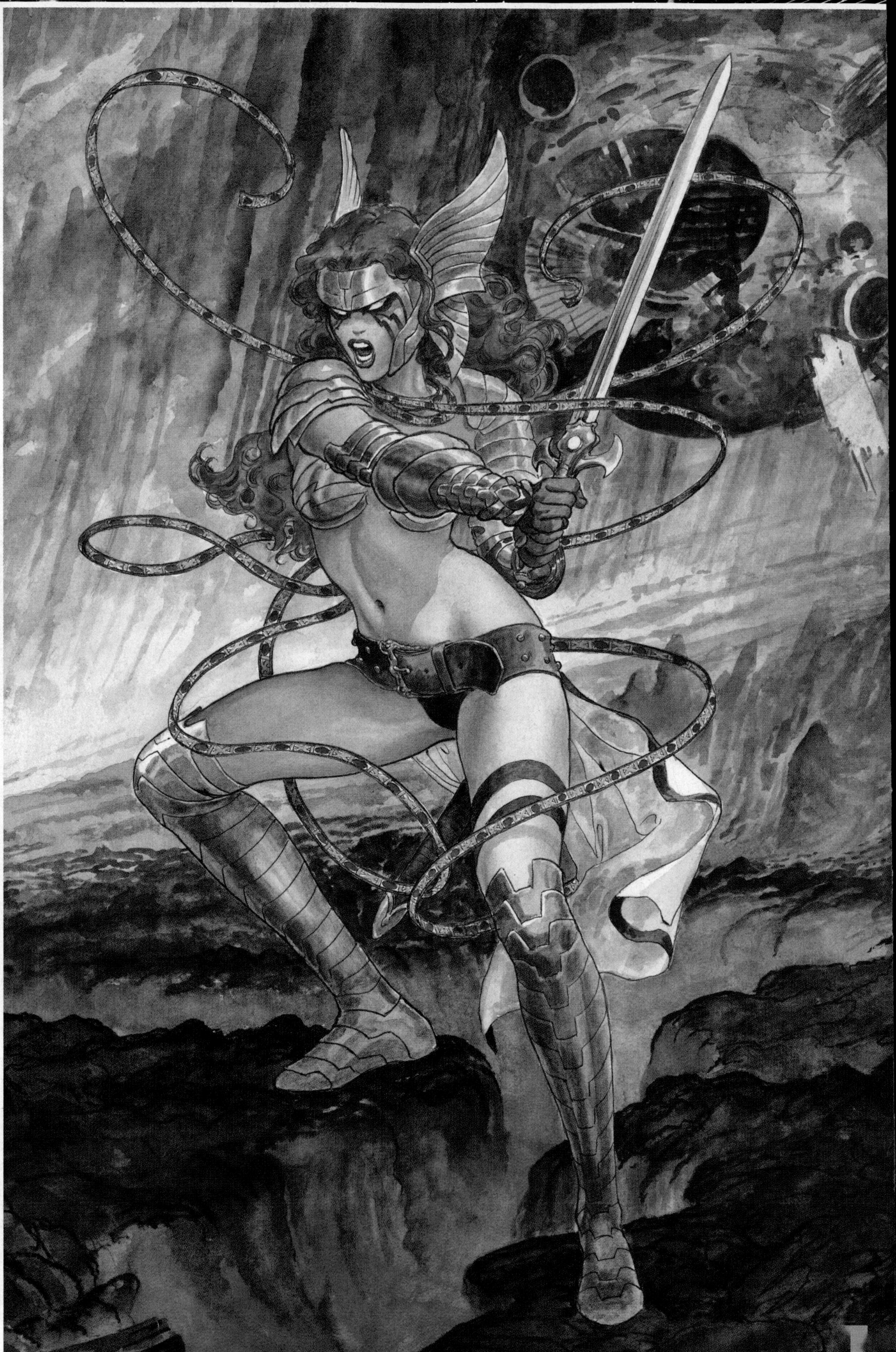

#5 VARIANT BY MILO MANARA

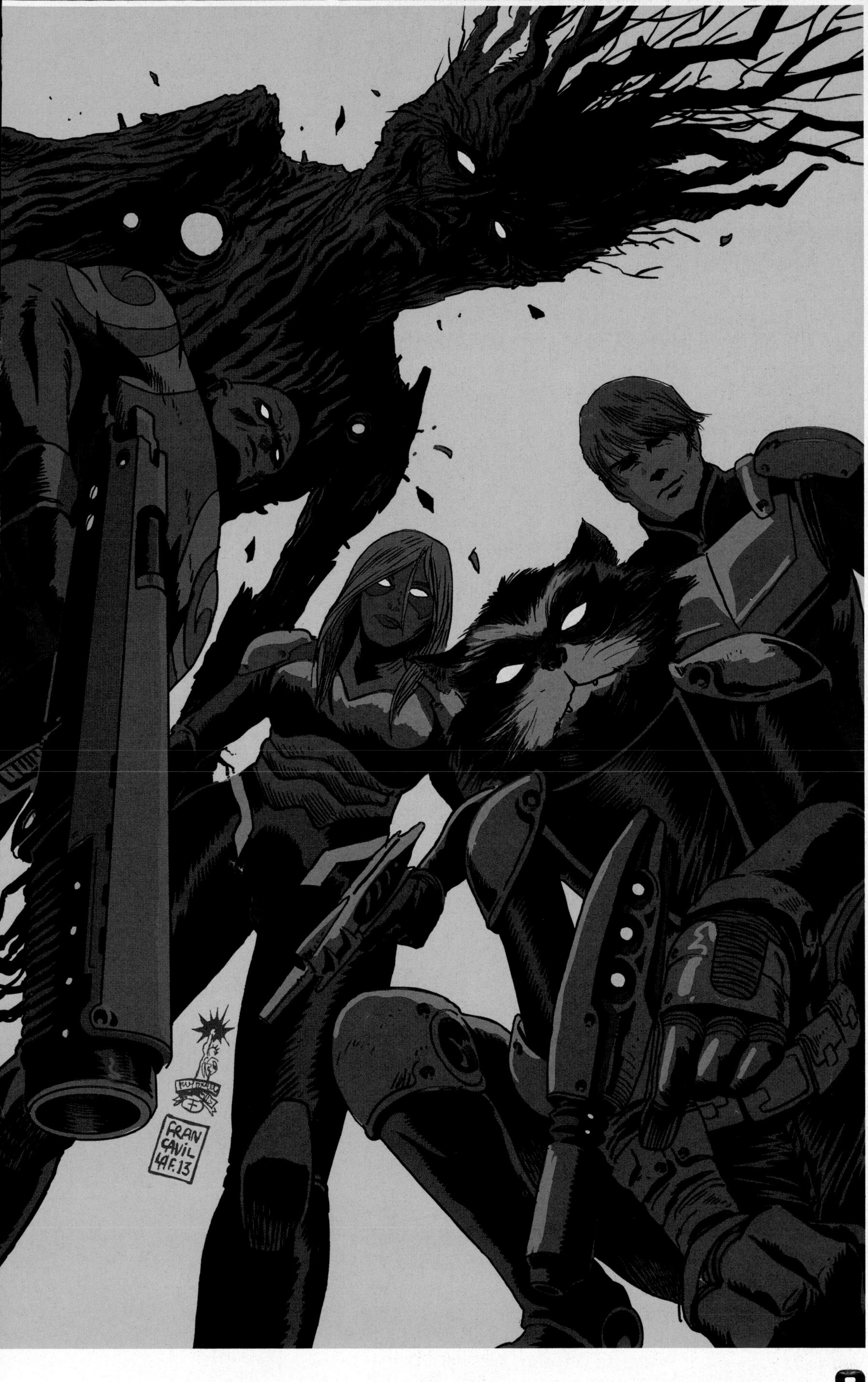

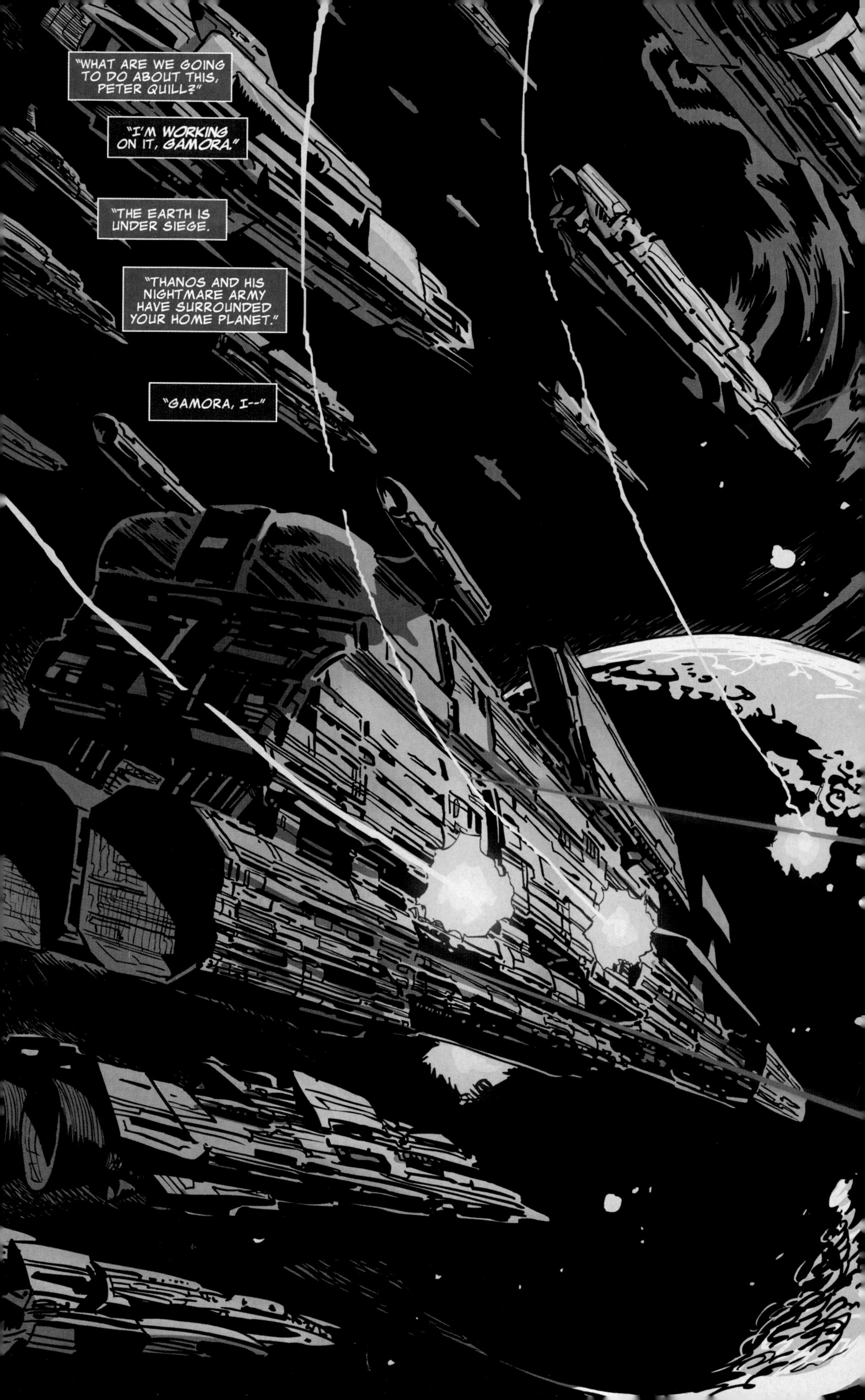
"WHAT ARE WE GOING TO DO ABOUT THIS, PETER QUILL?"
"I'M WORKING ON IT, GAMORA."
"THE EARTH IS UNDER SIEGE.
"THANOS AND HIS NIGHTMARE ARMY HAVE SURROUNDED YOUR HOME PLANET."
"GAMORA, I--"

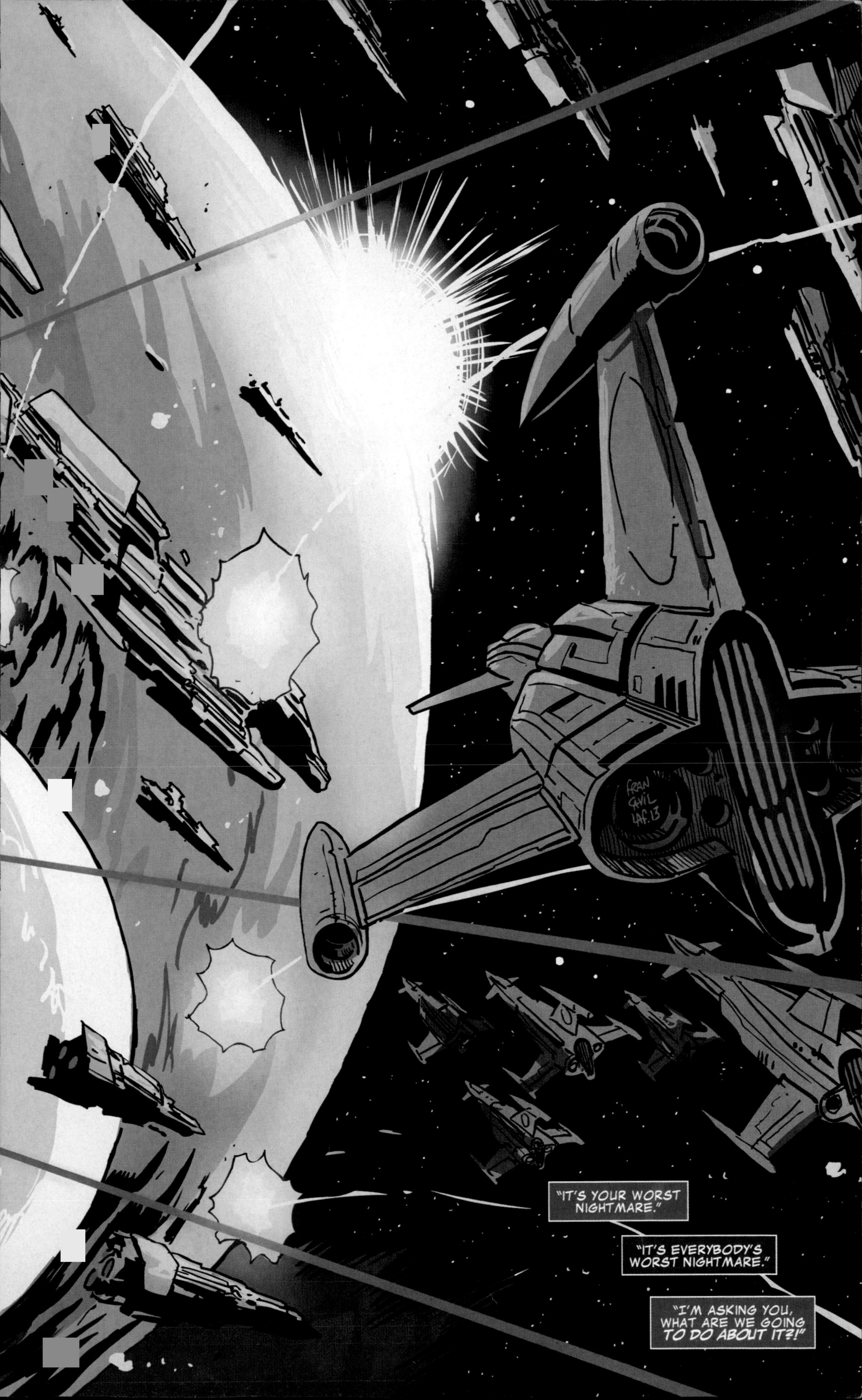
"IT'S YOUR WORST NIGHTMARE."
"IT'S EVERYBODY'S WORST NIGHTMARE."
"I'M ASKING YOU, WHAT ARE WE GOING TO DO ABOUT IT?!"

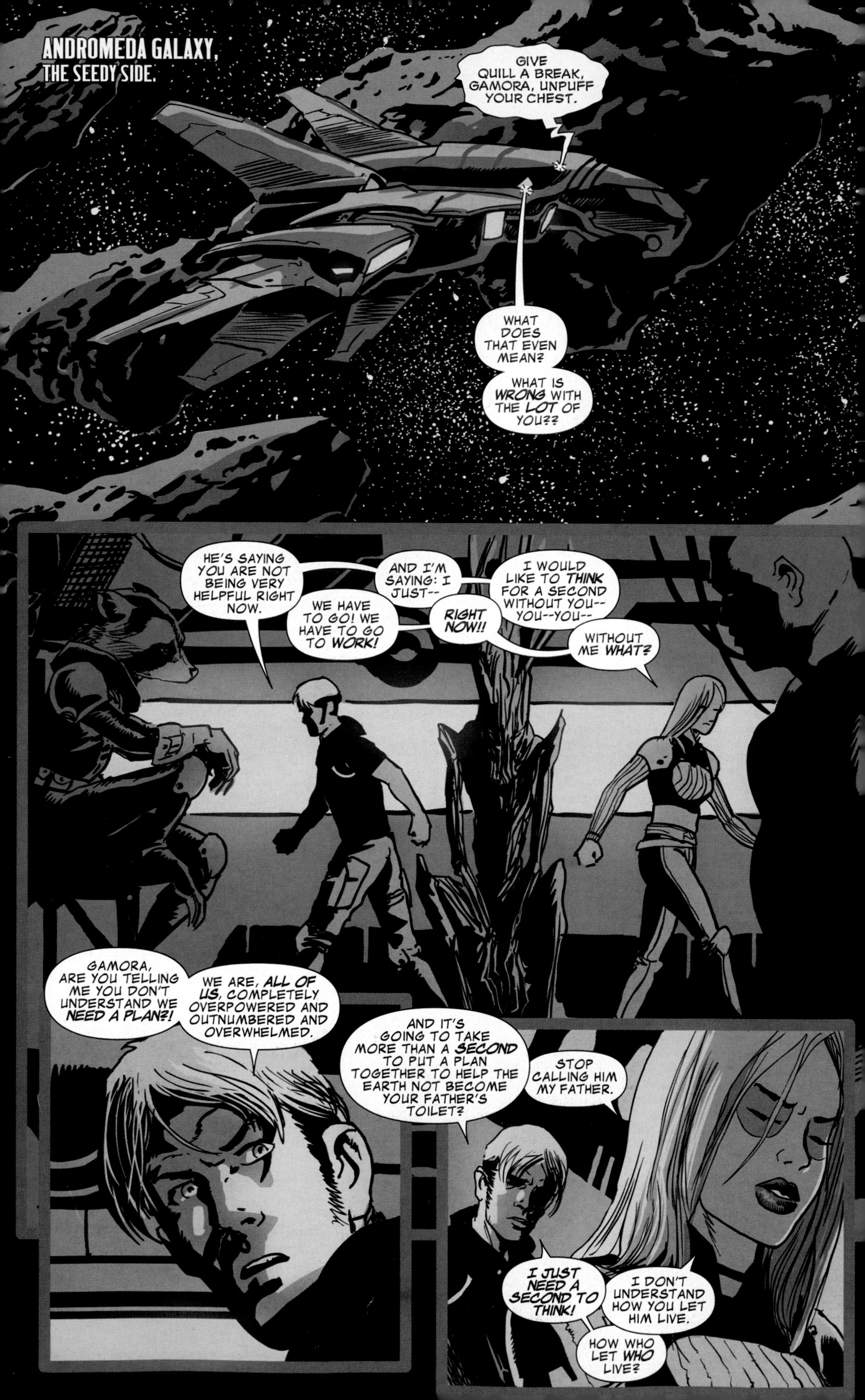
ANDROMEDA GALAXY, THE SEEDY SIDE.
GIVE QUILL A BREAK, GAMORA, UNPUFF YOUR CHEST.
WHAT DOES THAT EVEN MEAN?
WHAT IS WRONG WITH THE LOT OF YOU??
HE'S SAYING YOU ARE NOT BEING VERY HELPFUL RIGHT NOW.
AND I'M SAYING: I JUST--
I WOULD LIKE TO THINK FOR A SECOND WITHOUT YOU-- YOU--YOU--
WE HAVE TO GO! WE HAVE TO GO TO WORK!
RIGHT NOW!!
WITHOUT ME WHAT?
GAMORA, ARE YOU TELLING ME YOU DON'T UNDERSTAND WE NEED A PLAN?!
WE ARE, ALL OF US, COMPLETELY OVERPOWERED AND OUTNUMBERED AND OVERWHELMED.
AND IT'S GOING TO TAKE MORE THAN A SECOND TO PUT A PLAN TOGETHER TO HELP THE EARTH NOT BECOME YOUR FATHER'S TOILET?
STOP CALLING HIM MY FATHER.
I JUST NEED A SECOND TO THINK!
I DON'T UNDERSTAND HOW YOU LET HIM LIVE.
HOW WHO LET WHO LIVE?

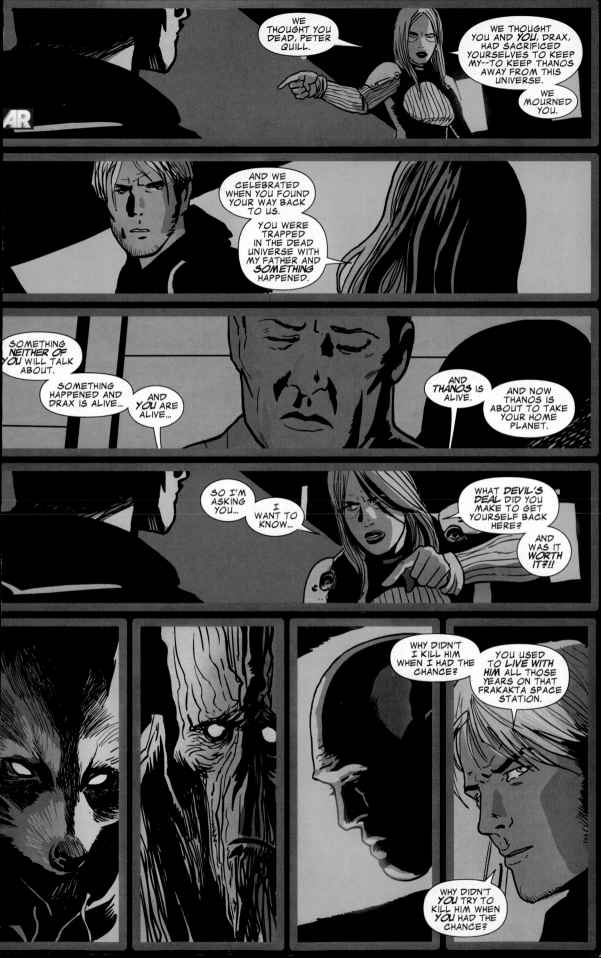

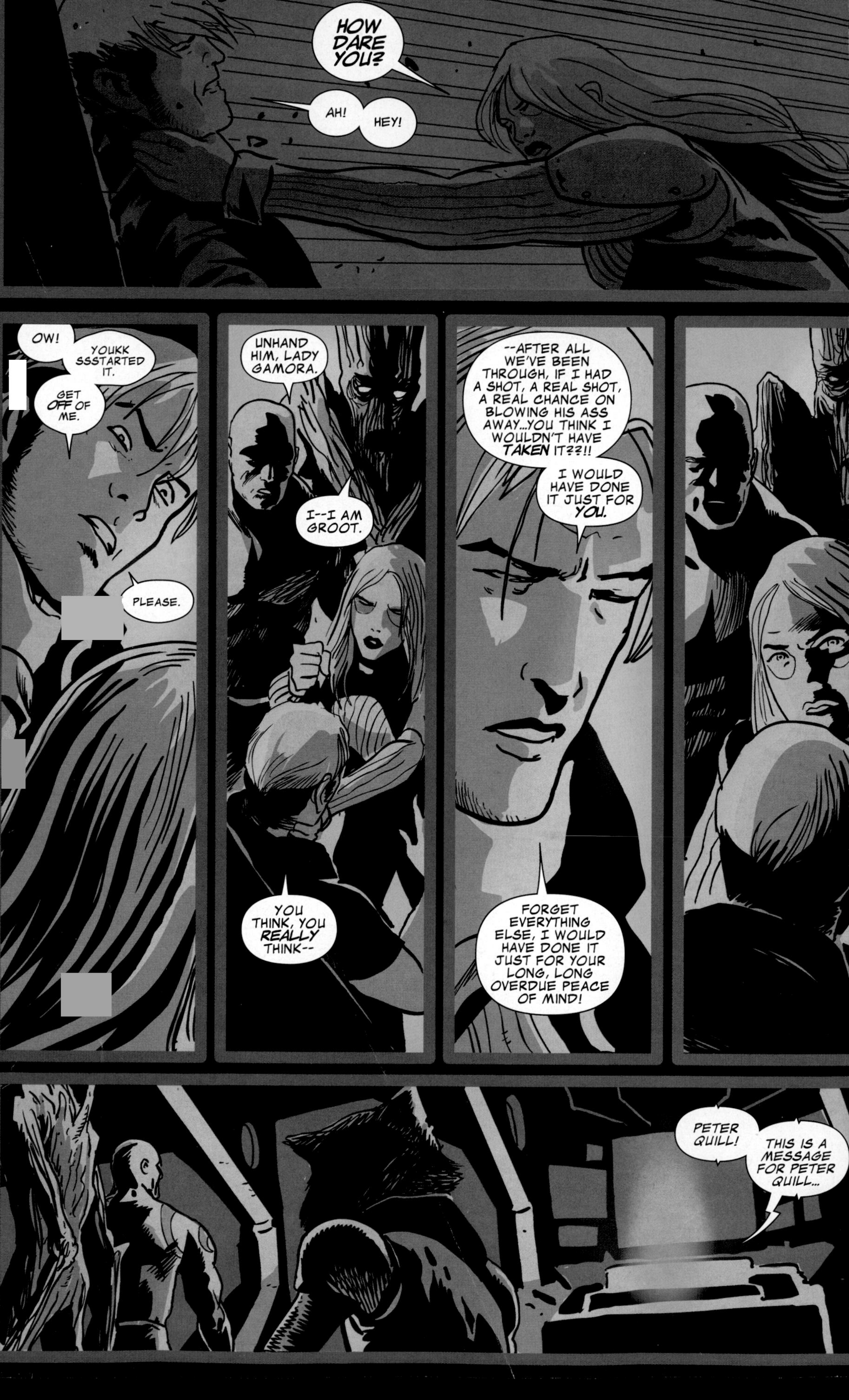
HOW DARE YOU?
AH!
HEY!
OW!
YOUKK SSSTARTED IT.
GET OFF OF ME.
PLEASE.
UNHAND HIM, LADY GAMORA.
I--I AM GROOT.
YOU THINK, YOU REALLY THINK--
--AFTER ALL WE'VE BEEN THROUGH, IF I HAD A SHOT, A REAL SHOT, A REAL CHANCE ON BLOWING HIS ASS AWAY...YOU THINK I WOULDN'T HAVE TAKEN IT??!!
I WOULD HAVE DONE IT JUST FOR YOU.
FORGET EVERYTHING ELSE, I WOULD HAVE DONE IT JUST FOR YOUR LONG, LONG OVERDUE PEACE OF MIND!
PETER QUILL!
THIS IS A MESSAGE FOR PETER QUILL...

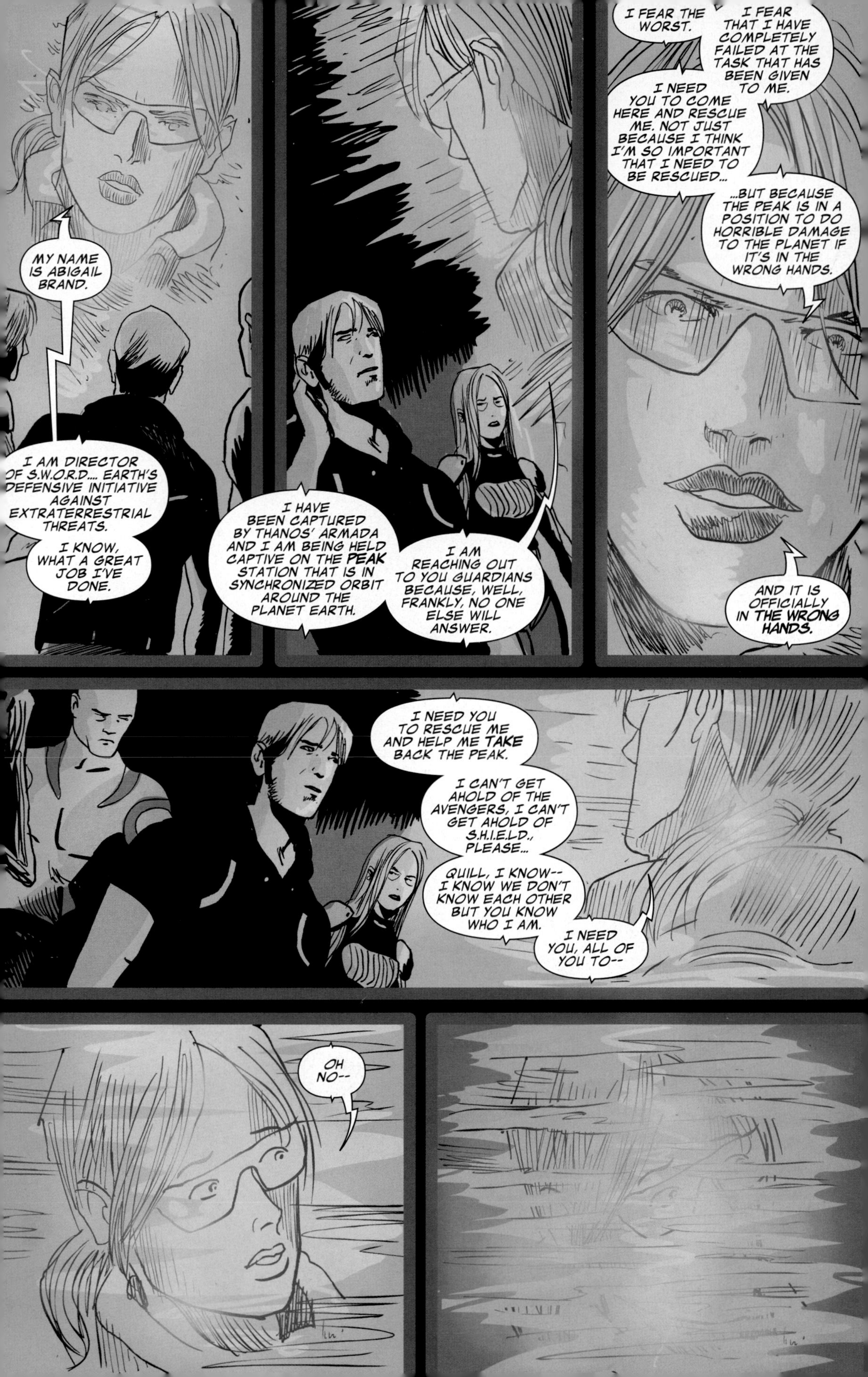
MY NAME IS ABIGAIL BRAND.
I AM DIRECTOR OF S.W.O.R.D.... EARTH'S DEFENSIVE INITIATIVE AGAINST EXTRATERRESTRIAL THREATS.
I KNOW, WHAT A GREAT JOB I'VE DONE.
I HAVE BEEN CAPTURED BY THANOS' ARMADA AND I AM BEING HELD CAPTIVE ON THE PEAK STATION THAT IS IN SYNCHRONIZED ORBIT AROUND THE PLANET EARTH.
I AM REACHING OUT TO YOU GUARDIANS BECAUSE, WELL, FRANKLY, NO ONE ELSE WILL ANSWER.
I FEAR THE WORST.
I FEAR THAT I HAVE COMPLETELY FAILED AT THE TASK THAT HAS BEEN GIVEN TO ME.
I NEED YOU TO COME HERE AND RESCUE ME. NOT JUST BECAUSE I THINK I'M SO IMPORTANT THAT I NEED TO BE RESCUED...
...BUT BECAUSE THE PEAK IS IN A POSITION TO DO HORRIBLE DAMAGE TO THE PLANET IF IT'S IN THE WRONG HANDS.
AND IT IS OFFICIALLY IN THE WRONG HANDS.
I NEED YOU TO RESCUE ME AND HELP ME TAKE BACK THE PEAK.
I CAN'T GET AHOLD OF THE AVENGERS, I CAN'T GET AHOLD OF S.H.I.E.L.D., PLEASE...
QUILL, I KNOW-- I KNOW WE DON'T KNOW EACH OTHER BUT YOU KNOW WHO I AM.
I NEED YOU, ALL OF YOU TO--
OH NO--

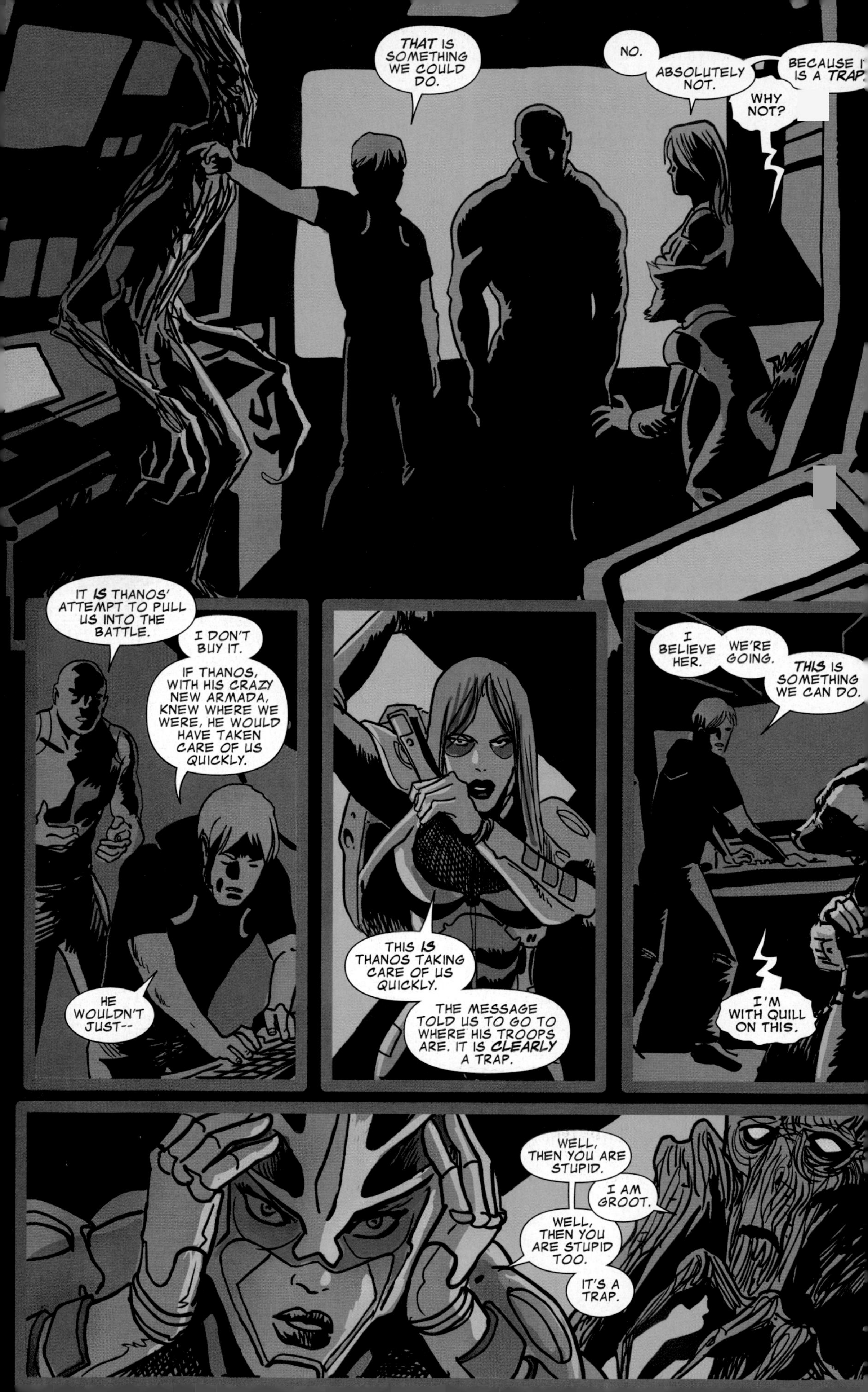
THAT IS SOMETHING WE COULD DO.
NO.
ABSOLUTELY NOT.
WHY NOT?
BECAUSE IT IS A TRAP.
IT IS THANOS' ATTEMPT TO PULL US INTO THE BATTLE.
I DON'T BUY IT.
IF THANOS, WITH HIS CRAZY NEW ARMADA, KNEW WHERE WE WERE, HE WOULD HAVE TAKEN CARE OF US QUICKLY.
HE WOULDN'T JUST--
THIS IS THANOS TAKING CARE OF US QUICKLY.
THE MESSAGE TOLD US TO GO TO WHERE HIS TROOPS ARE. IT IS CLEARLY A TRAP.
I BELIEVE HER.
WE'RE GOING.
THIS IS SOMETHING WE CAN DO.
I'M WITH QUILL ON THIS.
WELL, THEN YOU ARE STUPID.
I AM GROOT.
WELL, THEN YOU ARE STUPID TOO.
IT'S A TRAP.

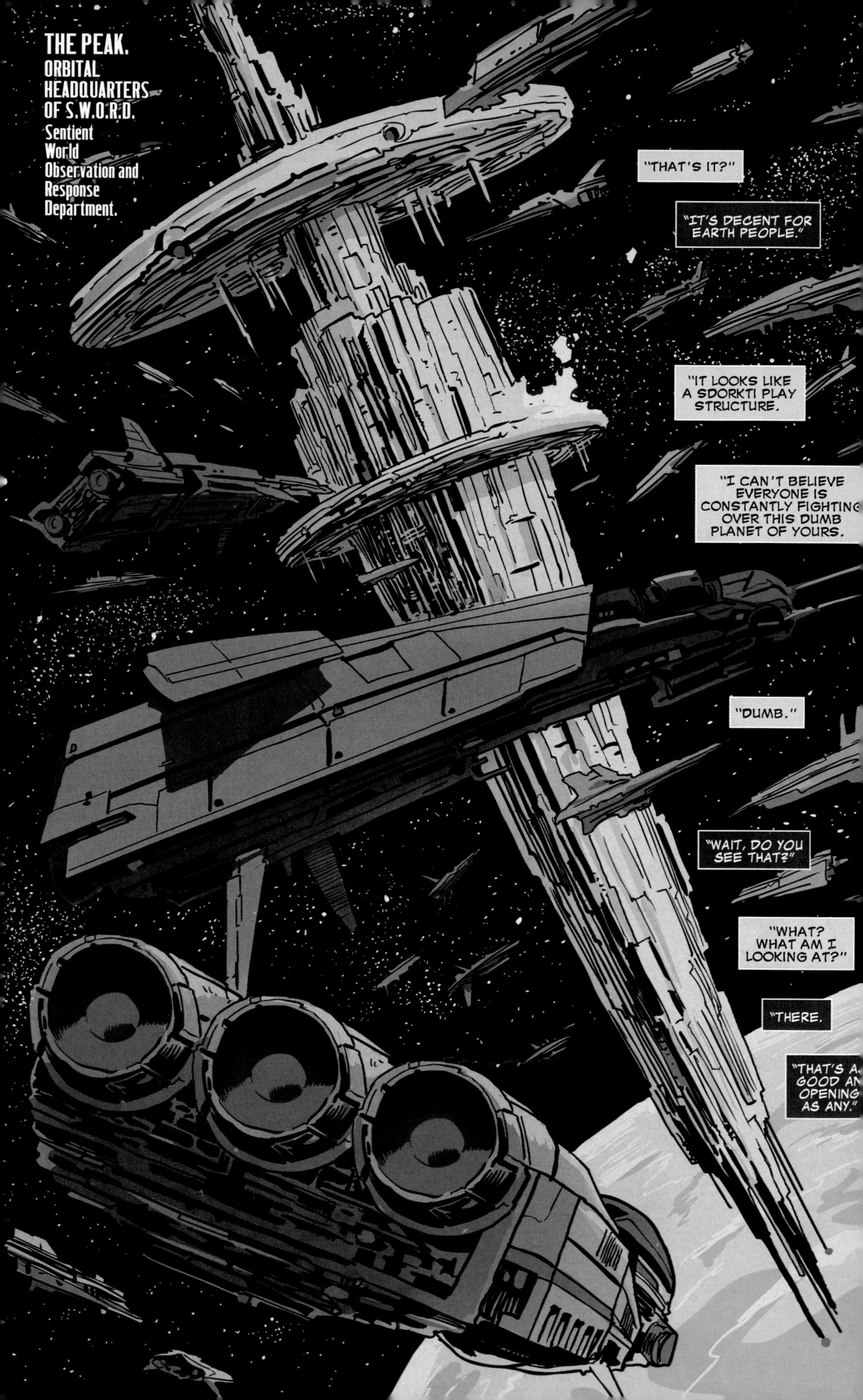
THE PEAK.
ORBITAL HEADQUARTERS OF S.W.O.R.D.
Sentient World Observation and Response Department.
"THAT'S IT?"
"IT'S DECENT FOR EARTH PEOPLE."
"IT LOOKS LIKE A SDORKTI PLAY STRUCTURE.
"I CAN'T BELIEVE EVERYONE IS CONSTANTLY FIGHTING OVER THIS DUMB PLANET OF YOURS.
"DUMB."
"WAIT, DO YOU SEE THAT?"
"WHAT? WHAT AM I LOOKING AT?"
"THERE.
"THAT'S A GOOD AN OPENING AS ANY."

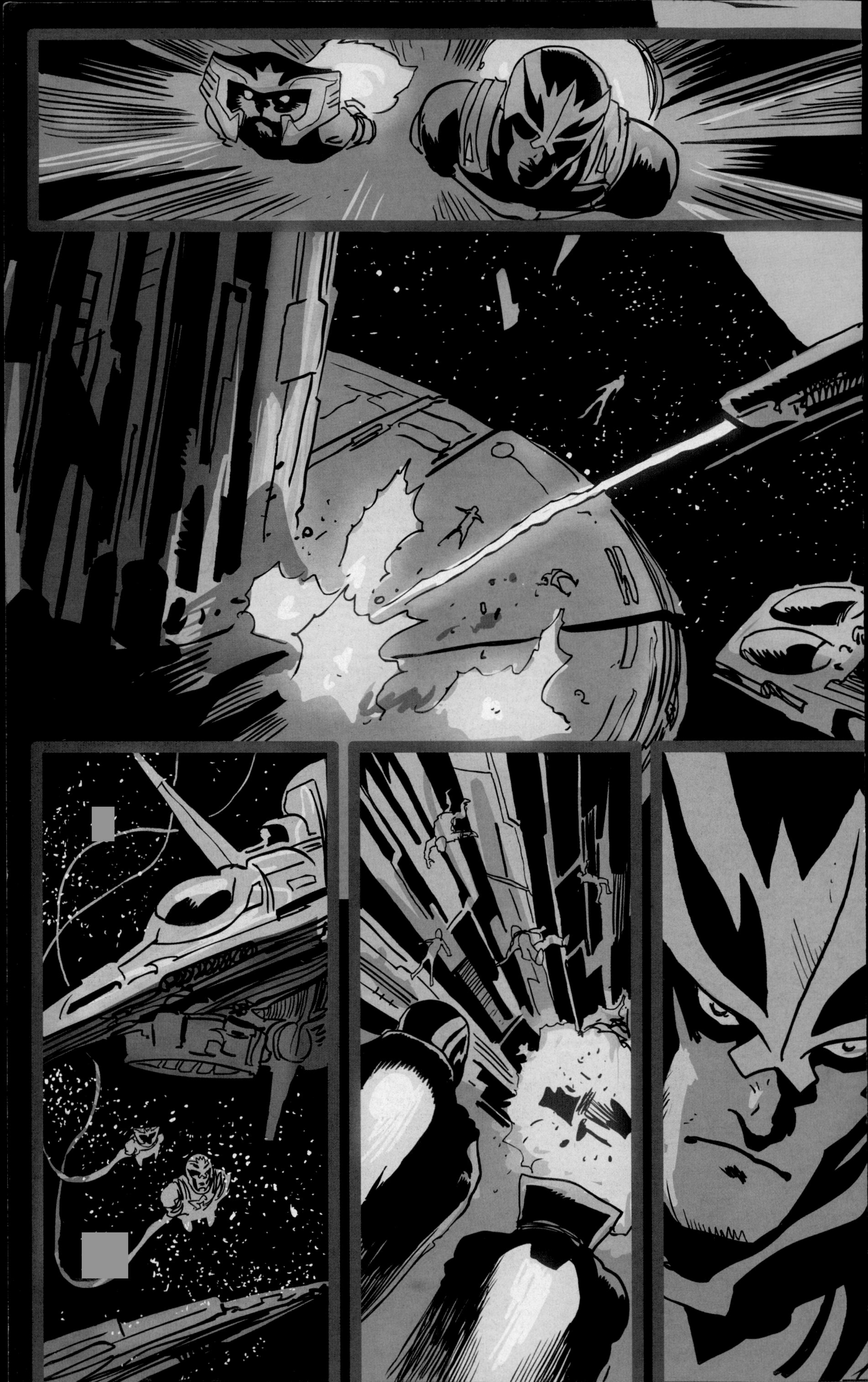

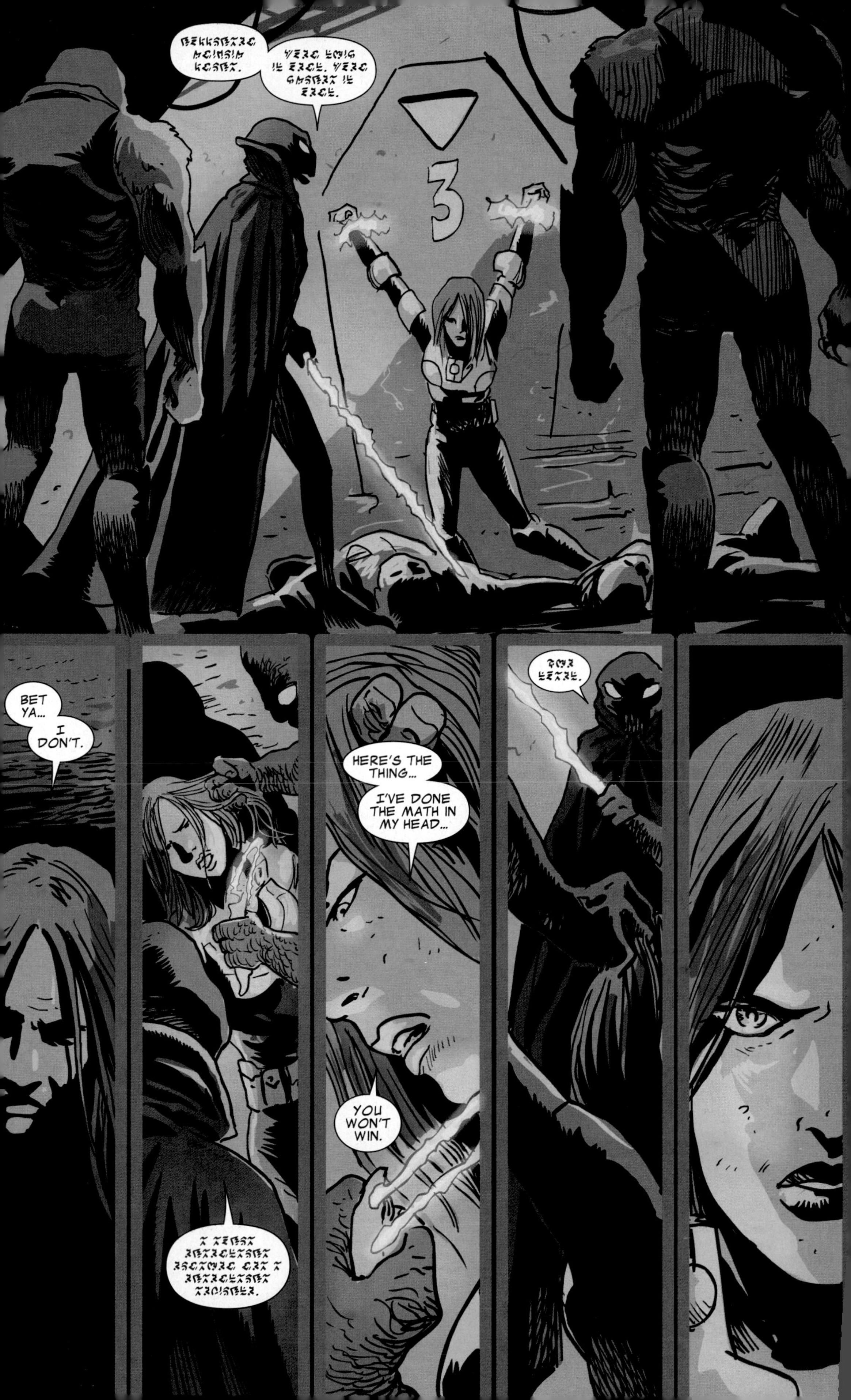
BET YA...
I DON'T.
HERE'S THE THING...
I'VE DONE THE MATH IN MY HEAD...
YOU WON'T WIN.

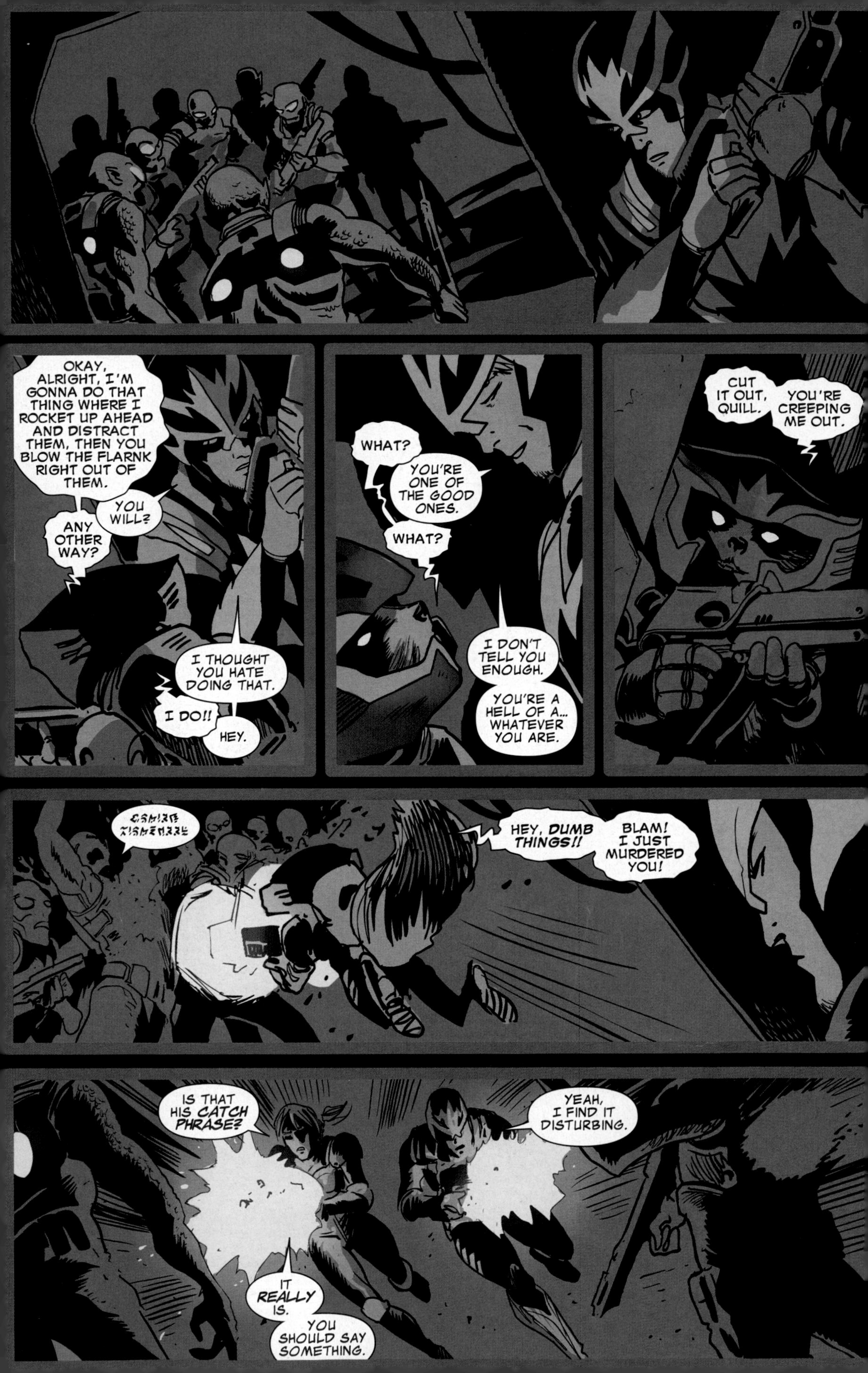
OKAY, ALRIGHT, I'M GONNA DO THAT THING WHERE I ROCKET UP AHEAD AND DISTRACT THEM, THEN YOU BLOW THE FLARNK RIGHT OUT OF THEM.
ANY OTHER WAY?
YOU WILL?
I THOUGHT YOU HATE DOING THAT.
I DO!!
HEY.
WHAT?
YOU'RE ONE OF THE GOOD ONES.
WHAT?
I DON'T TELL YOU ENOUGH.
YOU'RE A HELL OF A... WHATEVER YOU ARE.
CUT IT OUT, QUILL.
YOU'RE CREEPING ME OUT.
HEY, DUMB THINGS!!
BLAM! I JUST MURDERED YOU!
IS THAT HIS CATCH PHRASE?
YEAH, I FIND IT DISTURBING.
IT REALLY IS.
YOU SHOULD SAY SOMETHING.

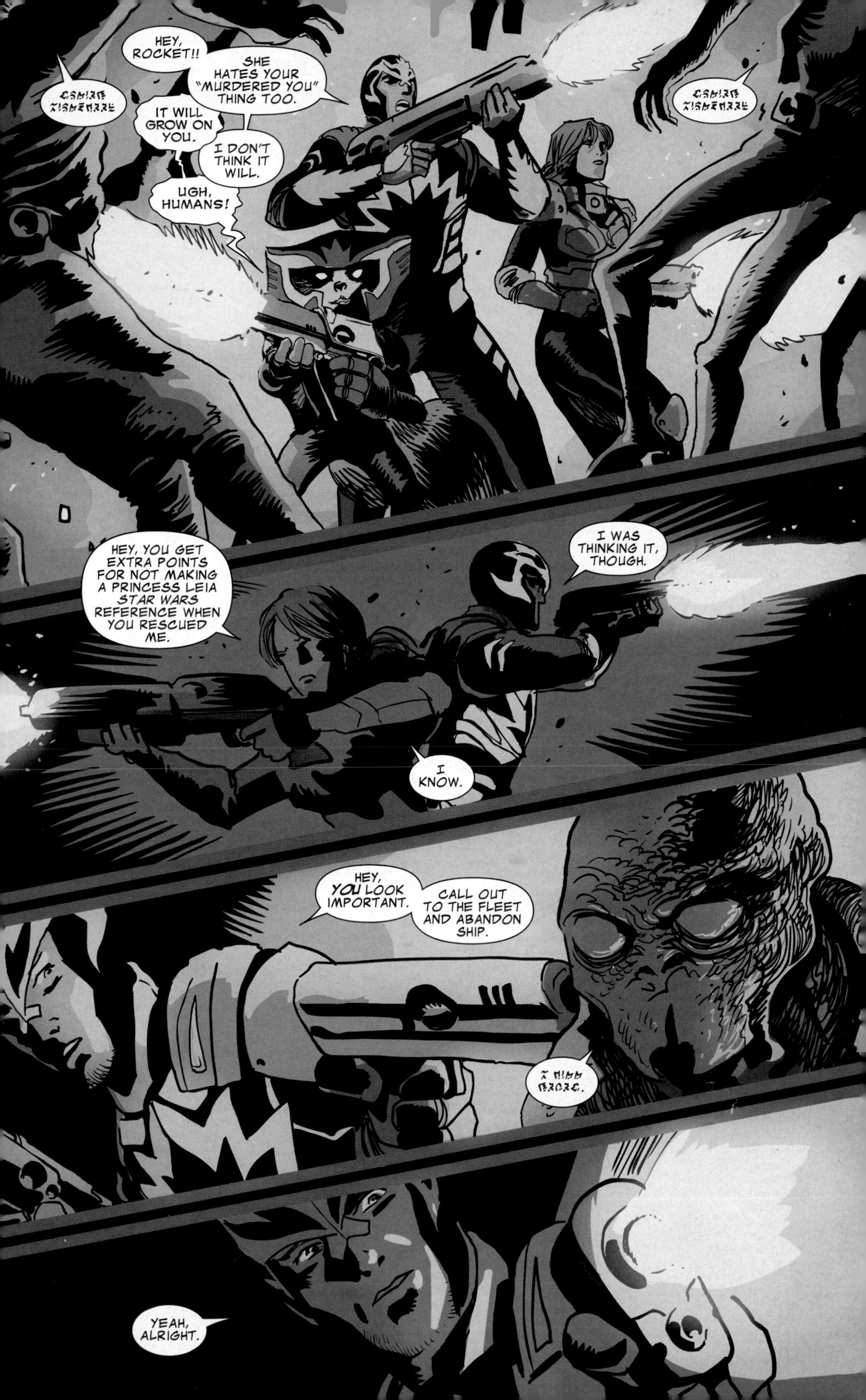
HEY, ROCKET!!
SHE HATES YOUR "MURDERED YOU" THING TOO.
IT WILL GROW ON YOU.
I DON'T THINK IT WILL.
UGH, HUMANS!
HEY, YOU GET EXTRA POINTS FOR NOT MAKING A PRINCESS LEIA STAR WARS REFERENCE WHEN YOU RESCUED ME.
I WAS THINKING IT, THOUGH.
I KNOW.
HEY, YOU LOOK IMPORTANT.
CALL OUT TO THE FLEET AND ABANDON SHIP.
YEAH, ALRIGHT.

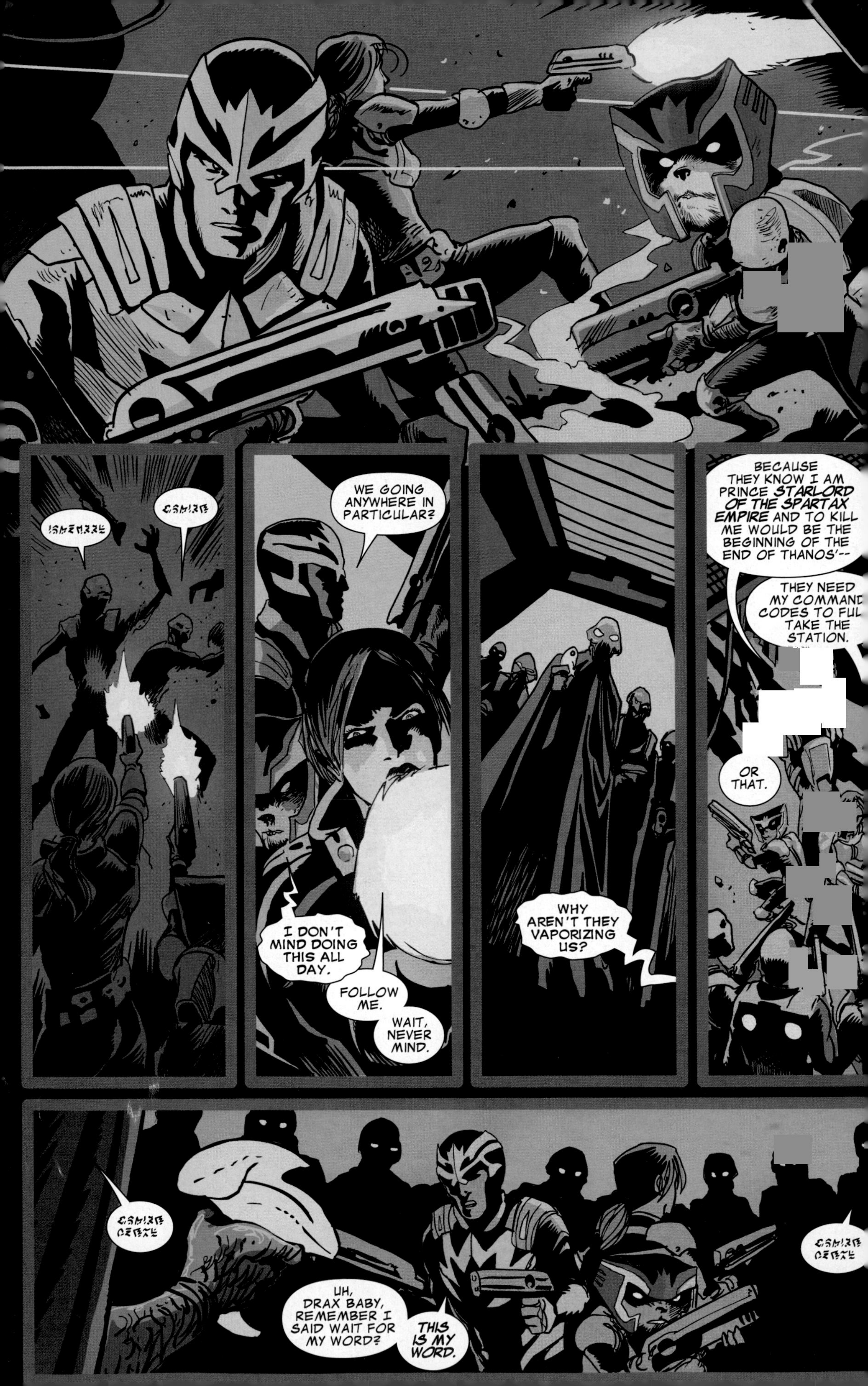
WE GOING ANYWHERE IN PARTICULAR?
I DON'T MIND DOING THIS ALL DAY.
FOLLOW ME.
WAIT, NEVER MIND.
WHY AREN'T THEY VAPORIZING US?
BECAUSE THEY KNOW I AM PRINCE STARLORD OF THE SPARTAX EMPIRE AND TO KILL ME WOULD BE THE BEGINNING OF THE END OF THANOS'--
THEY NEED MY COMMAND CODES TO FUL TAKE THE STATION.
OR THAT.
UH, DRAX BABY, REMEMBER I SAID WAIT FOR MY WORD?
THIS IS MY WORD.

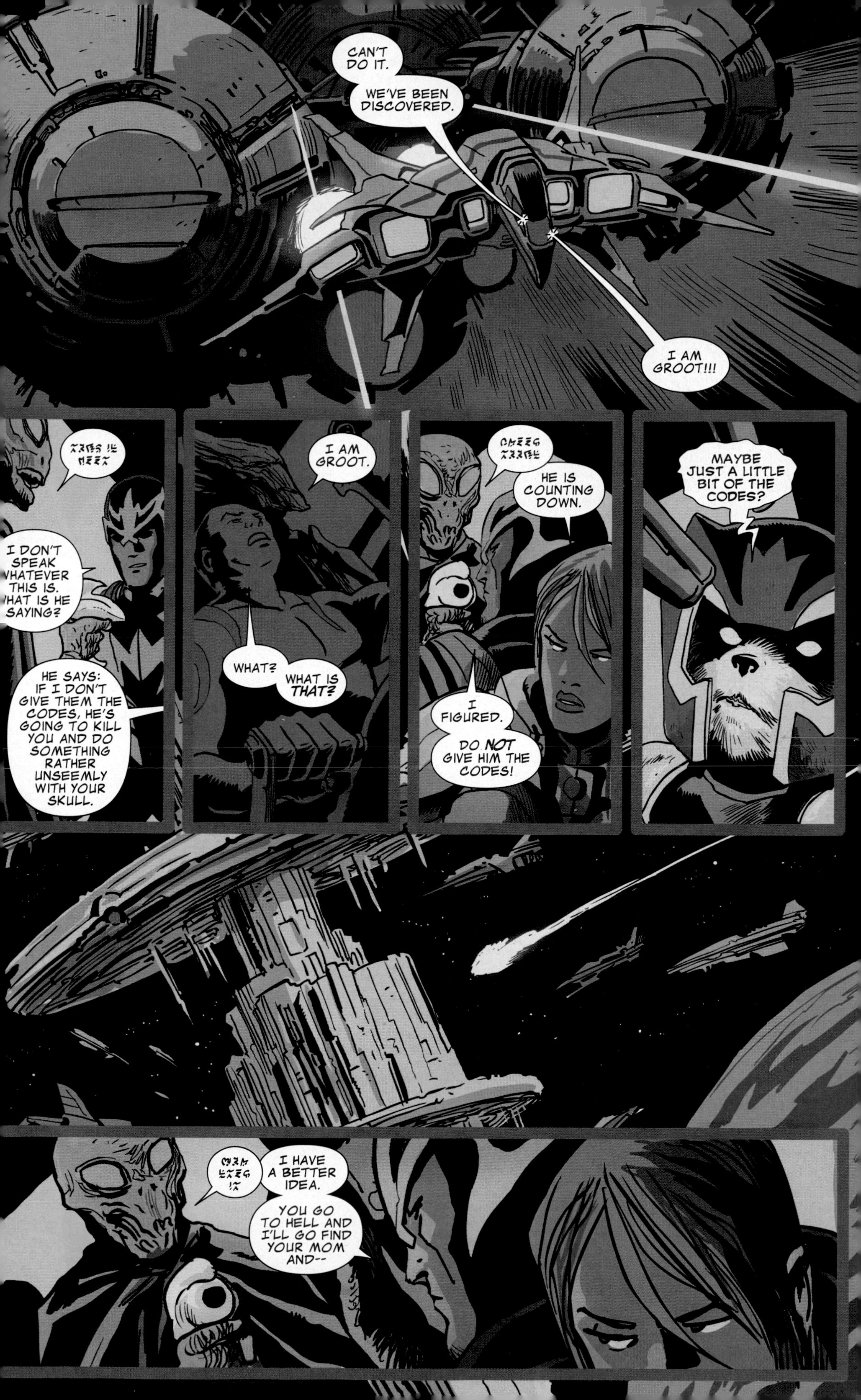
CAN'T DO IT.
WE'VE BEEN DISCOVERED.
I AM GROOT!!!
I DON'T SPEAK WHATEVER THIS IS. WHAT IS HE SAYING?
HE SAYS: IF I DON'T GIVE THEM THE CODES, HE'S GOING TO KILL YOU AND DO SOMETHING RATHER UNSEEMLY WITH YOUR SKULL.
I AM GROOT.
WHAT?
WHAT IS THAT?
HE IS COUNTING DOWN.
I FIGURED.
DO NOT GIVE HIM THE CODES!
MAYBE JUST A LITTLE BIT OF THE CODES?
I HAVE A BETTER IDEA.
YOU GO TO HELL AND I'LL GO FIND YOUR MOM AND--

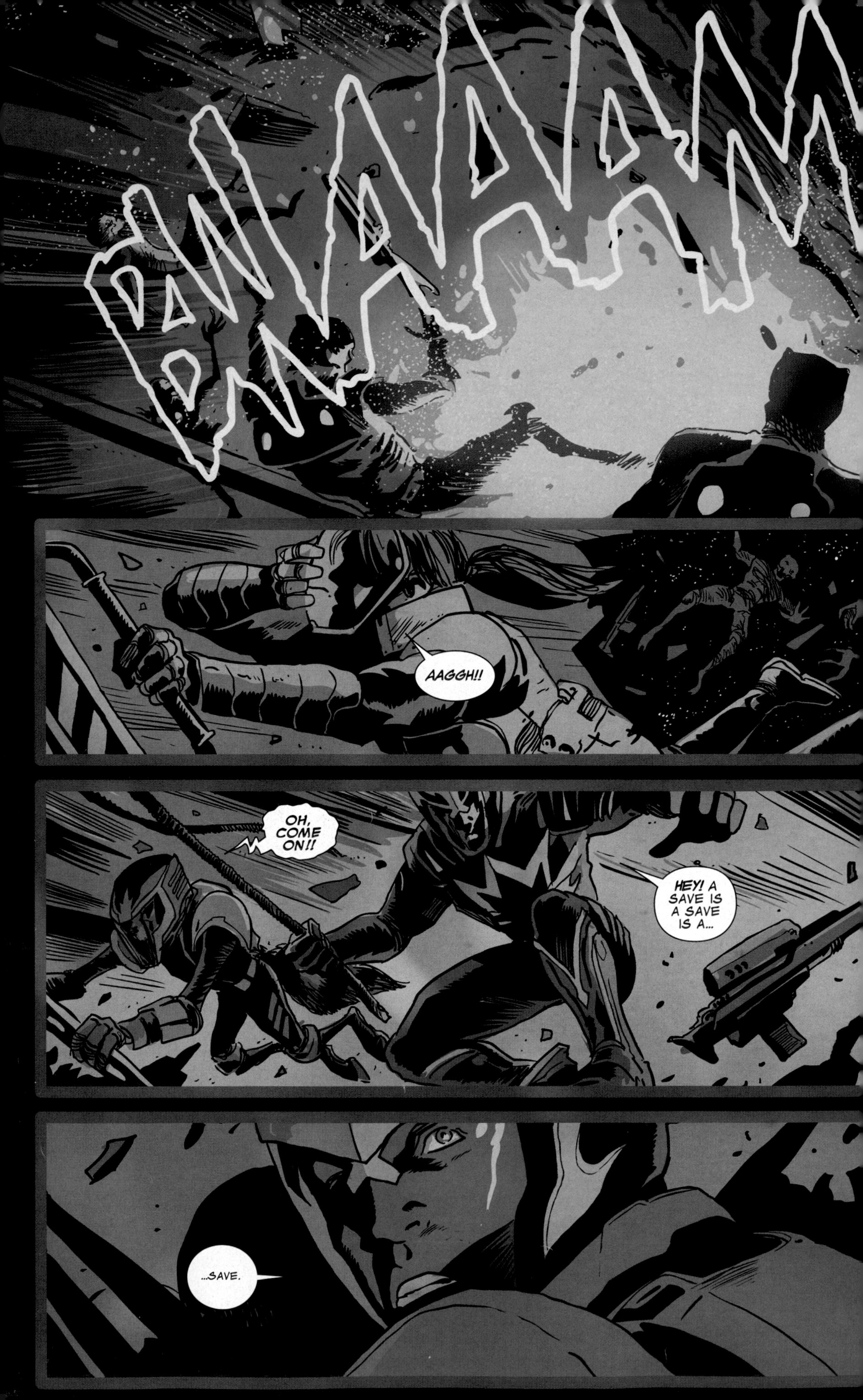
BWAAAM
AAGGH!!
OH, COME ON!!
HEY! A SAVE IS A SAVE IS A...
...SAVE.

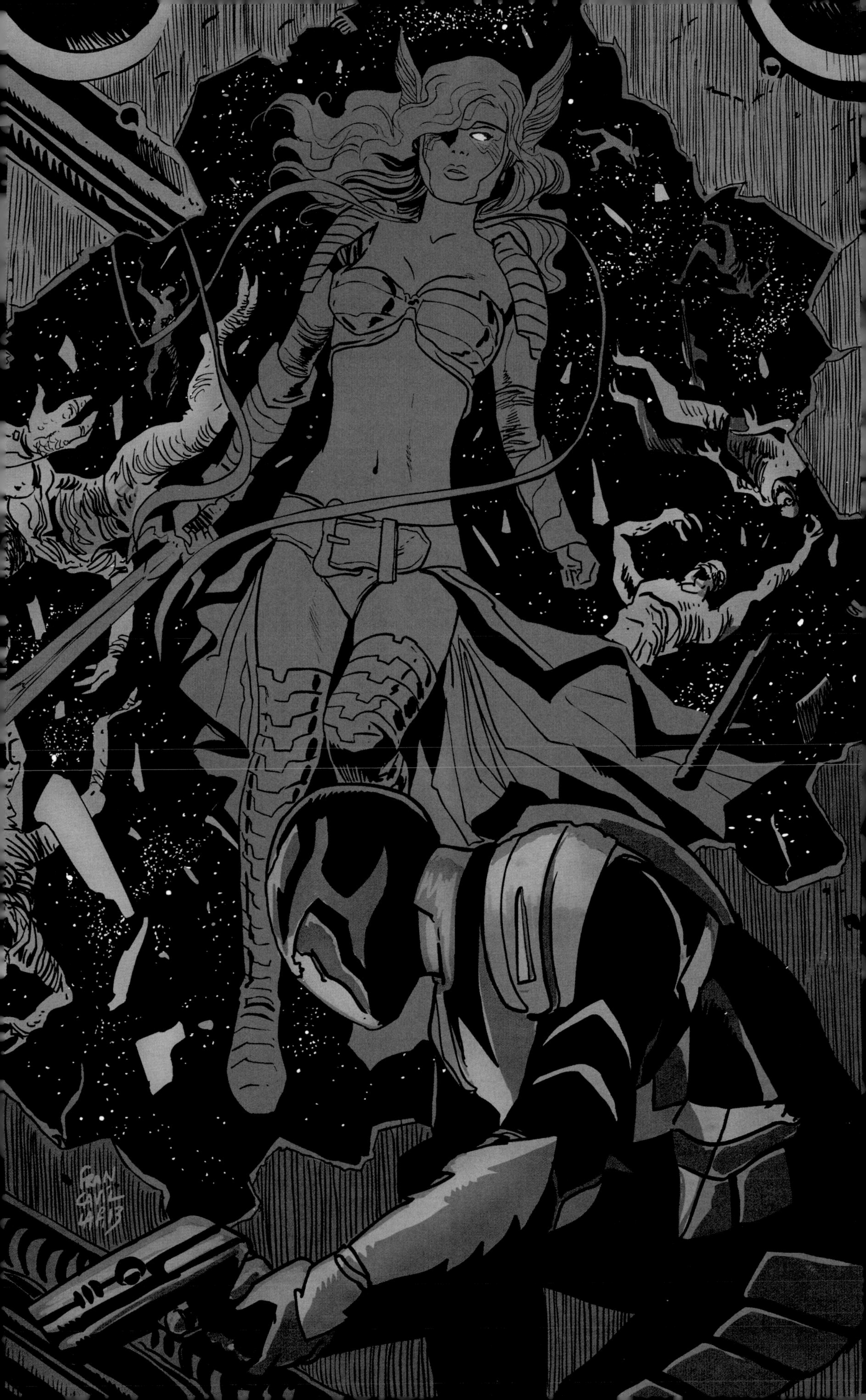

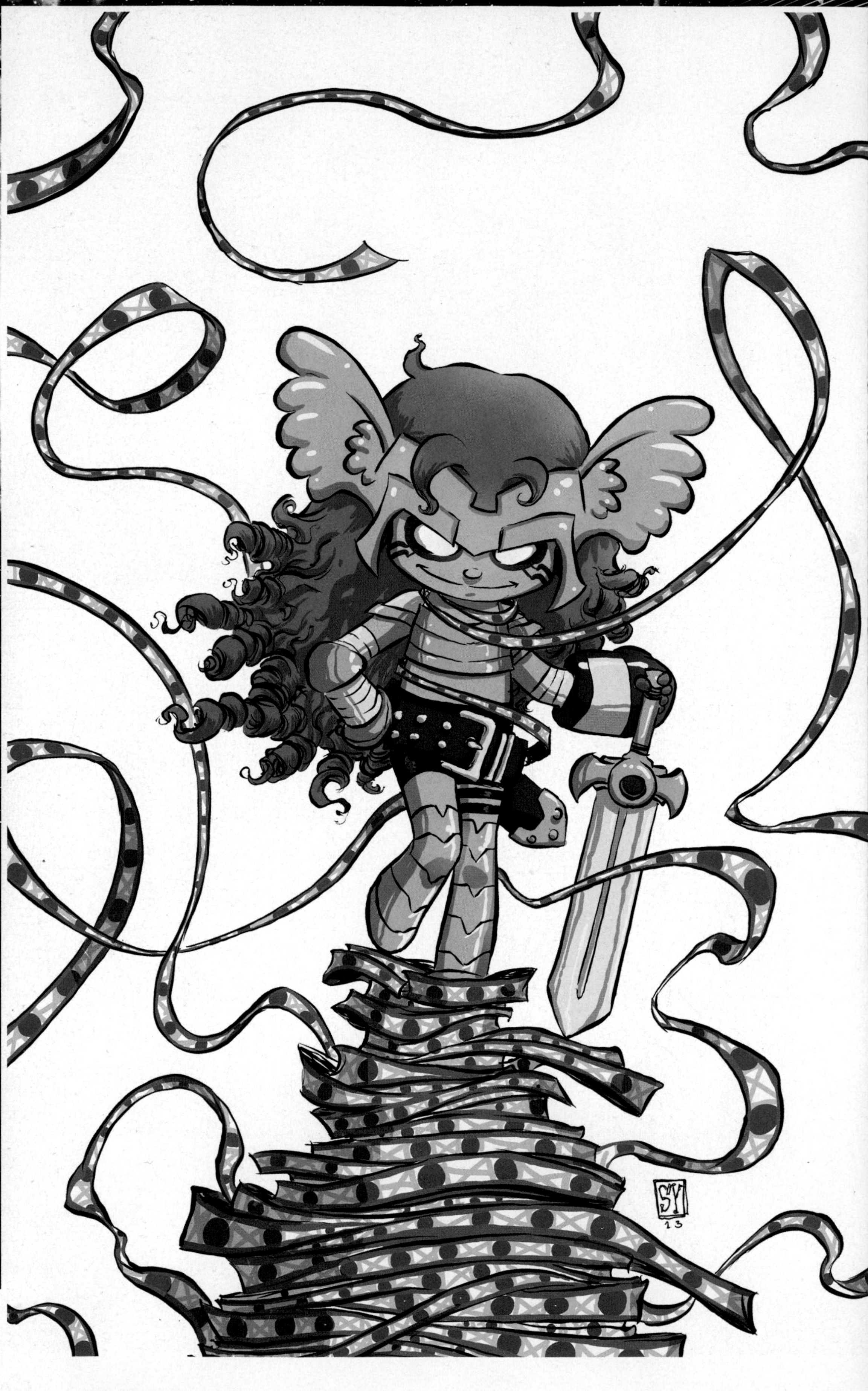
SY
13

#5 VARIANT BY SKOTTIE YOUNG

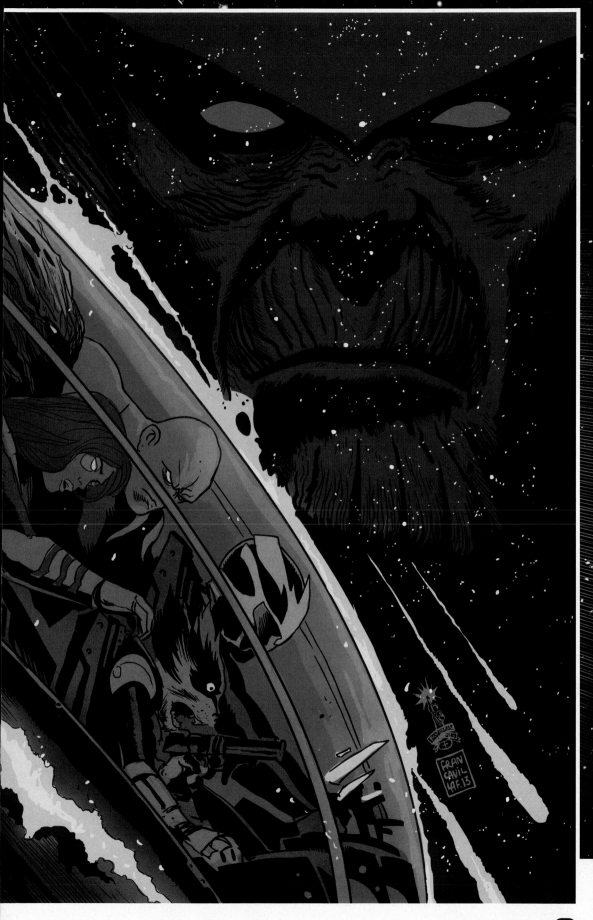

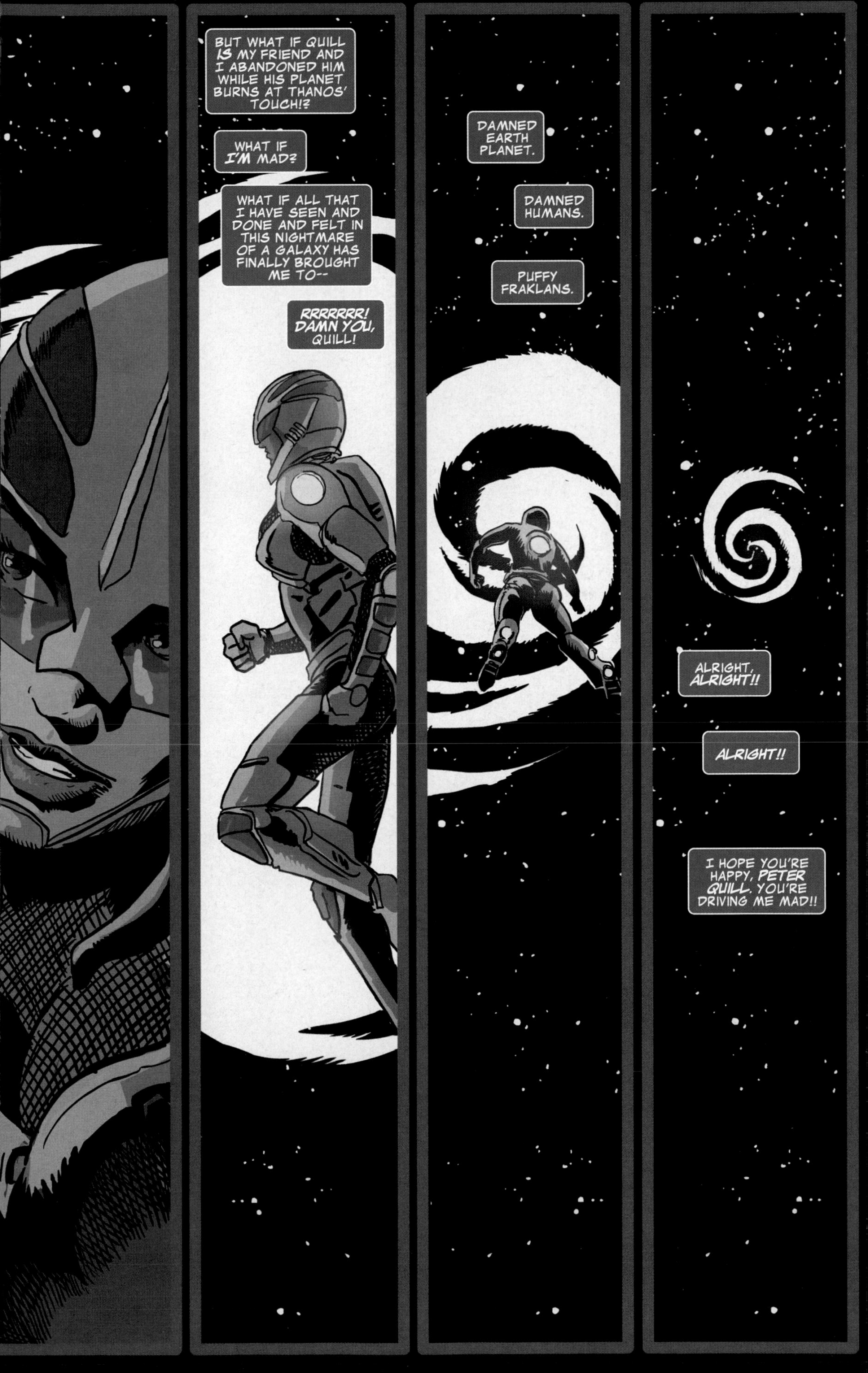
BUT WHAT IF QUILL IS MY FRIEND AND I ABANDONED HIM WHILE HIS PLANET BURNS AT THANOS' TOUCH!?
WHAT IF I'M MAD?
WHAT IF ALL THAT I HAVE SEEN AND DONE AND FELT IN THIS NIGHTMARE OF A GALAXY HAS FINALLY BROUGHT ME TO--
RRRRRRR! DAMN YOU, QUILL!
DAMNED EARTH PLANET.
DAMNED HUMANS.
PUFFY FRAKLANS.
ALRIGHT, ALRIGHT!!
ALRIGHT!!
I HOPE YOU'RE HAPPY, PETER QUILL. YOU'RE DRIVING ME MAD!!

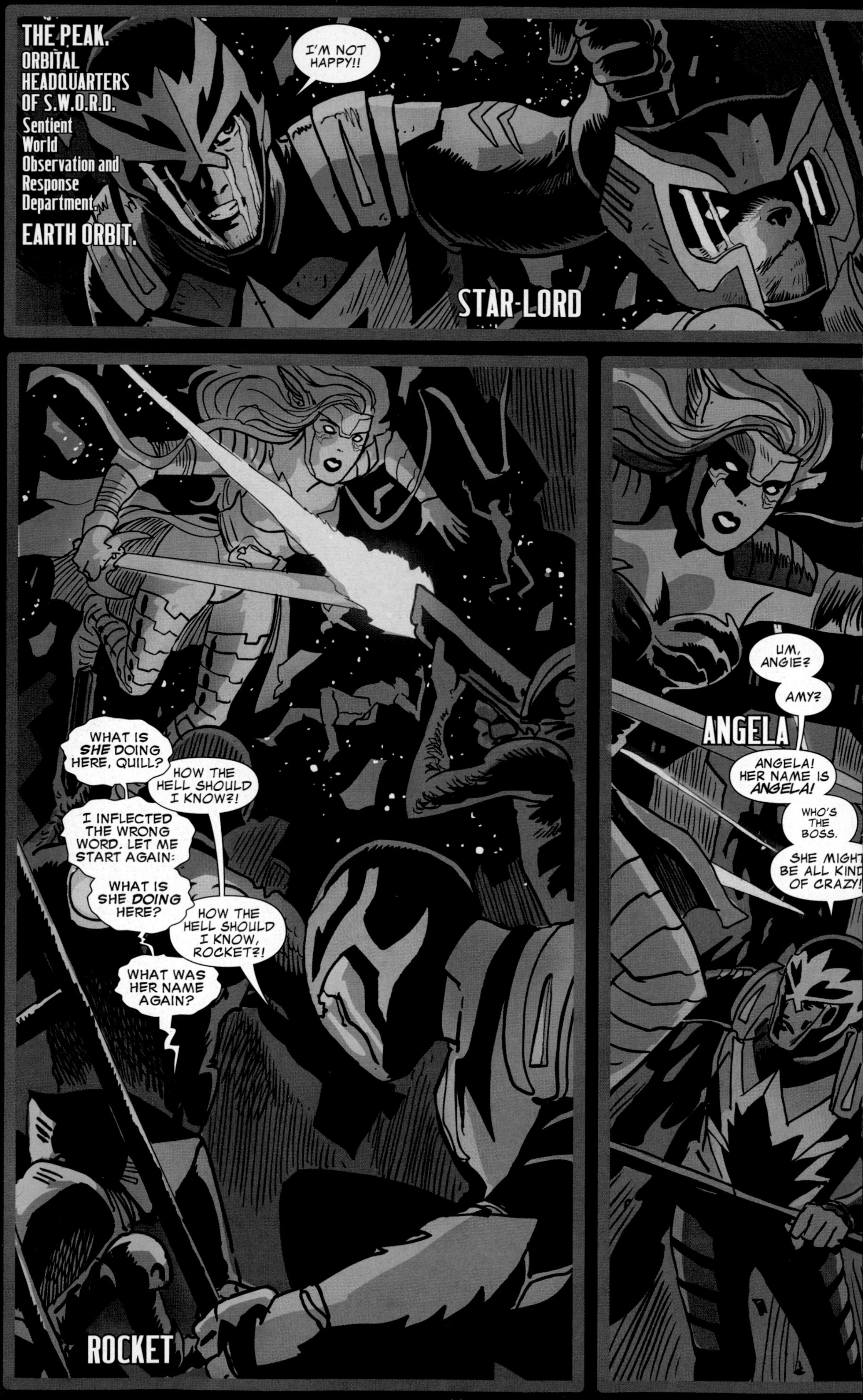
THE PEAK.
ORBITAL HEADQUARTERS OF S.W.O.R.D.
Sentient World Observation and Response Department.
EARTH ORBIT.
I'M NOT HAPPY!!
STAR-LORD
WHAT IS SHE DOING HERE, QUILL?
HOW THE HELL SHOULD I KNOW?!
I INFLECTED THE WRONG WORD. LET ME START AGAIN:
WHAT IS SHE DOING HERE?
HOW THE HELL SHOULD I KNOW, ROCKET?!
WHAT WAS HER NAME AGAIN?
ROCKET
UM, ANGIE?
AMY?
ANGELA
ANGELA! HER NAME IS ANGELA!
WHO'S THE BOSS.
SHE MIGHT BE ALL KIND OF CRAZY!

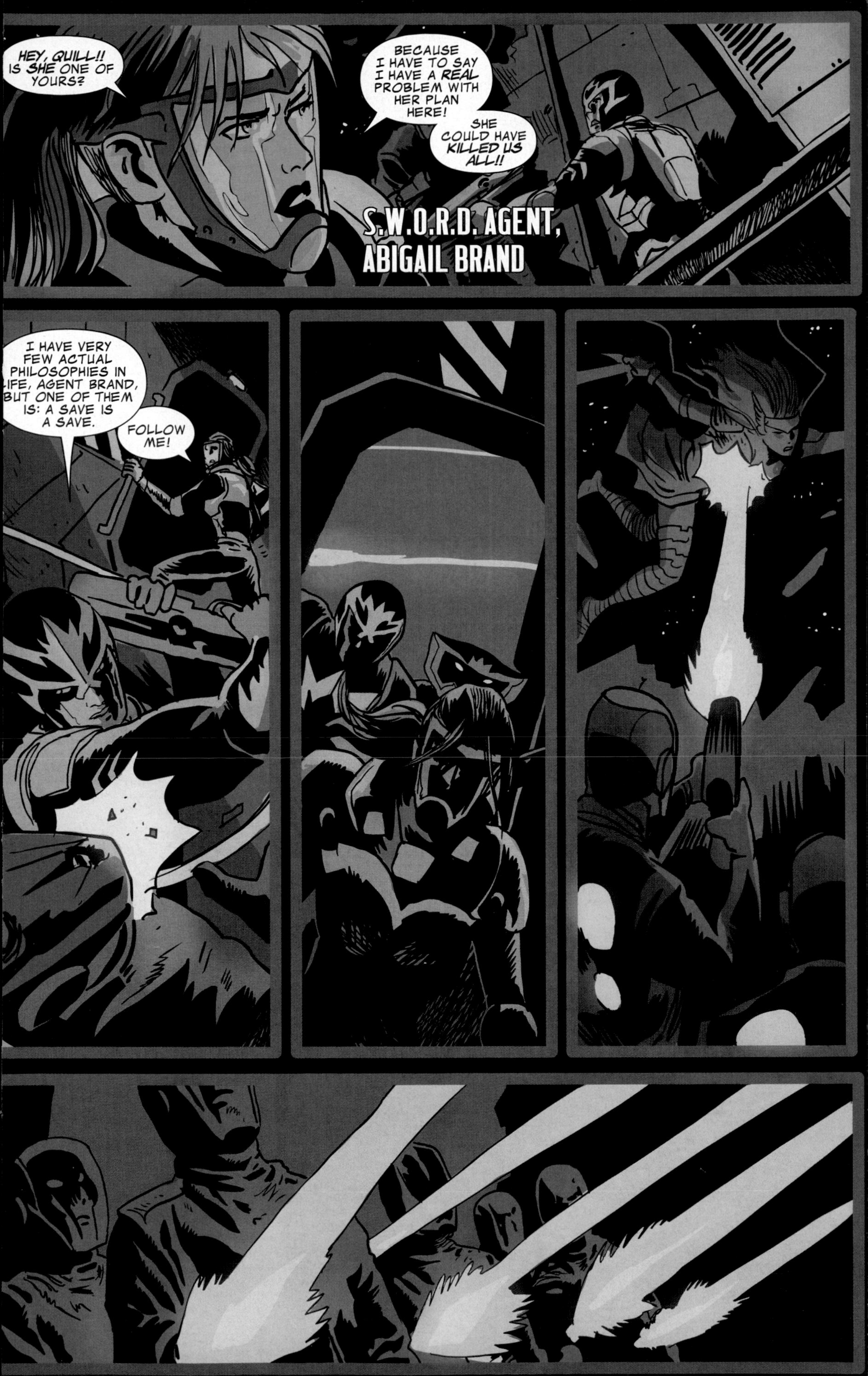
HEY, QUILL!! IS SHE ONE OF YOURS?
BECAUSE I HAVE TO SAY I HAVE A REAL PROBLEM WITH HER PLAN HERE!
SHE COULD HAVE KILLED US ALL!!
S.W.O.R.D. AGENT, ABIGAIL BRAND
I HAVE VERY FEW ACTUAL PHILOSOPHIES IN LIFE, AGENT BRAND, BUT ONE OF THEM IS: A SAVE IS A SAVE.
FOLLOW ME!

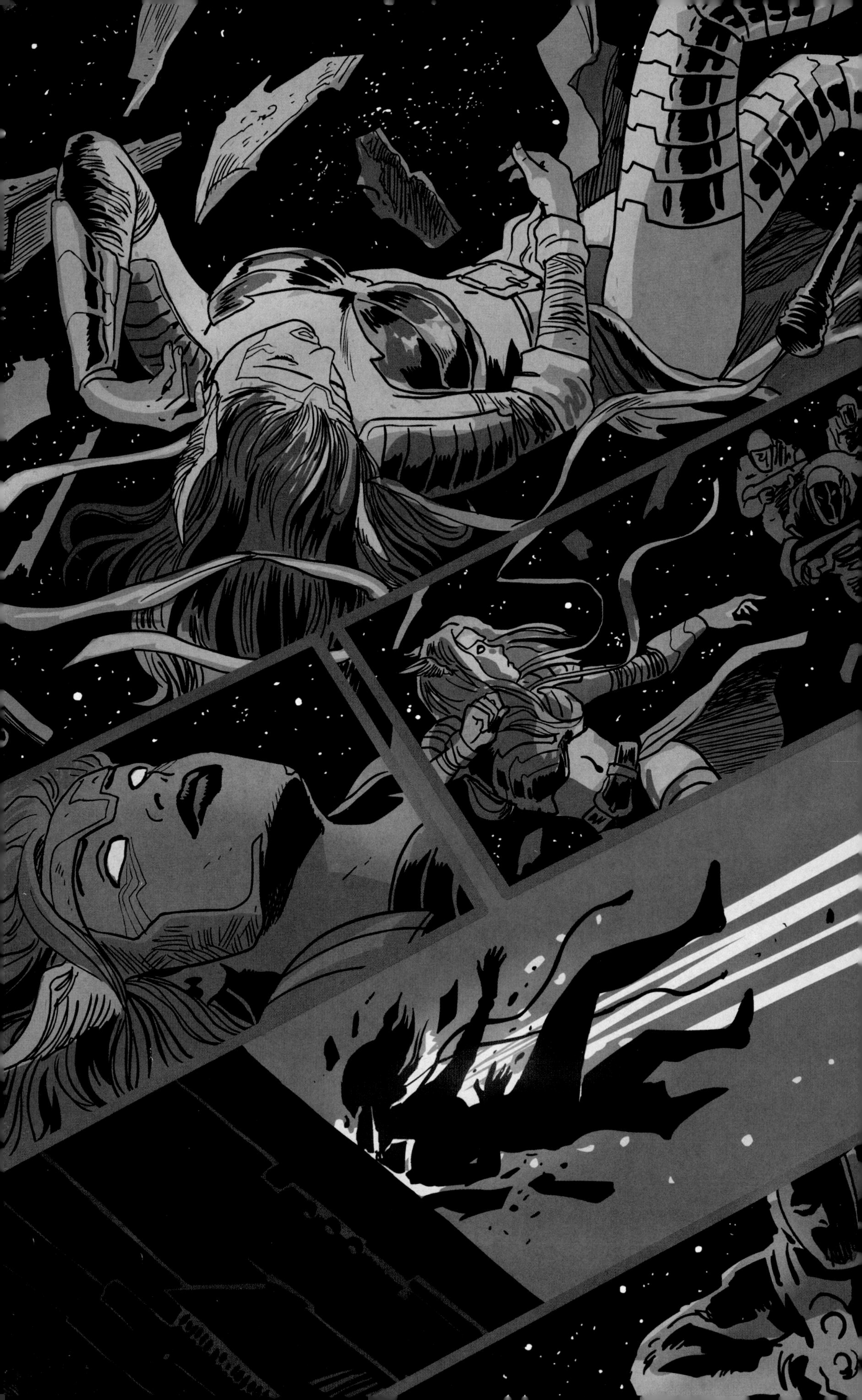

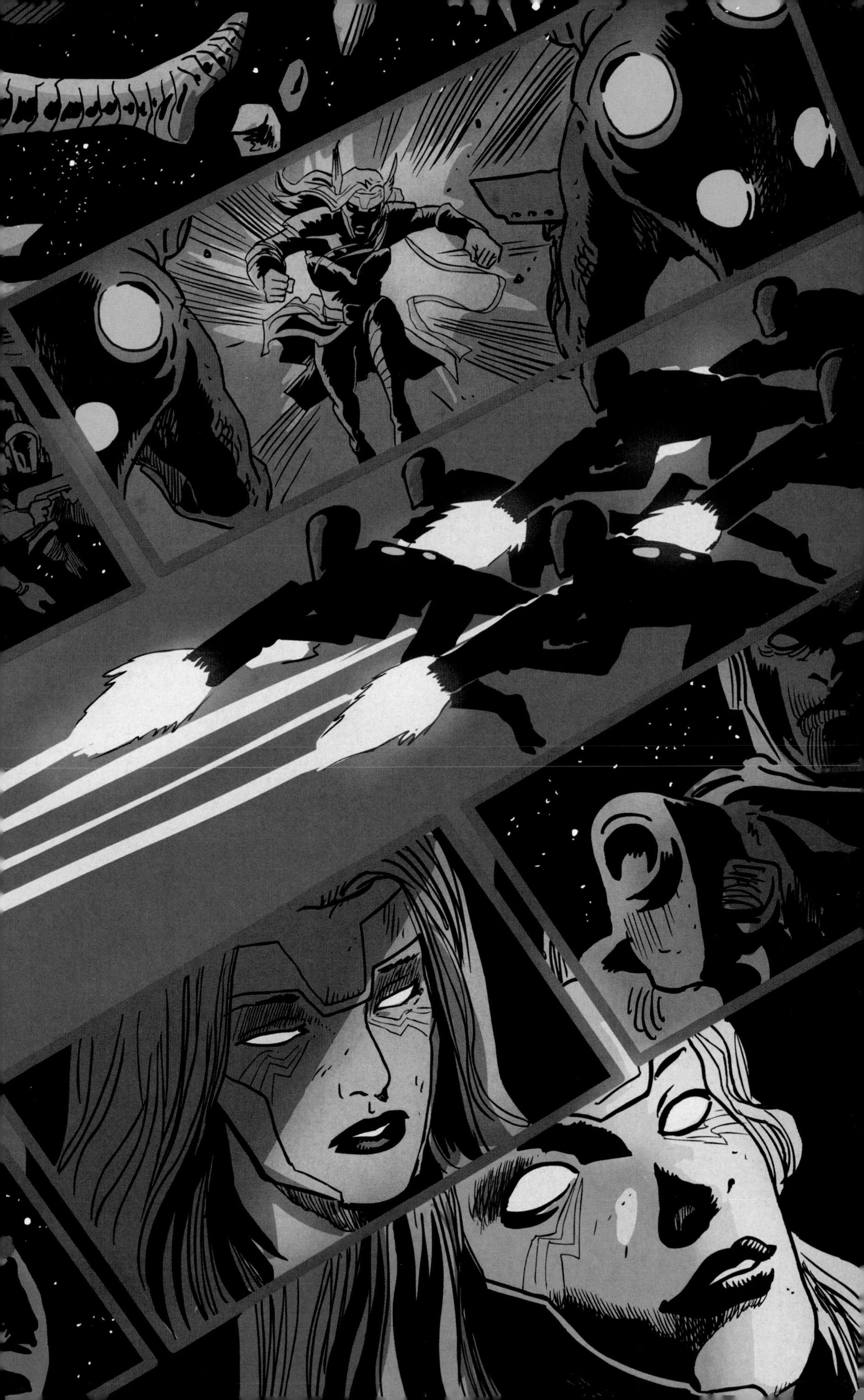

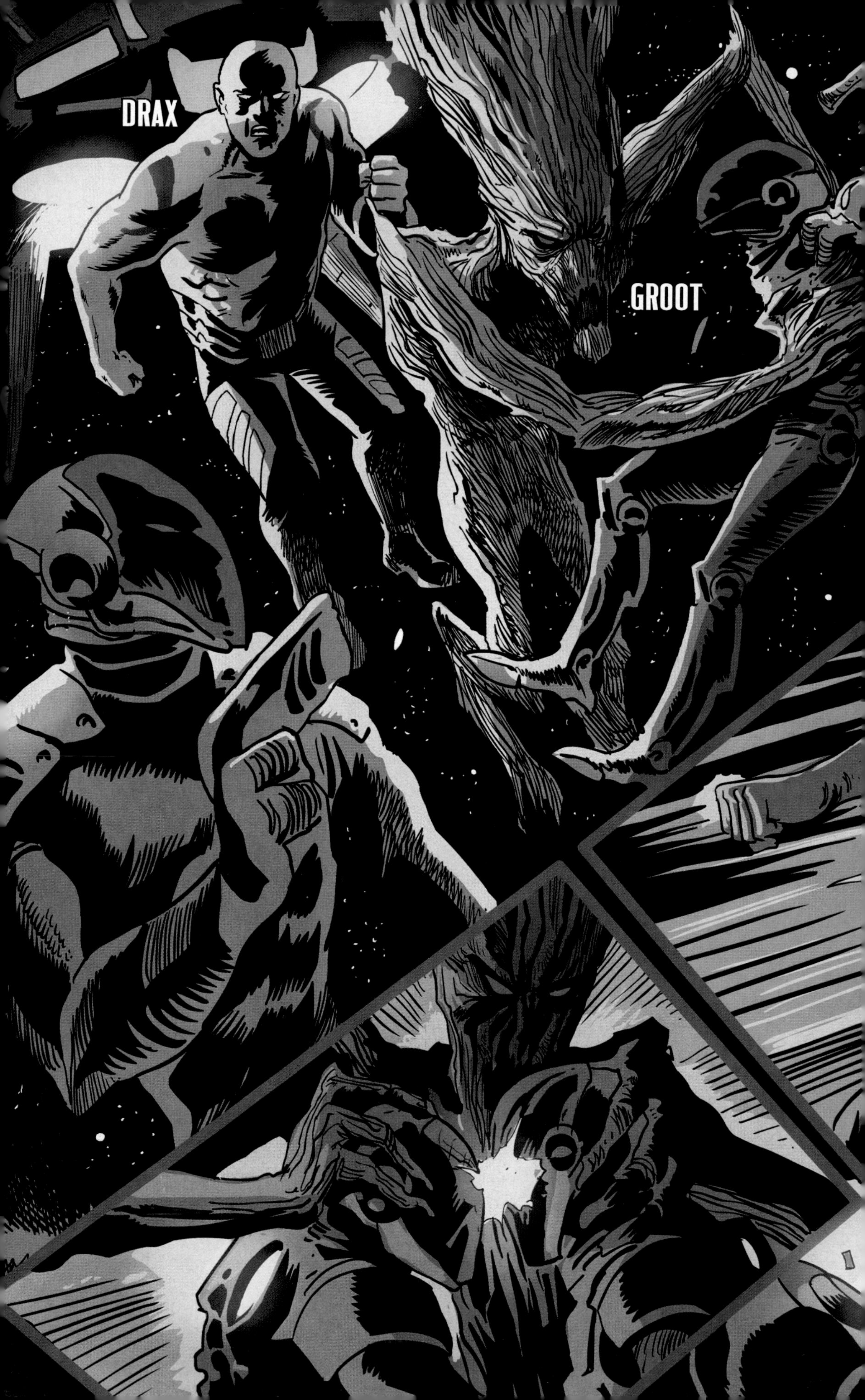
DRAX
GROOT

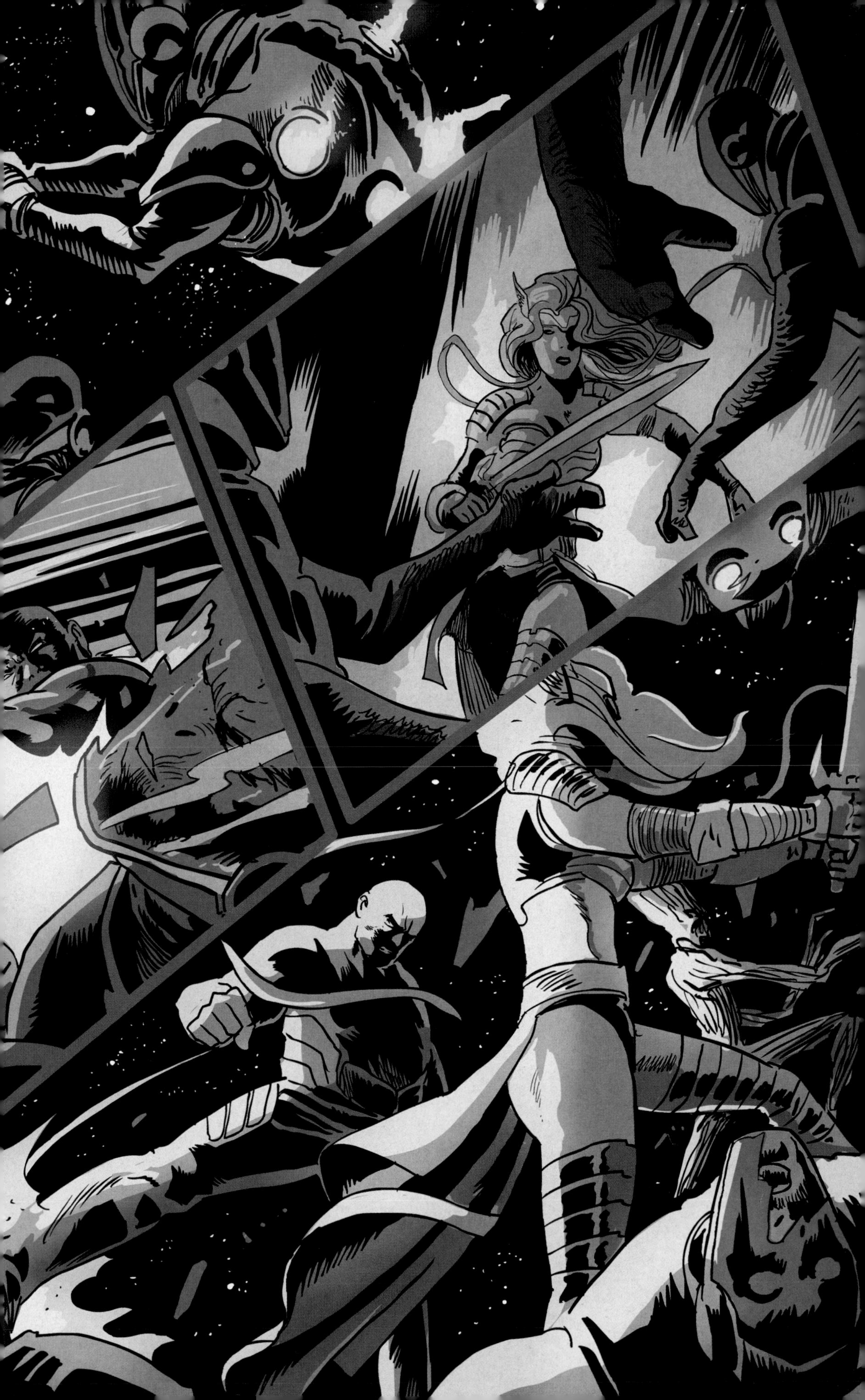

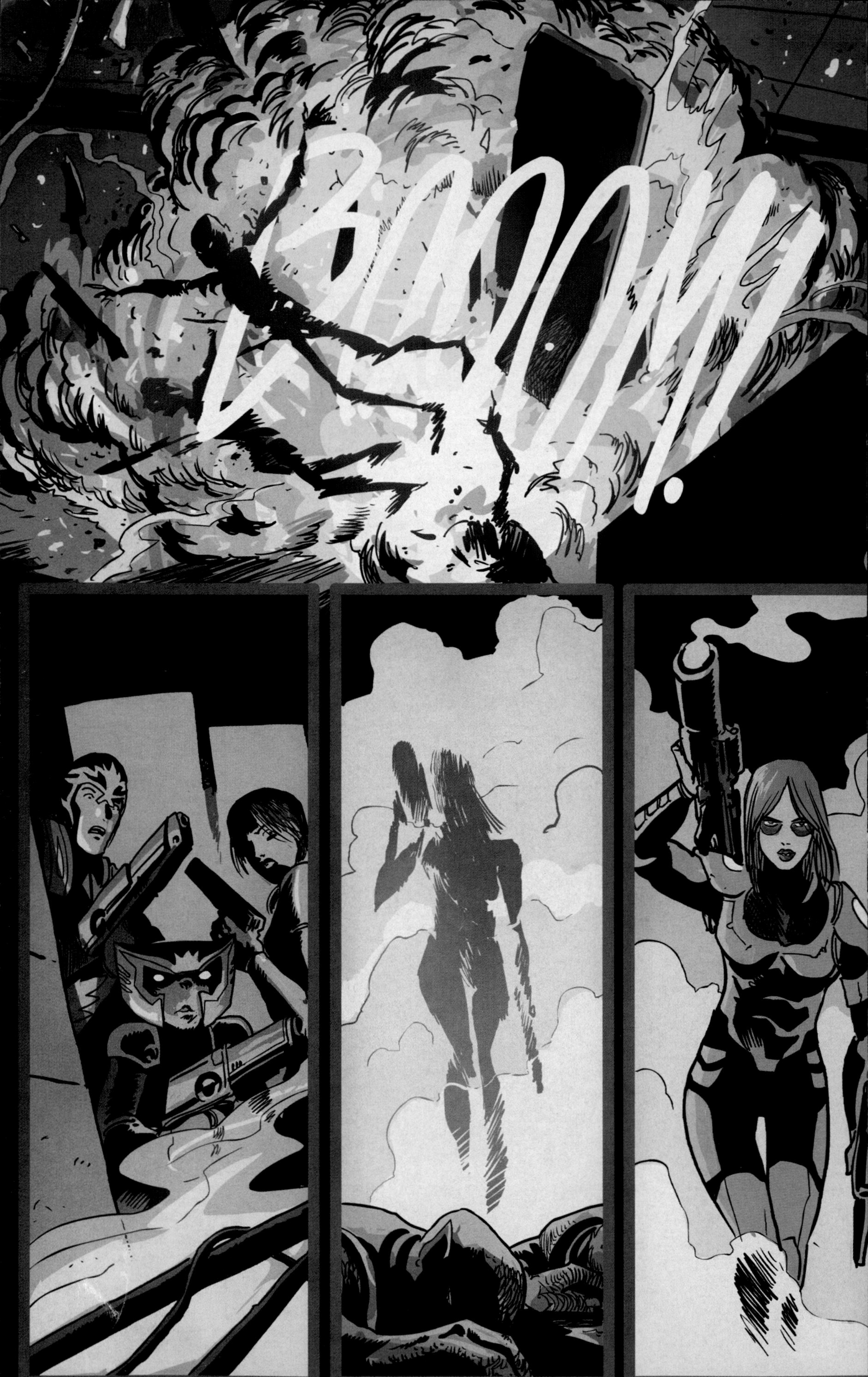
BOOM!

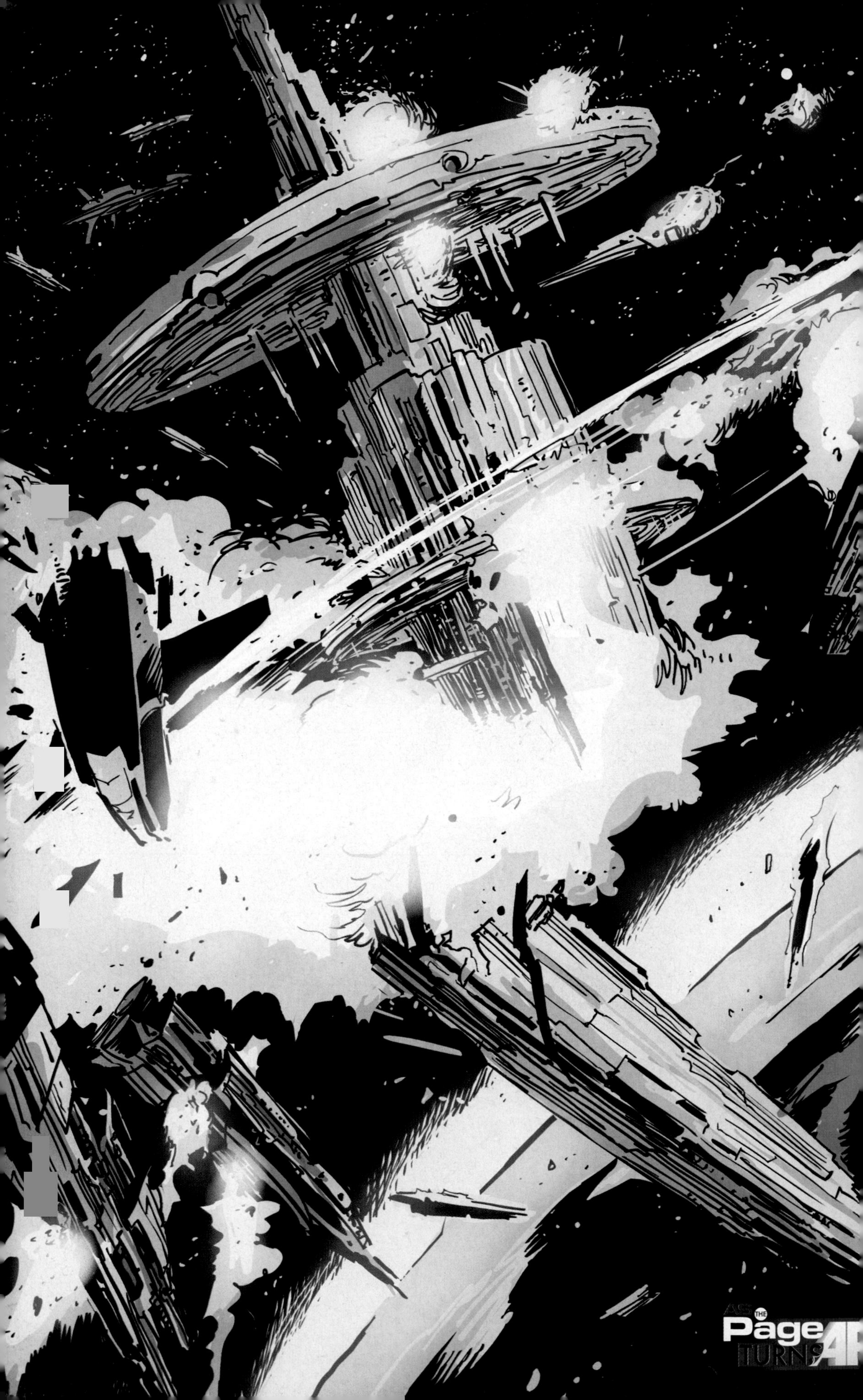

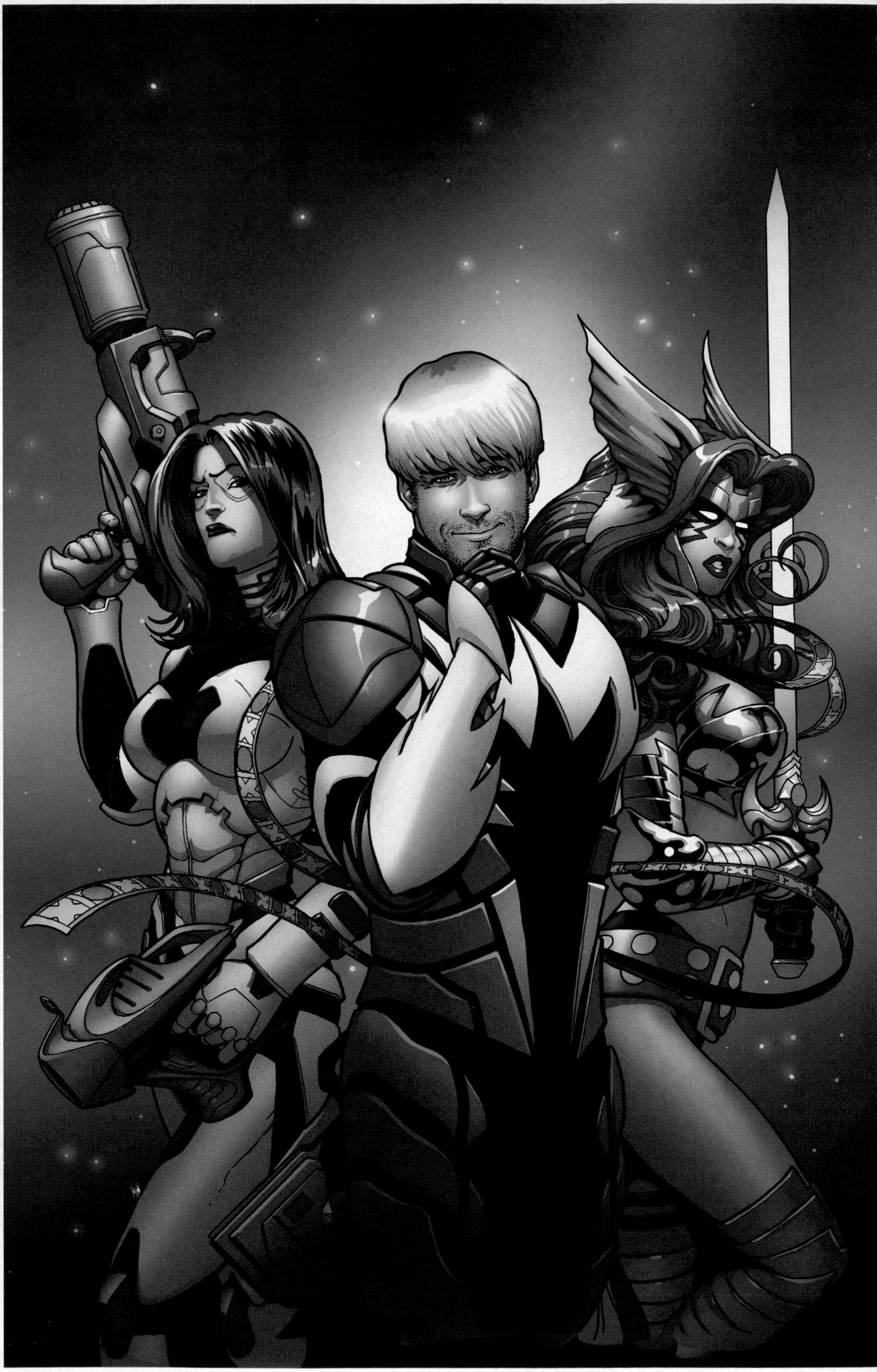

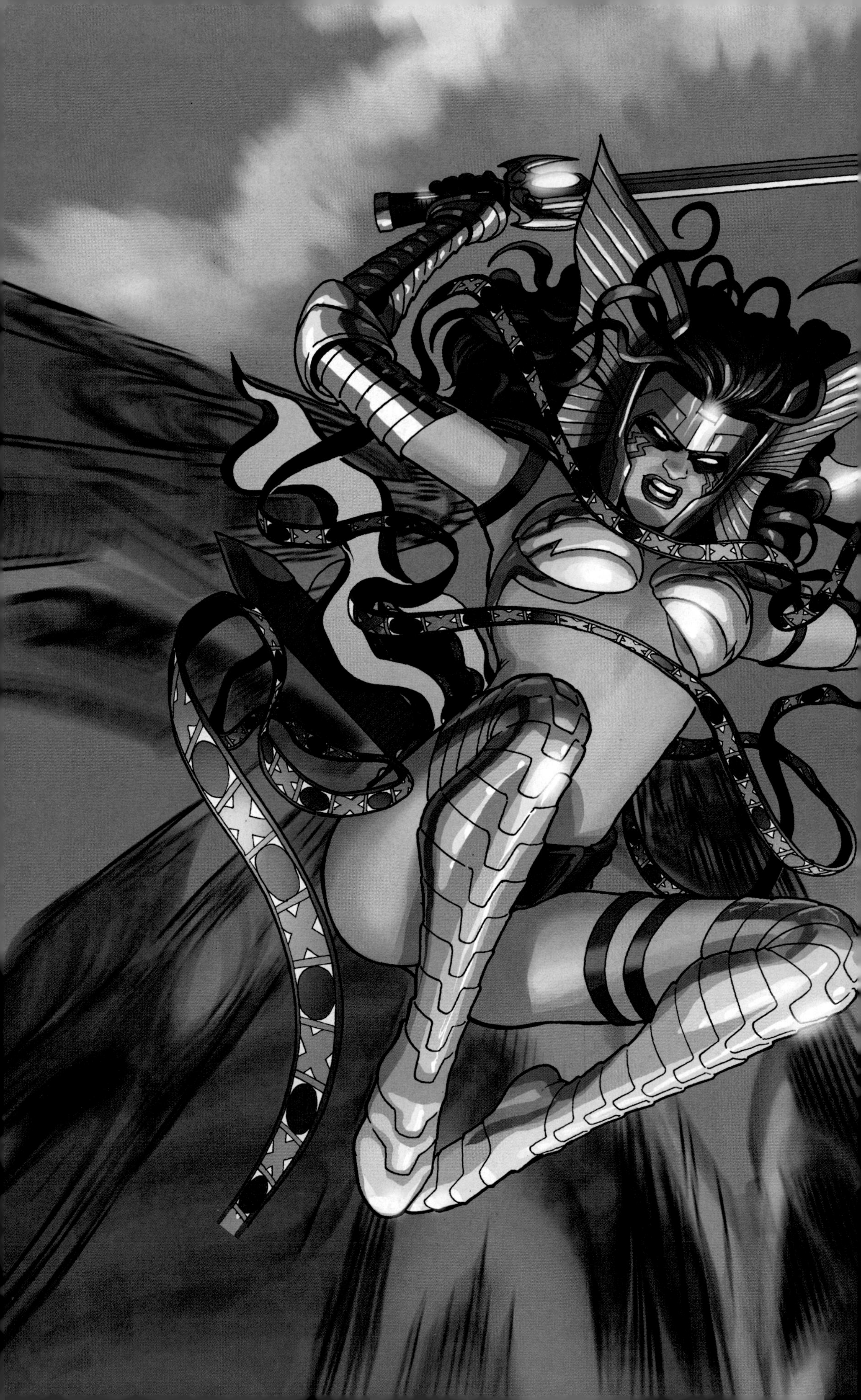

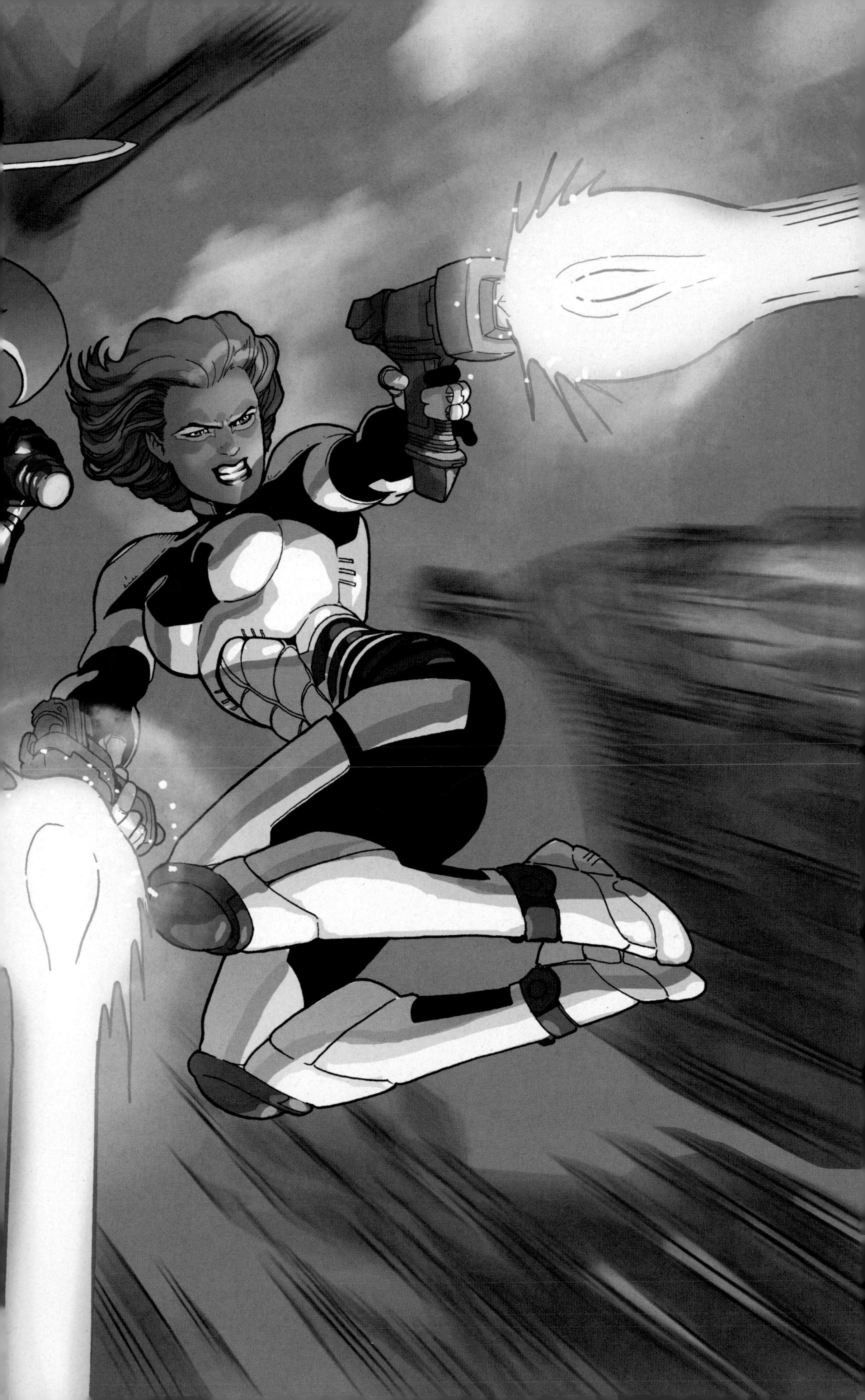

PREVIOUSLY IN *INFINITY*:
Thanos' army came very close to taking the Earth, but the Guardians helped save the planet. The Mad Titan has disappeared.

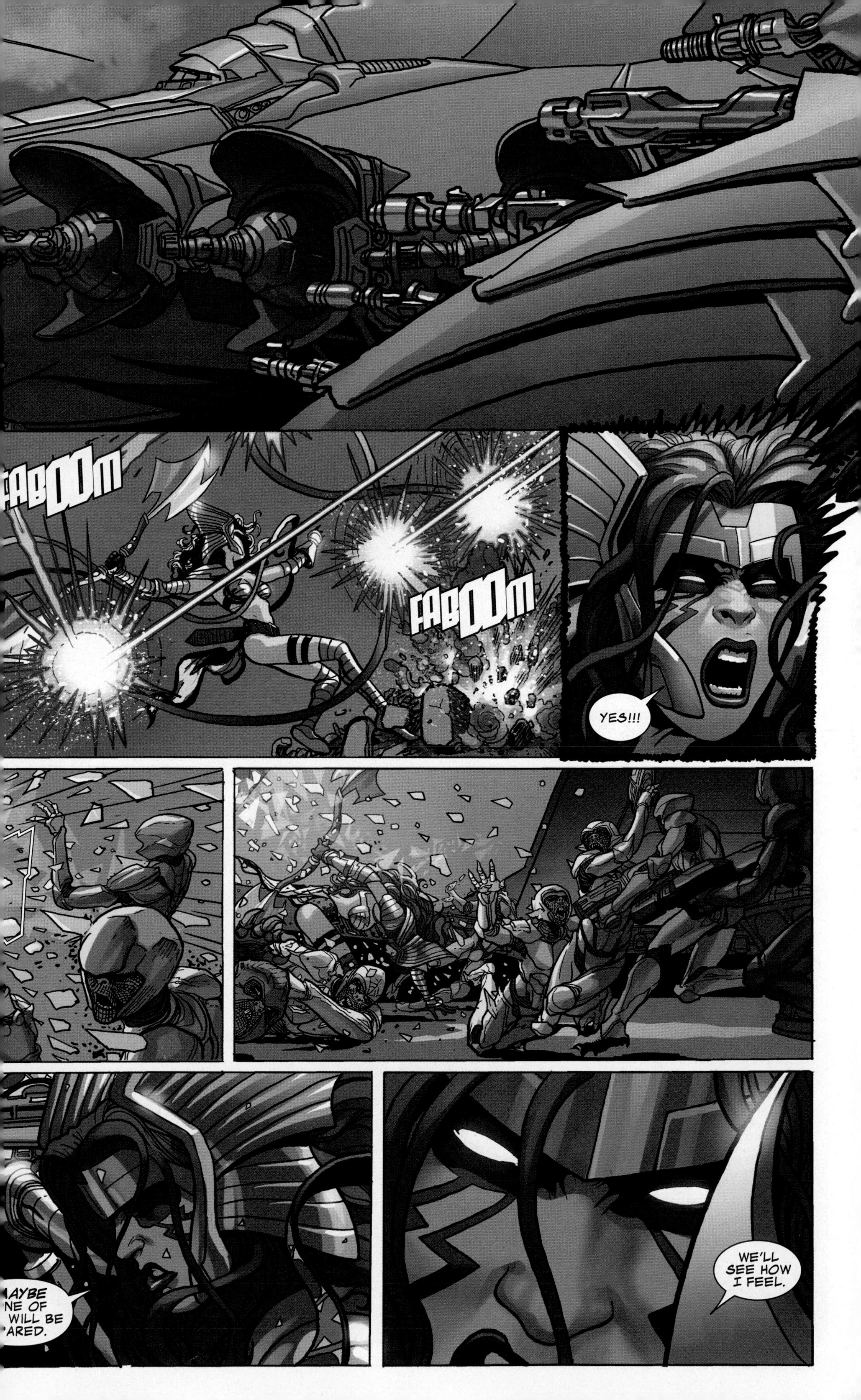
FABOOM
FABOOM
YES!!!
AYBE
NE OF
WILL BE
ARED.
WE'LL
SEE HOW
I FEEL.

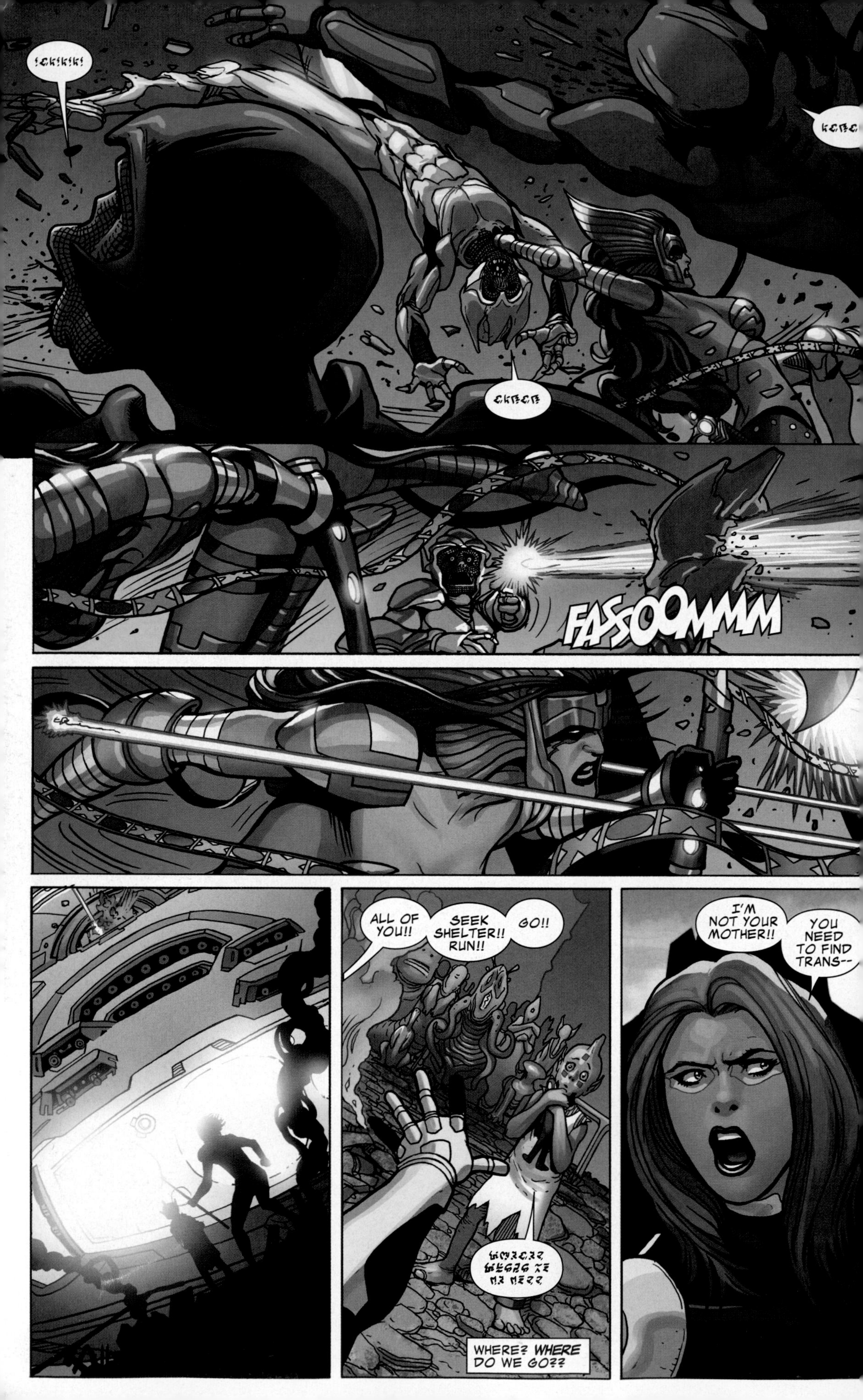
FASOOMMM
ALL OF YOU!!
SEEK SHELTER!! RUN!!
GO!!
WHERE? WHERE DO WE GO??
I'M NOT YOUR MOTHER!!
YOU NEED TO FIND TRANS--

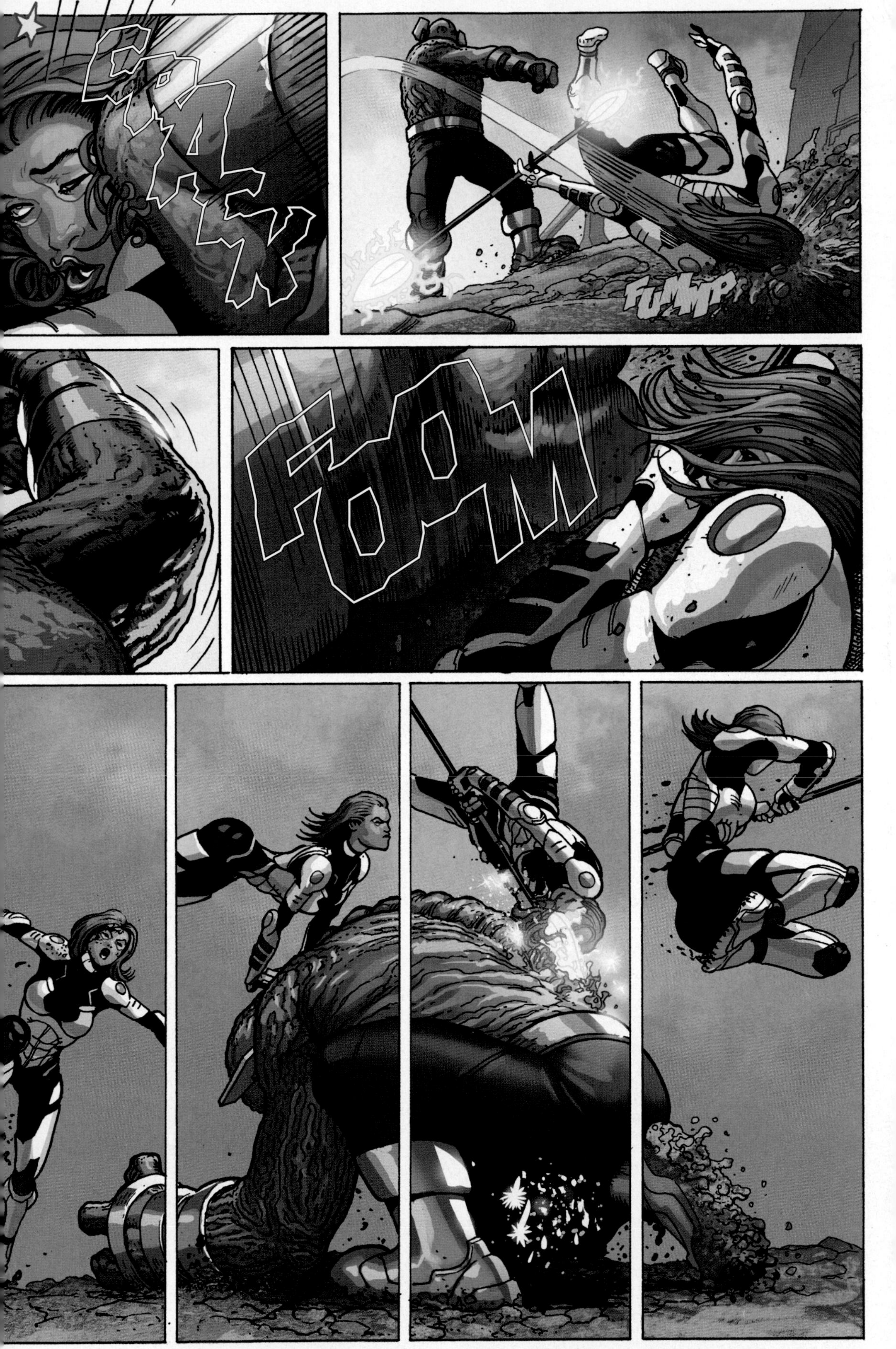
CRACK
FUMMP
FOOM

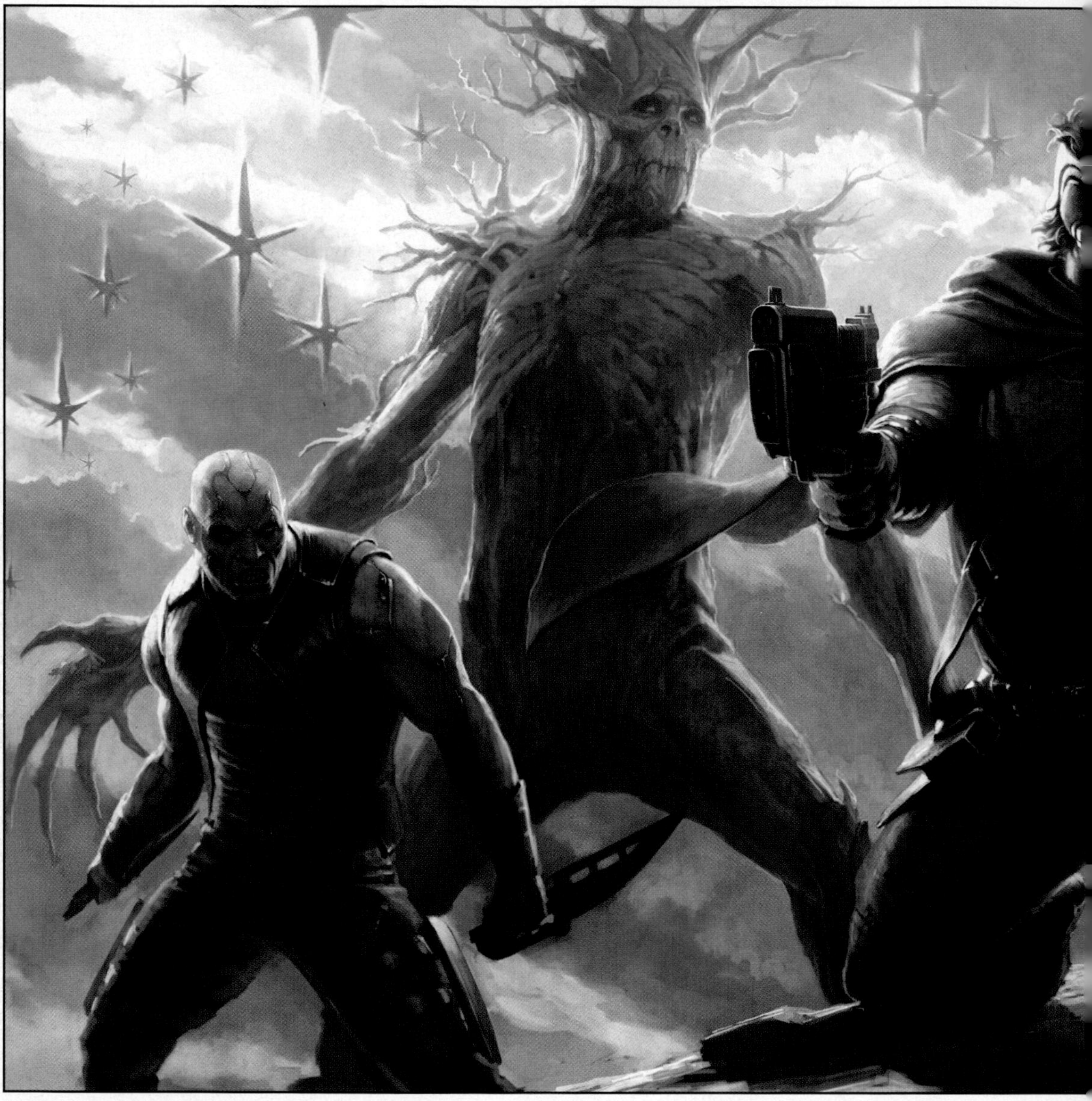

***#2-4* COMBINED VARIANTS** BY CHARLIE WEN

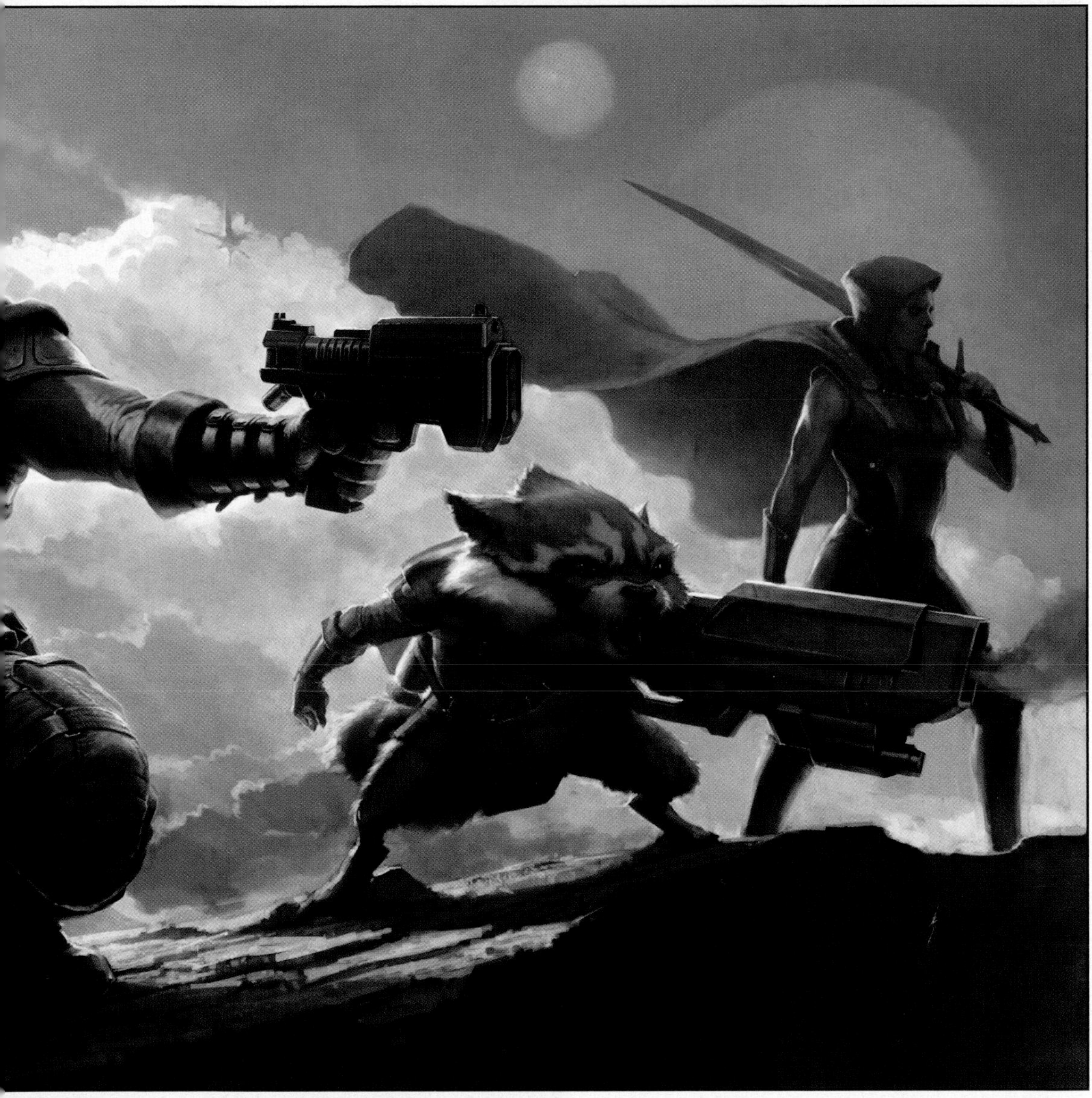

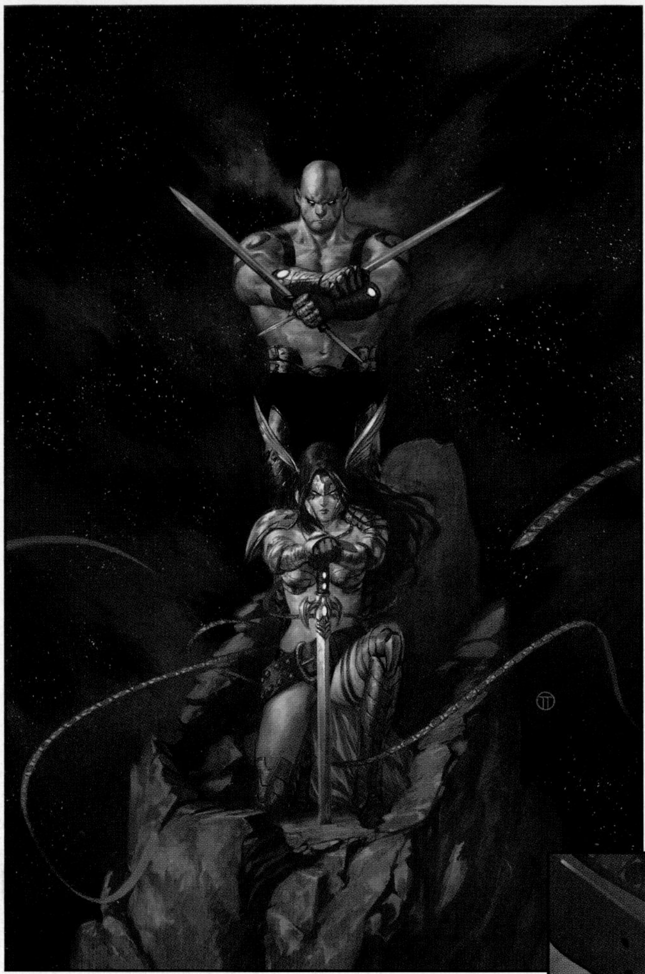

***#5* DRAGON'S LAIR VARIANT**
BY JULIAN TOTINO TEDESCO

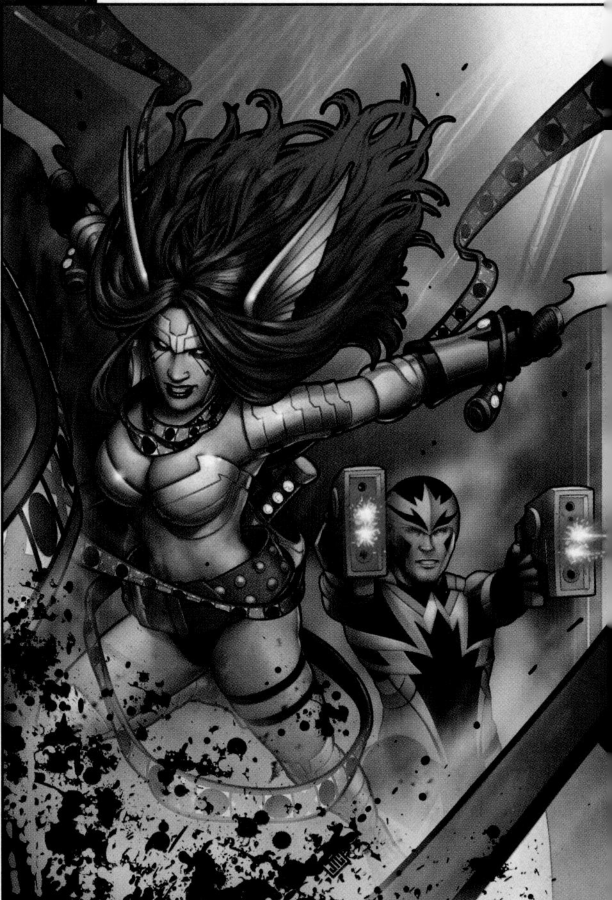

***#5* HASTINGS VARIANT**
BY JOHN TYLER CHRISTOPHER

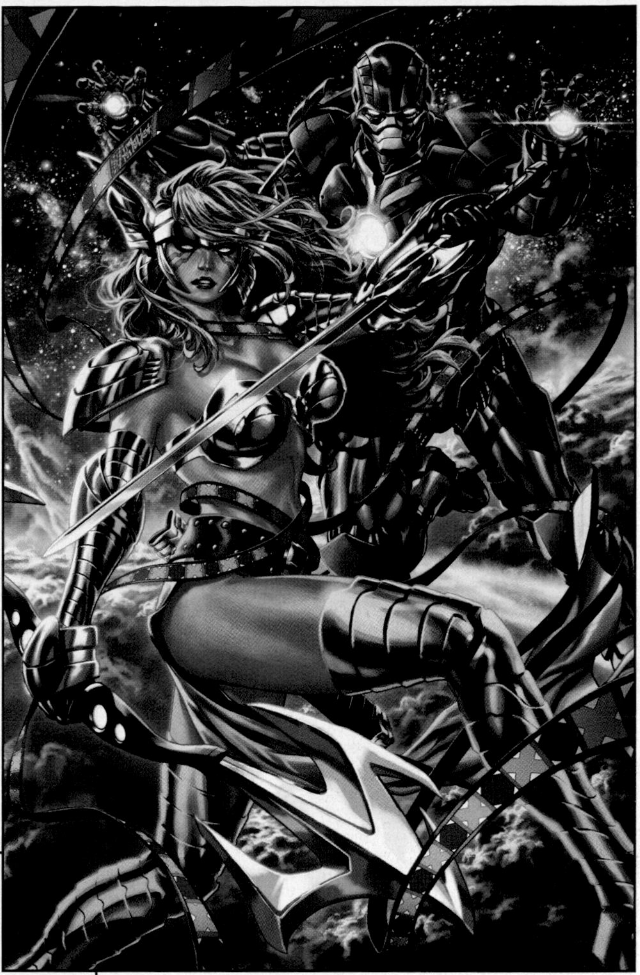

#5 MIDTOWN VARIANT
BY MARK BROOKS

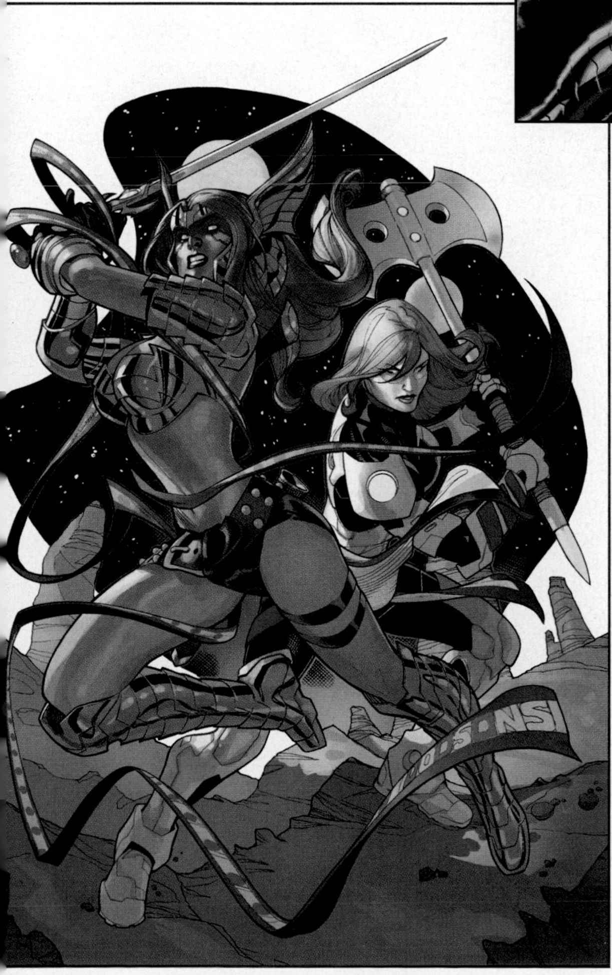

#5 MILE HIGH VARIANT
BY TERRY DODSON & RACHEL DODSON

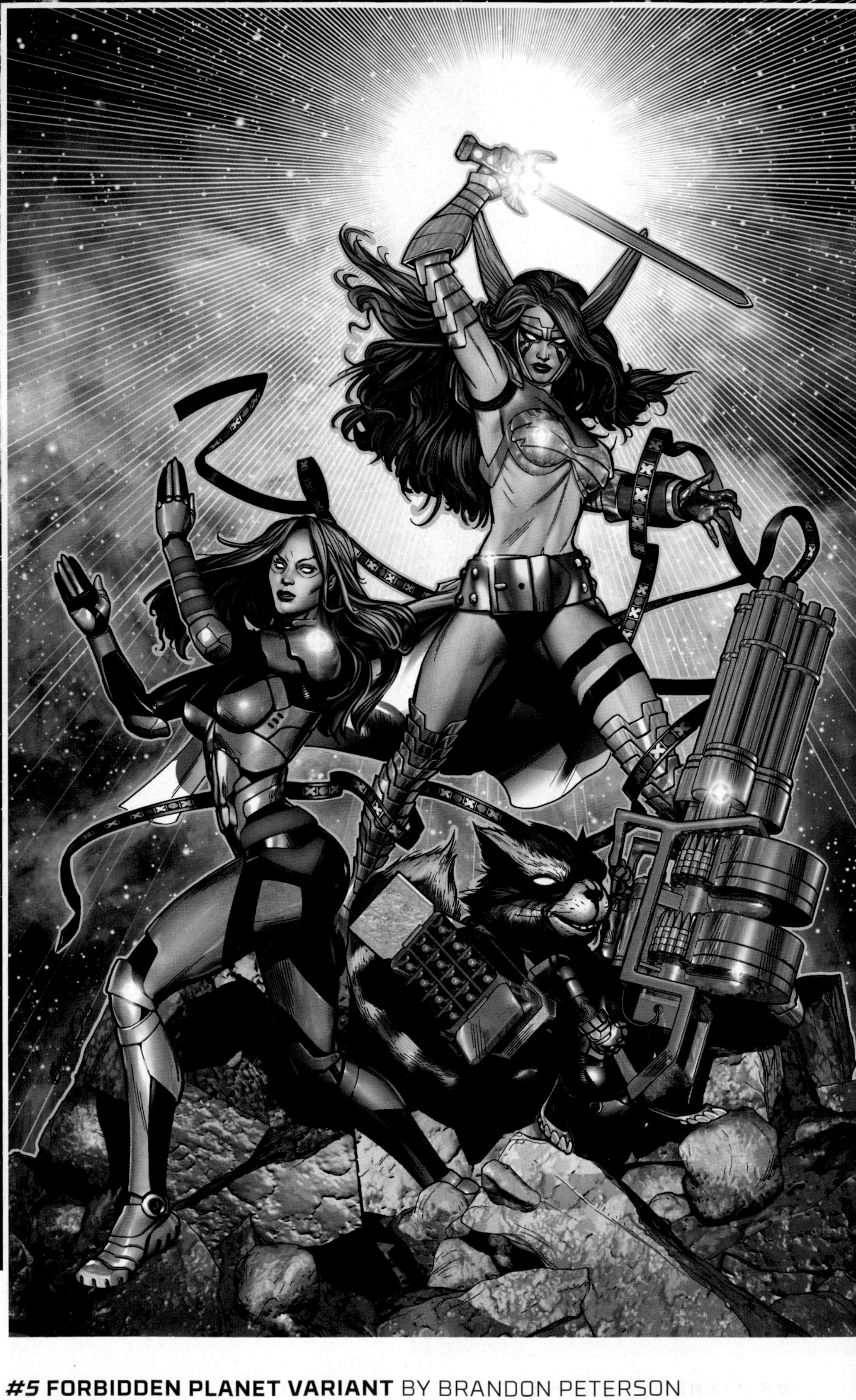

#5 FORBIDDEN PLANET VARIANT BY BRANDON PETERSON